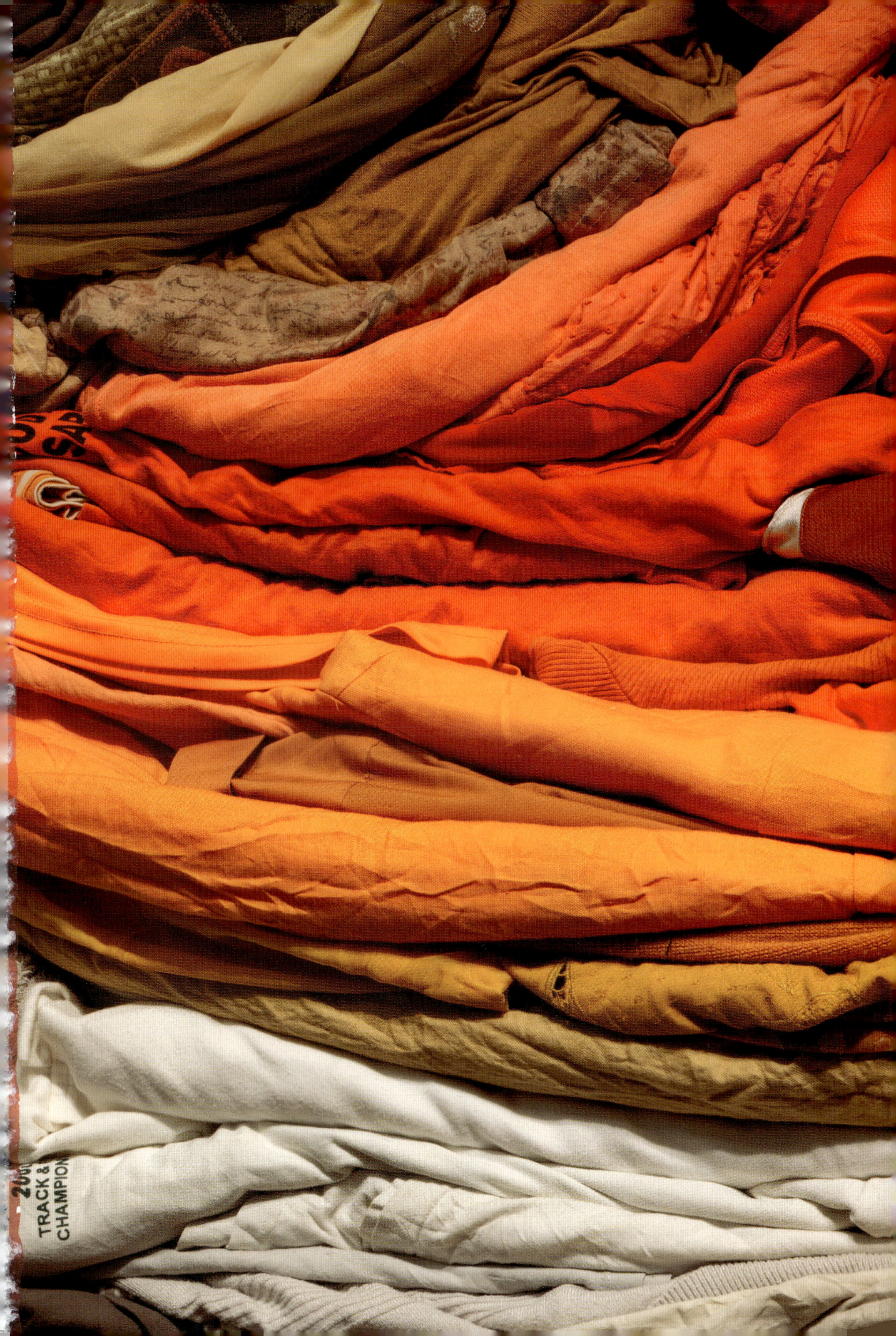
TRACK &
CHAMPION

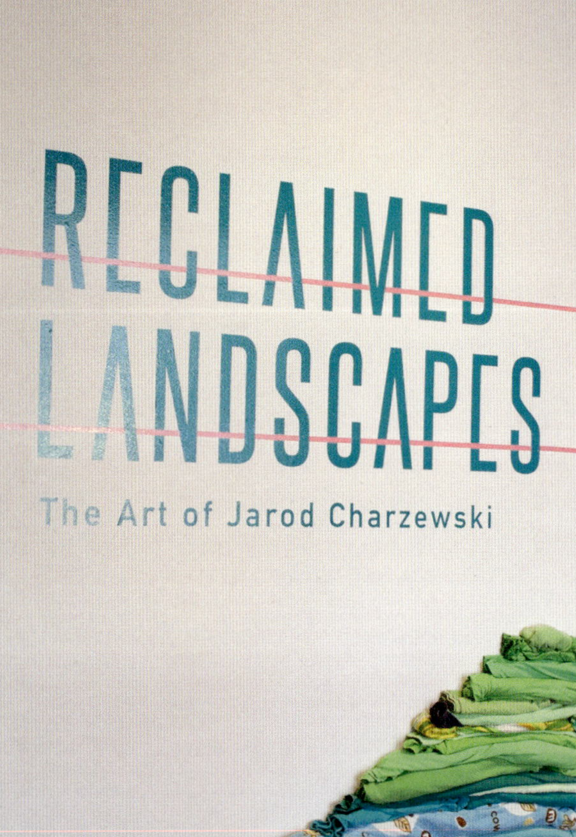

RECLAIMED
LANDSCAPES
The Art of Jarod Charzewski

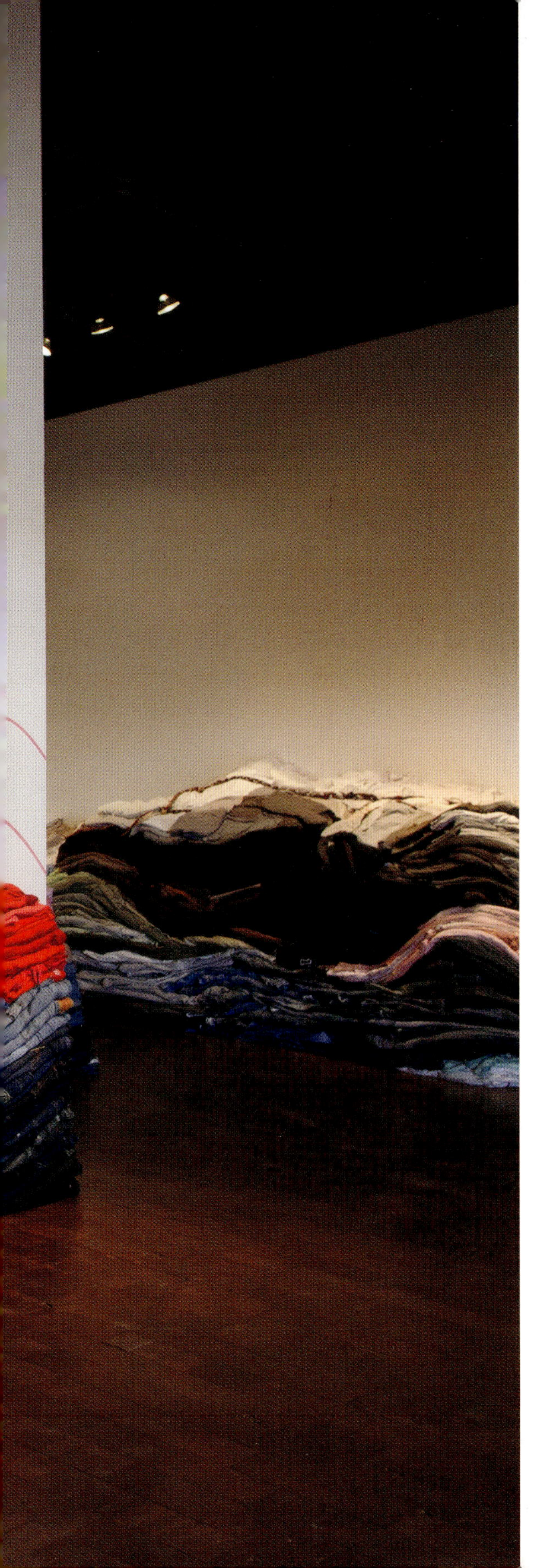

RECLAIMED LANDSCAPES
the art of Jarod Charzewski

6,000 pounds of fabric

4,000 pounds of wires

500 pounds of rubber

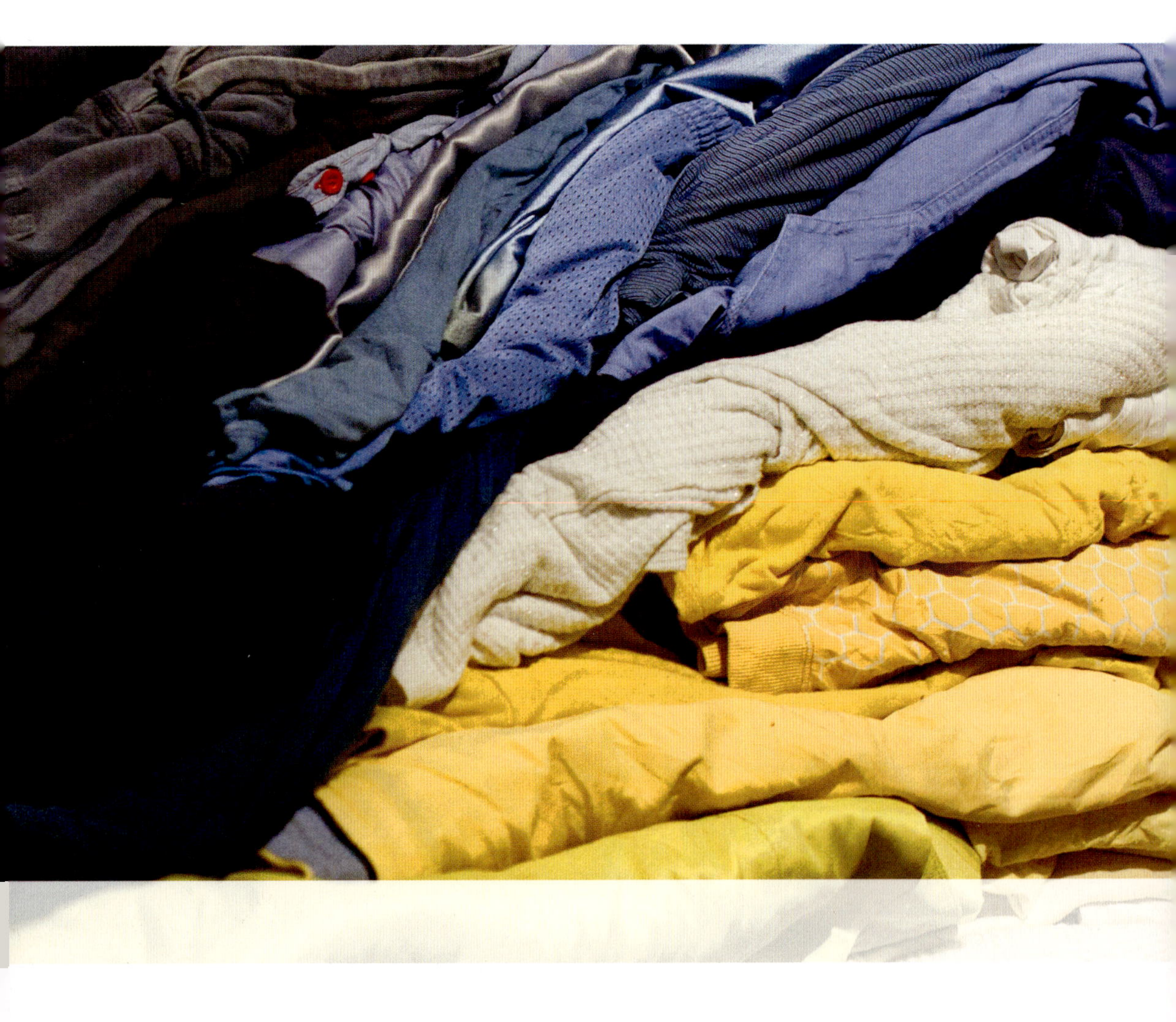

RECLAIMED LANDSCAPES

the art of Jarod Charzewski

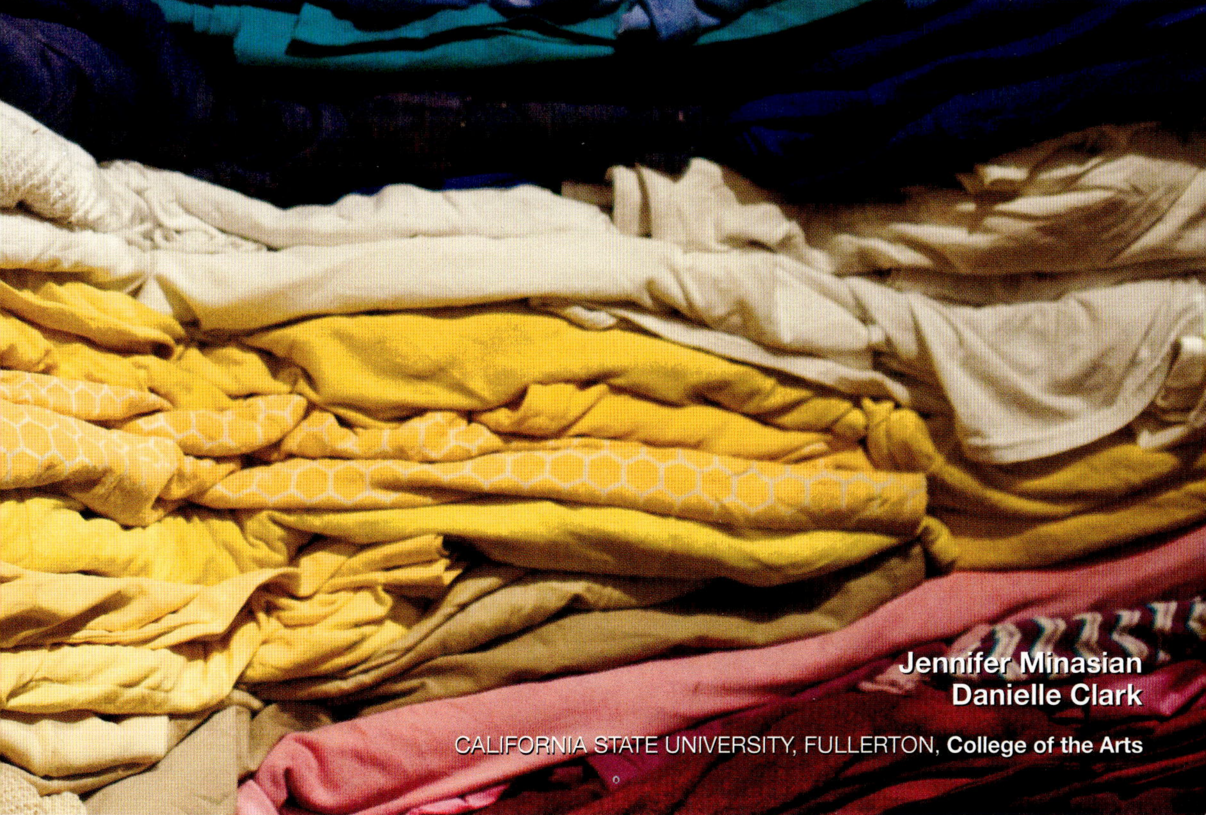

Jennifer Minasian
Danielle Clark

CALIFORNIA STATE UNIVERSITY, FULLERTON, College of the Arts

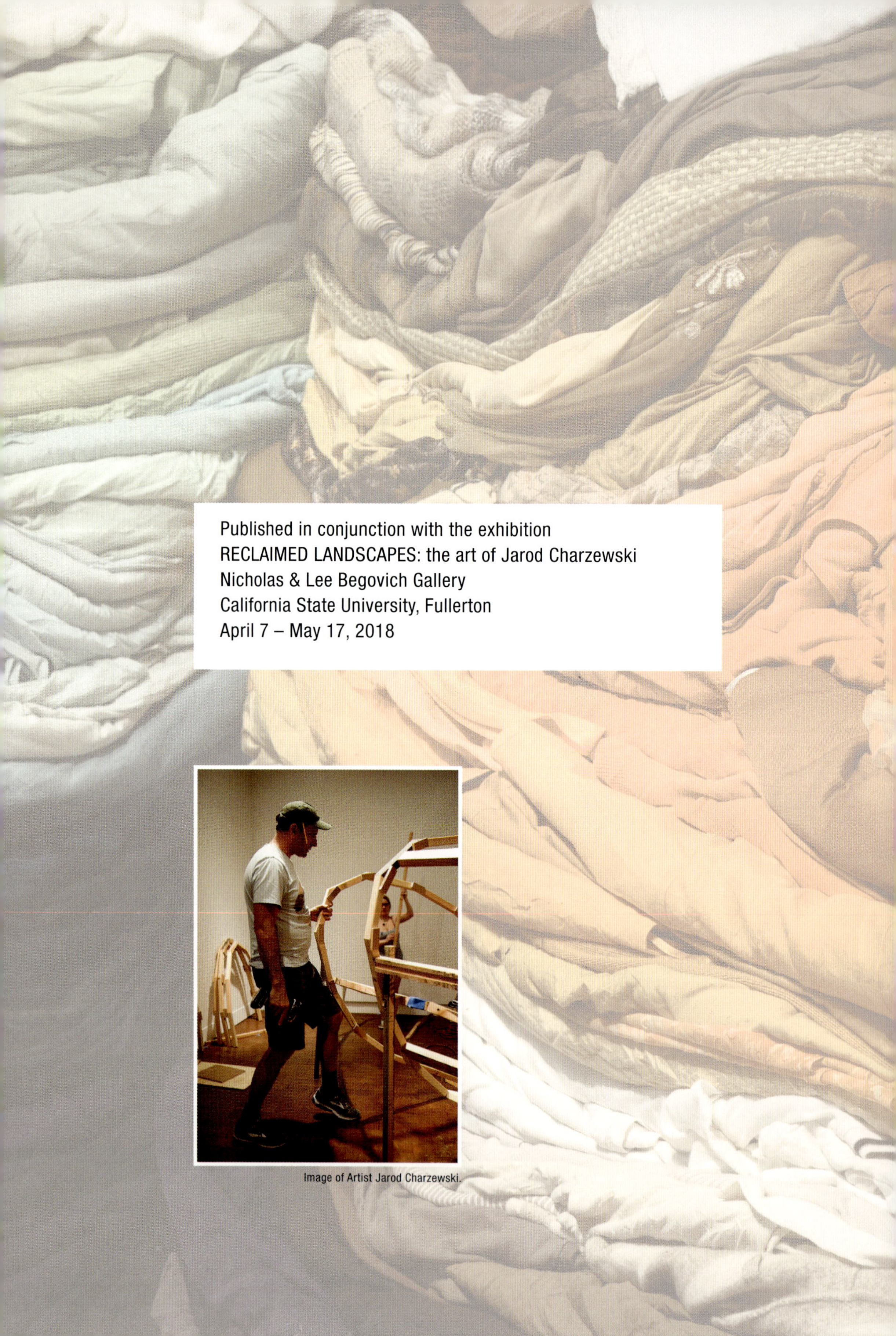

Published in conjunction with the exhibition
RECLAIMED LANDSCAPES: the art of Jarod Charzewski
Nicholas & Lee Begovich Gallery
California State University, Fullerton
April 7 – May 17, 2018

Image of Artist Jarod Charzewski.

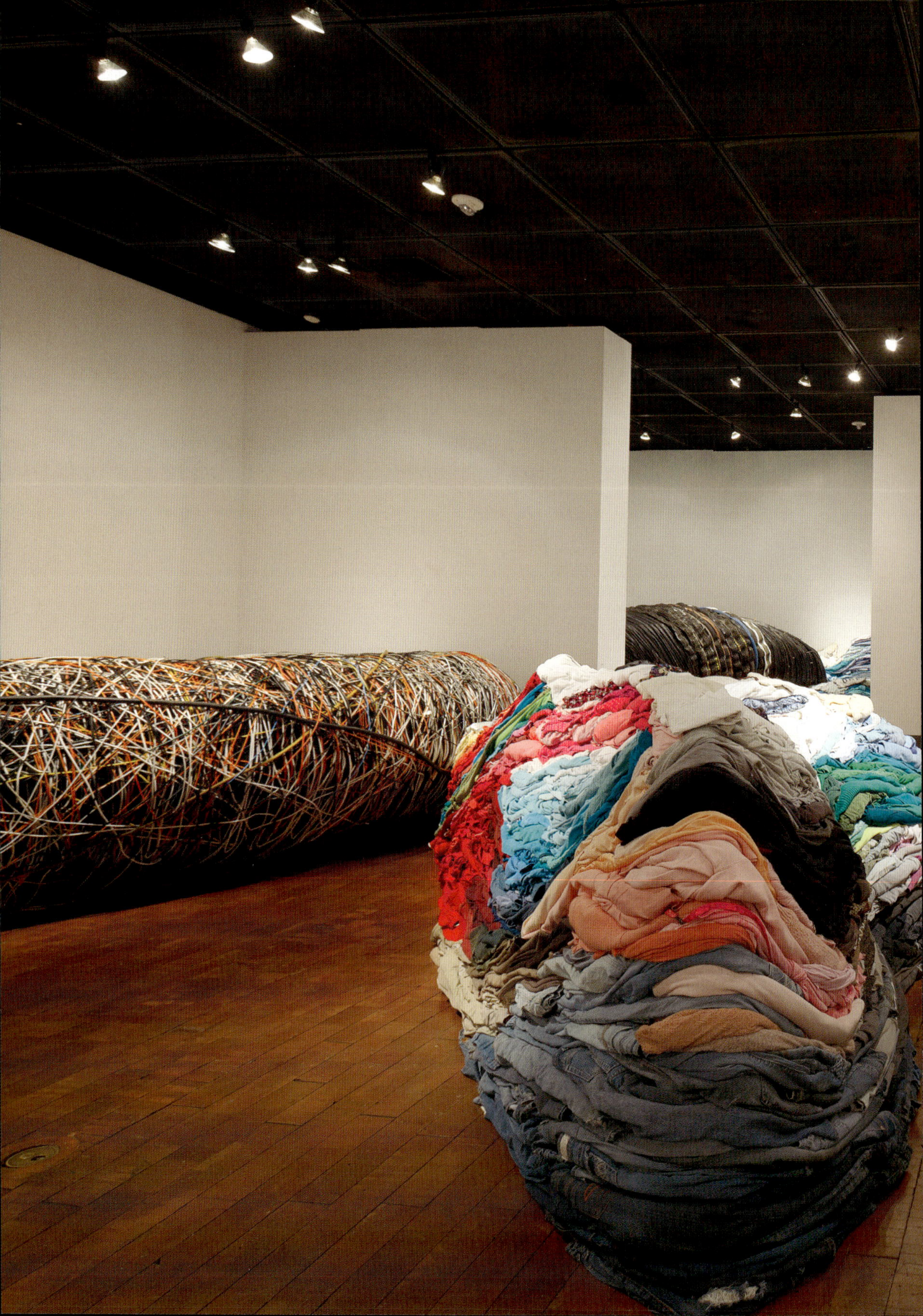

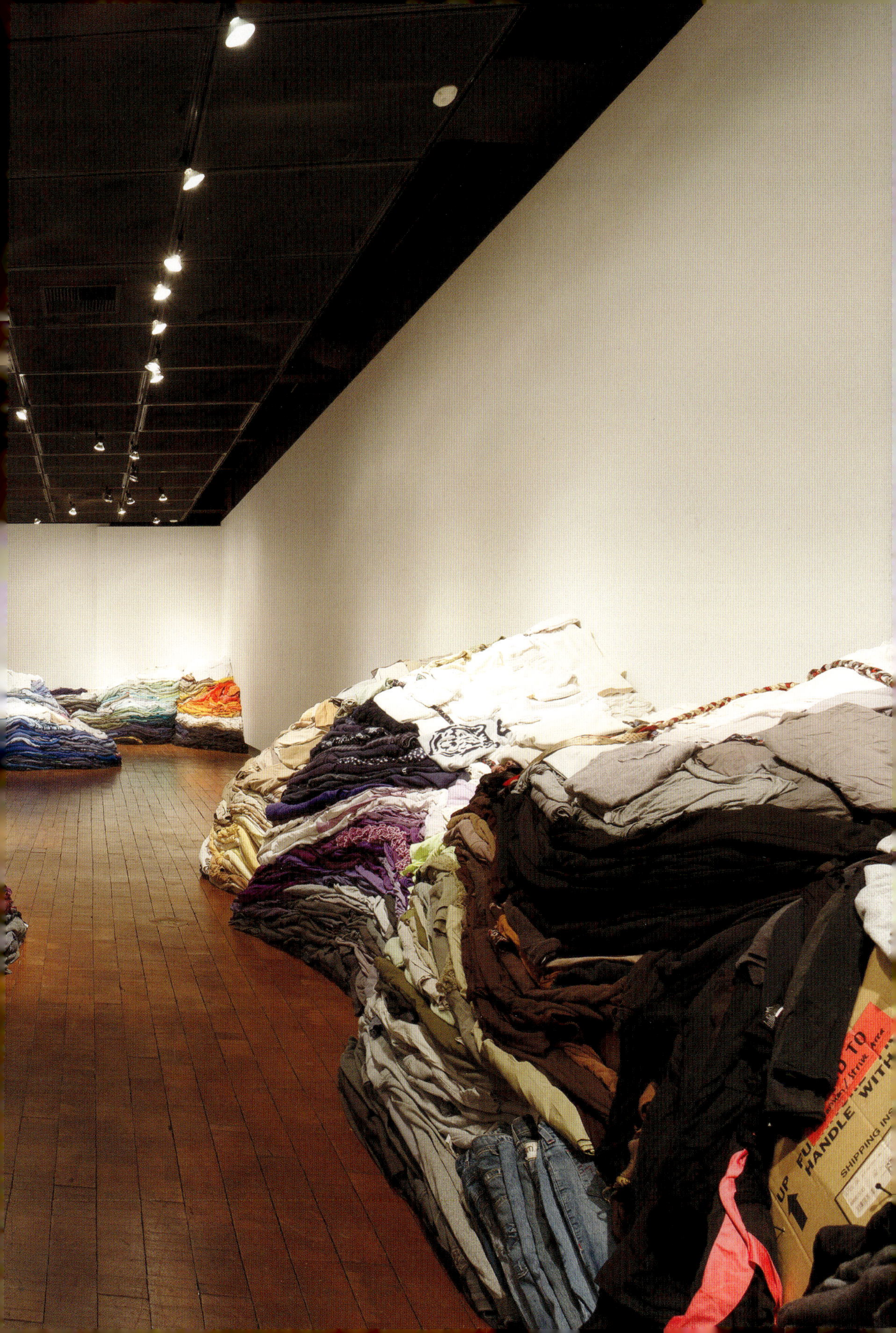

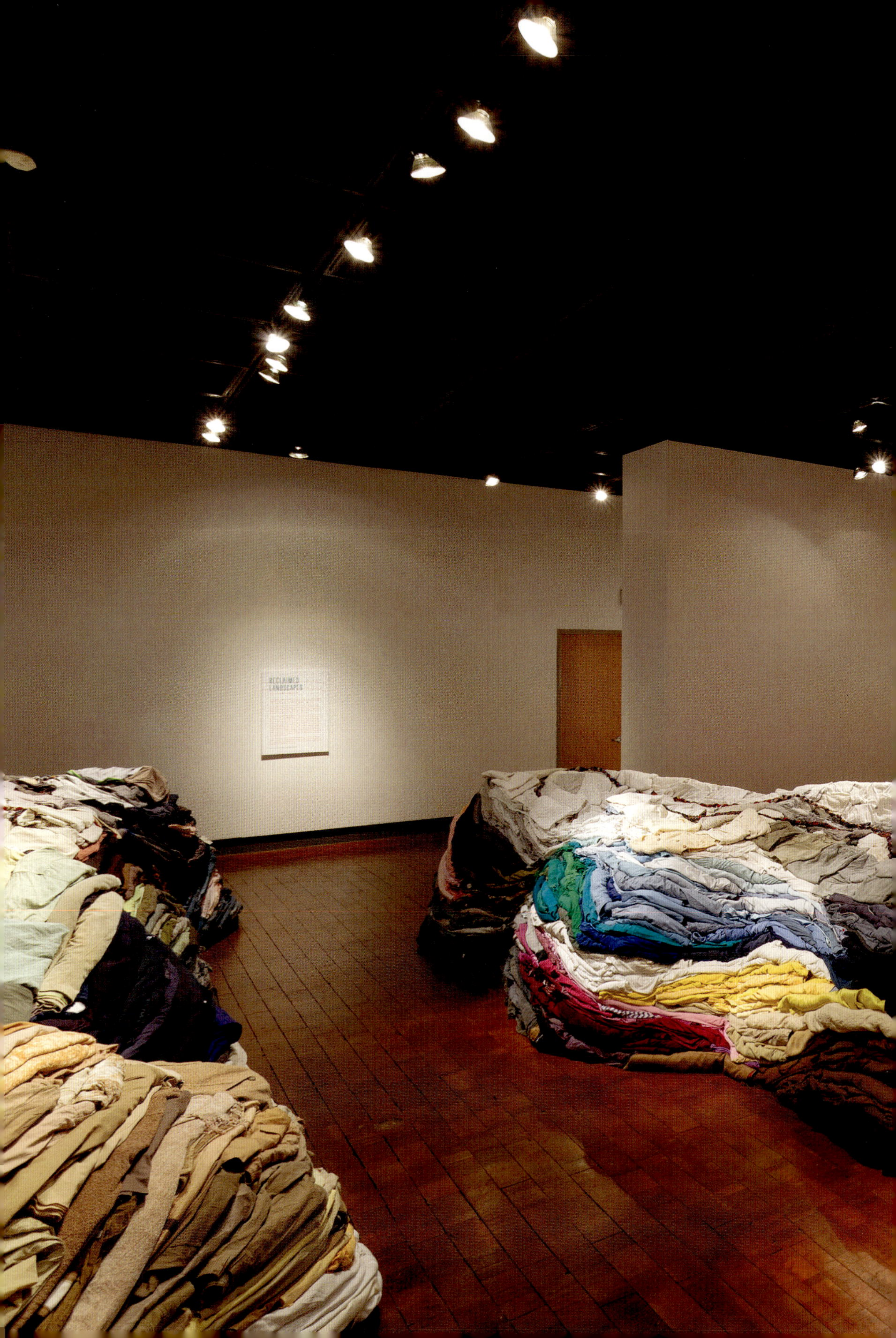
RECLAIMED
LANDSCAPES

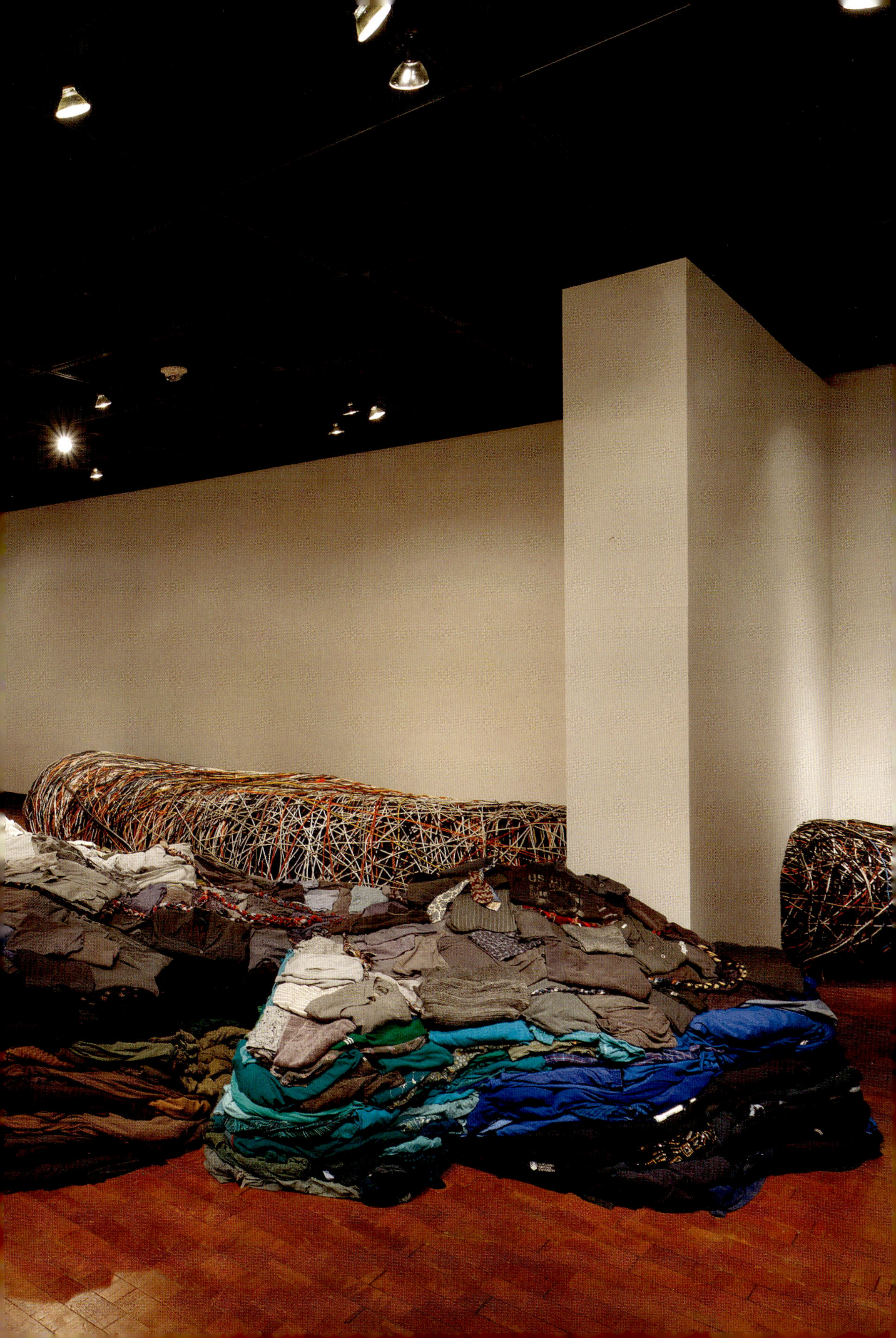

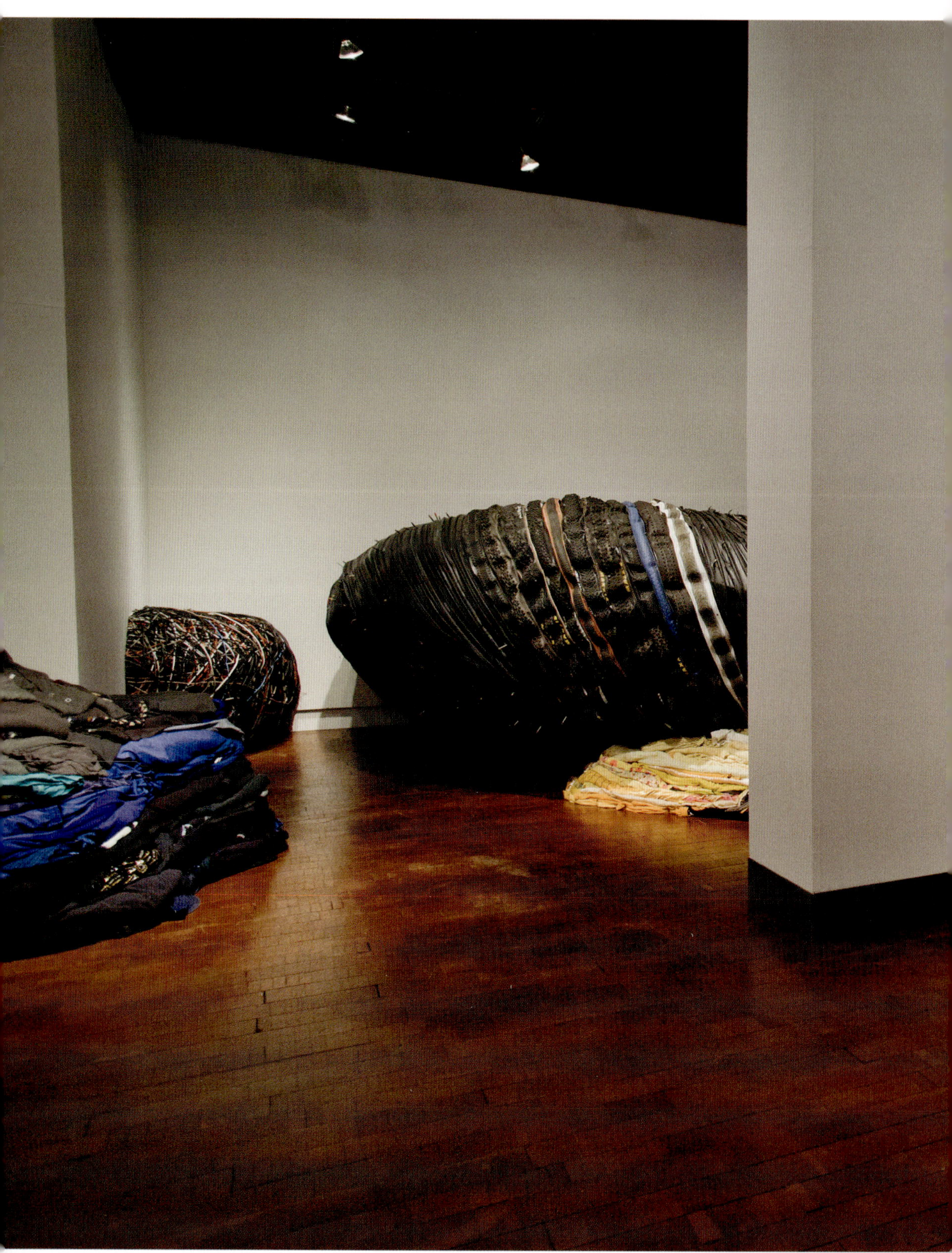

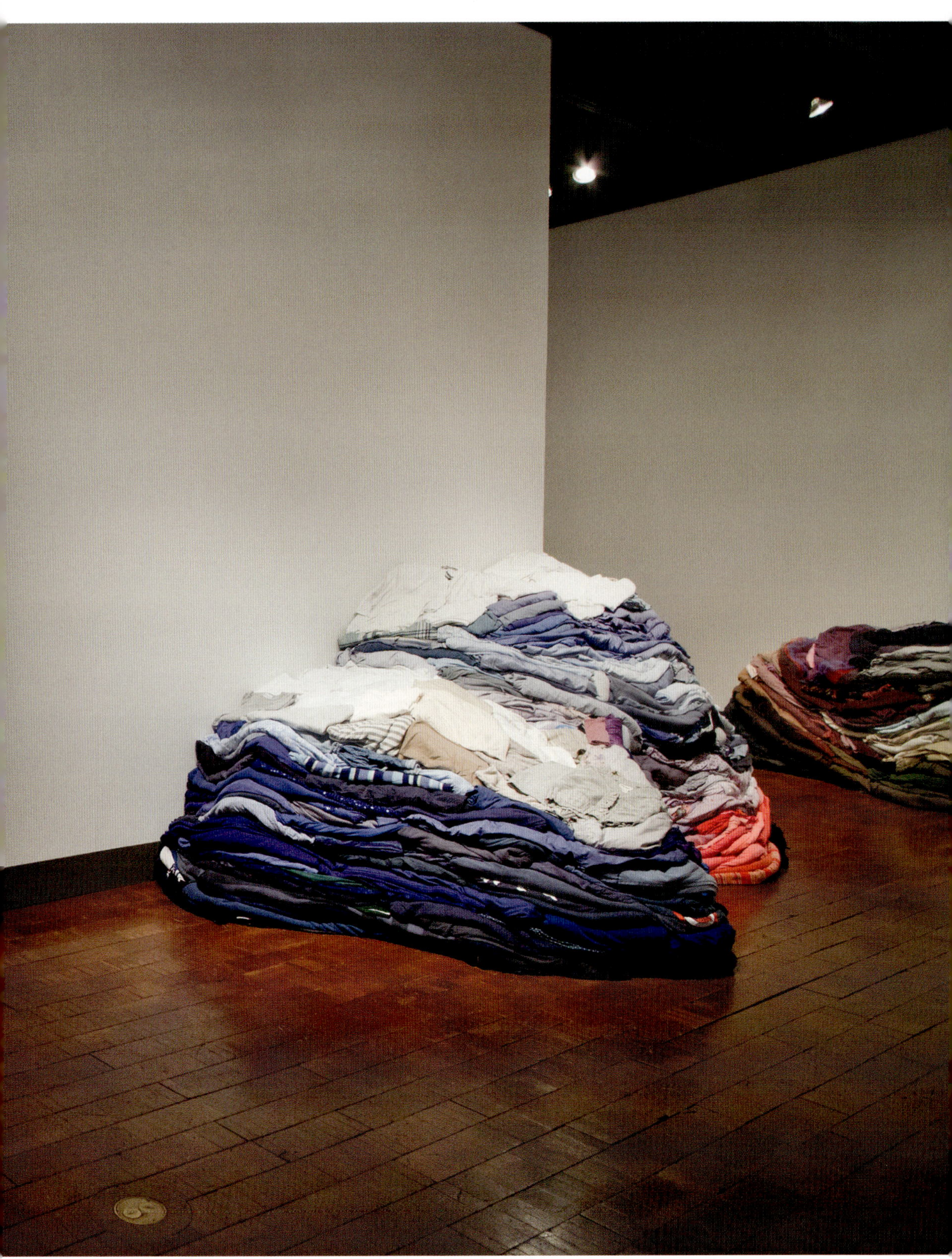

FOREWORD

Karen Crews Hendon

The idea of walking in beauty, or, *the beauty way*, is a traditional insight of many cultures around the globe. No matter the language, the expression references acting in harmony with the environment and all its relations. When referencing our placement among other living creatures, human beings are not pictured at the apex of a pyramid, but instead are shown in the center of a circle to represent their position as a stewardship for all life. In practice, the beauty way is simple: leave the environment in better condition than how it was found. While some may find this perspective complicated or idealistic in a modern world, others are championing the ways of sustainable living and find the act of reducing their carbon footprint to be a process of respect, reciprocation, compassion, and liberation.

Now more than ever, moral concern is rising about our natural resources and the long-term impacts of industrial processes, materials, and byproducts. Source materials are becoming public knowledge and consumers are faced with complex decisions regarding the types of products they choose for their daily needs. Ideas of worth and importance are changing and the qualities of our belongings are scrutinized in conjunction with their possible consequences. Questions such as *Is this worth it? Who created this? How was it made? What is the lifespan?* are more prevalent. We are relearning and reconsidering how to place authenticity and value on consumer goods, especially if we become aware that they were made at the detriment of a community or the environment. With Fair Trade movements and certifications established well over fifty years ago, we are still confronted with trade injustices and not enough strong environmental policies. Now, twelve years since the 2006 climate documentary *An Inconvenient Truth* was created by former presidential candidate Al Gore and his team, much of the evidence discussed in the documentary regarding global degradation continues to be supported by scientific research. While the film brought social awareness and education to the public about the subject, many of the same issues continue to be subjects of heated debate during a time of political polarization.

As American news media expose more information related to frustrating toxic problems, hazardous landfills, frequent chemical spills, pipeline leaks, and the abundance of waste that has accumulated for decades on land and sea, many people recognize the need for major reform. Companies that boast their high consumption patterns and growing investment rates have rarely been the same ones that measure their own waste generation management. Our inventive pursuits for convenience have led not only to incredible positive discoveries but also to considerable destruction. While it has been documented that wealthier economies tend to produce more waste and have the resources to reverse this behavior, it could be considered ironic that those with less are conserving more. Aside from the statistics that economists offer, social influences and marketing promos can lead to some of the quickest actions.

In growing numbers, people are becoming more mindful or "do-good" consumers. Supporting ethically conscious companies that both disclose the lifecycle of their products and have a reciprocal maker-to-consumer relationship allows buyers to feel actively engaged in making our world a better place. Whether one converts to trends such as the tiny-house movement or becomes a new minimalist (thanks to Matt D'Avella, Joshua Fields Millburn, and Ryan Nicodemus's 2015 film collaboration *Minimalism: A Documentary About the Important Things*), individuals are learning how to maximize multiple needs with as little as possible to lighten their load, seek new forms of happiness, and tend to the damage done to our environment and communities. Discussions on how individuals can be consumer-conscious and implement eco-friendly lifestyles are leading to major social networks, eco-webs, and community cooperatives inspired by the co-creation of an upcycled future.

While doing research for the exhibition *Reclaimed Landscapes* at the Begovich Gallery, curators Jennifer Minasian and Danielle Clark gathered appalling statistics about social-cultural waste. Their aim was to demonstrate how visual art can give these frightful numbers the strongest visibility and impact on viewers. Minasian and Clark, both passionate and mindful advocates, decided to uncover alternate views of these inconvenient truths with installation artist Jarod Charzewski. Their research and contributions led to much community awareness, detailing how much fabric weaves in and out of our landfills from the surplus of rejected clothing as a result of fast fashion. Introducing Jarod's work to California State University, Fullerton, was as ambitious as it looks. We quickly learned how the epic proportions of the artwork parallel the allegories of the artist's concepts. Through the mounds of clothing, bike tires, and electronic wires, Jarod demonstrates how these discarded objects created for fashion, transportation, and communication accompany our lives and, at times, define us, but ultimately outlive us in destructive ways. Being present near his work, viewers encountered the overwhelming energy of hyper-accumulation. They experienced how the man-made colors, layers, and textures meld, bulge, and push against one another, mimicking the layers and movement of our Earth. While we may already be aware that our landfills are a problem, the artist investigates specifically what kinds of objects contribute to the mass and how we can be empowered to change it. As our students meticulously folded and added clothing layer by layer, they realized firsthand how one person can make a difference and be either part of the detriment or part of the solution. We can indeed be stewards of the Earth, of our home, as we share it with all forms of life.

The *Reclaimed Landscapes* project also illuminated what a complex process it is to reuse or breakdown unnatural materials. In Orange County, or anywhere in California, disposing of the type of rubber used for bike tires—a subject rarely on our radar—put us to the test. Learning that tire recycling plants will only take nine bike tires at a time (and will charge per tire) unless you have a hauler's bond (worth $10,000.00) presented a challenge. With 200 pounds of bike tires to recycle at the culmination of this exhibition, this experience gave us a new respect for haulers 1-800 GOT JUNK and the city of Fontana, where a precision tire-crumb facility, Rubber Recovery, grinds up and recycles tire rubber for playground surfacing, rubber molding, synthetic turf, and other rubber goods.

Perhaps a good lesson for all who visited this exhibition and those who will continue to read about it in this 100-percent recyclable book, printed with soy-based ink, is that we will never look at clothes, bicycles, electronics, or anything in our possession as we once did. The objects we choose to live with have lives and histories of their own. Jarod Charzewski teaches us that we no longer have to hide or bury our imperishable secrets—just the compostable ones! Whether it's reducing waste by utilizing compost; initiating community gardens; replacing plastic with cloth bags or glass containers; partnering with neighborhood cleanup projects; experimenting with DIY household cleaning recipes; buying bulk instead of prepackaged goods; hosting clothing swaps; or utilizing ride-shares and alternative transportation, a few basic steps yield considerable economic, social, and environmental outcomes for a more compassionate way of living. While it's important to continue to educate ourselves as to where our supplies come from, how they were made, and the effects of their use, it's also as important to connect with others through community to create mutual support in these efforts. For this, we are grateful to Jarod, Jennifer, and Danielle, who together created community here at CSUF and guided us toward new definitions for the meaning and impact we need to shape a world we love.

— **Karen Crews Hendon**
Interim Director, Begovich Gallery
California State University, Fullerton

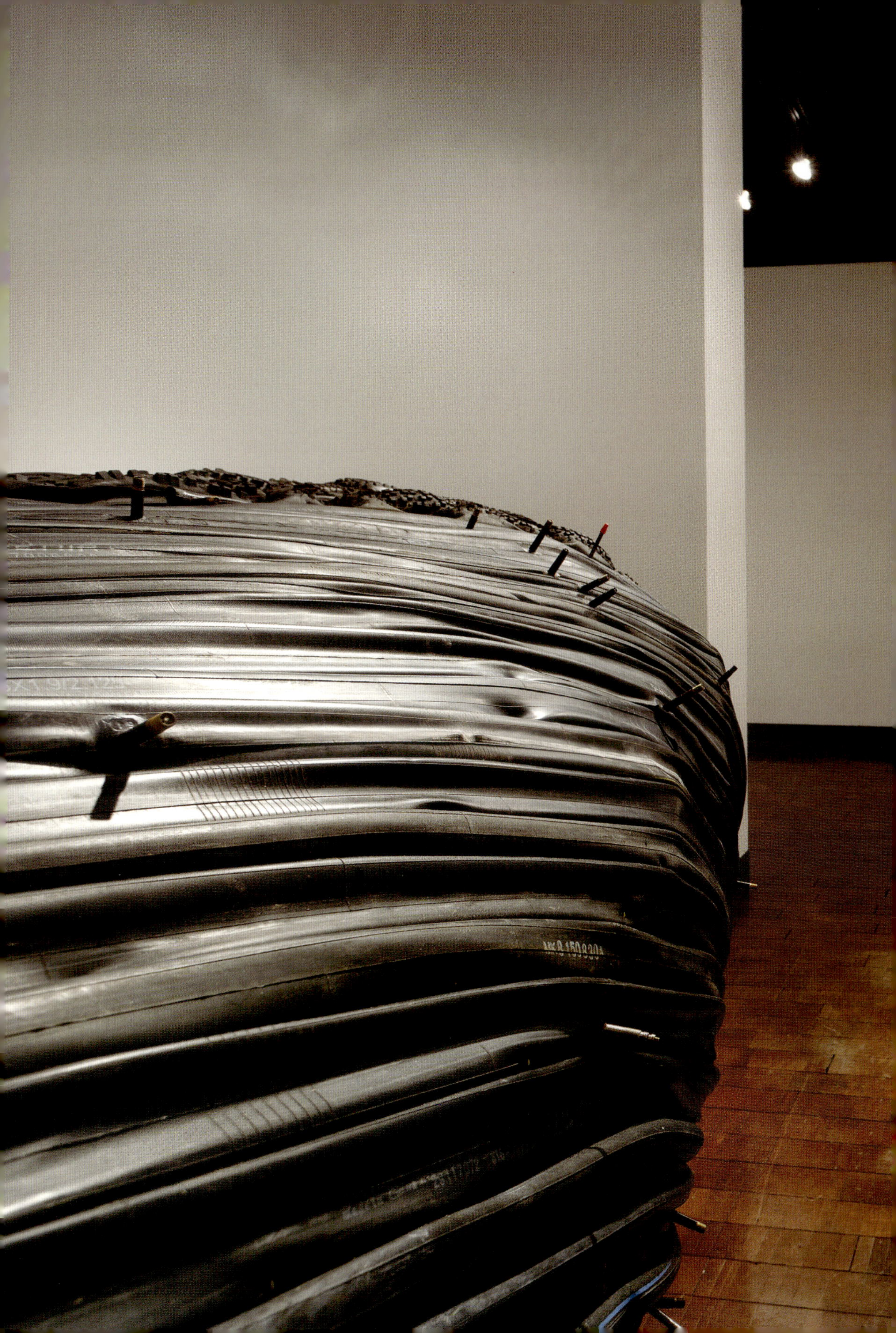

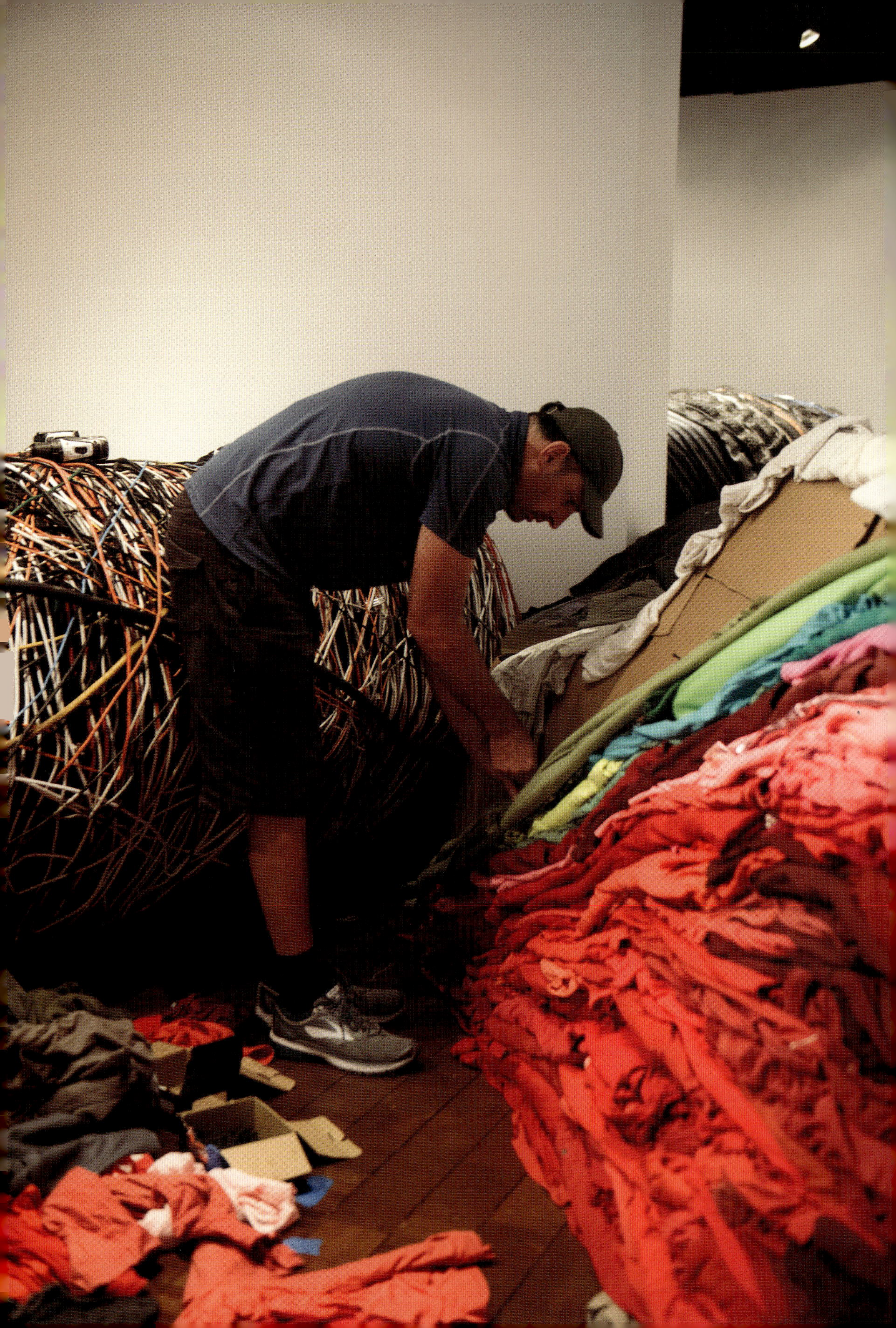

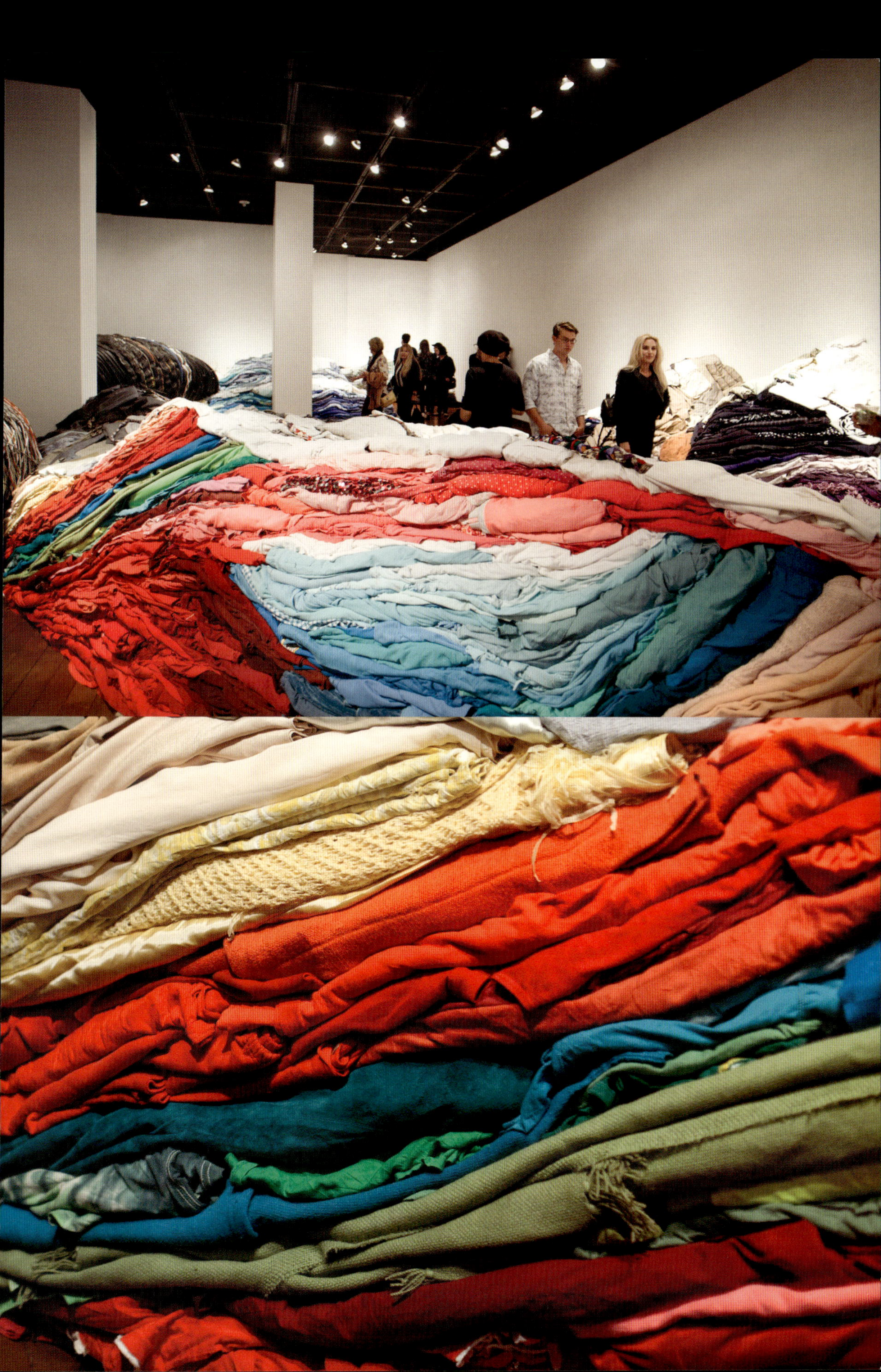

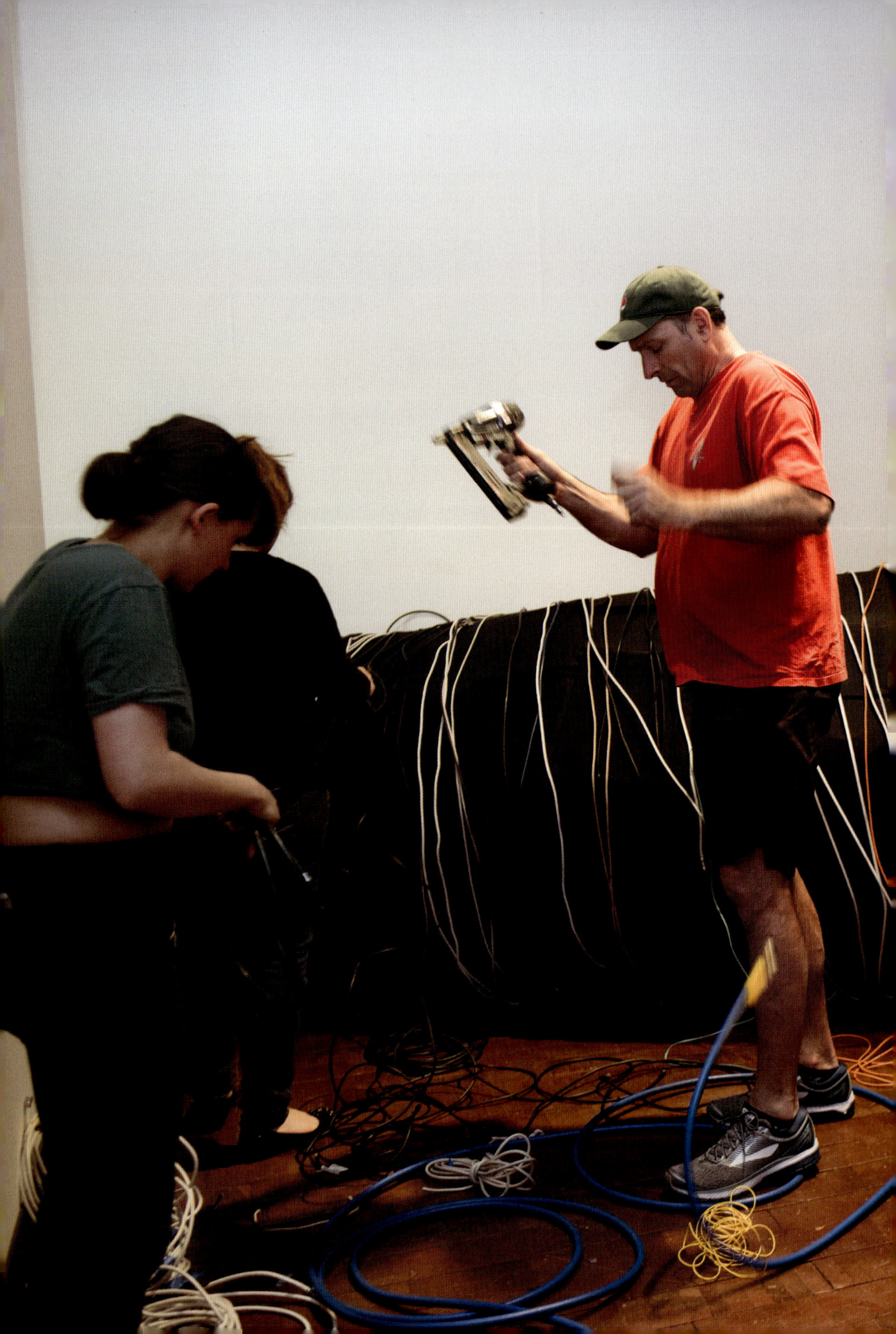

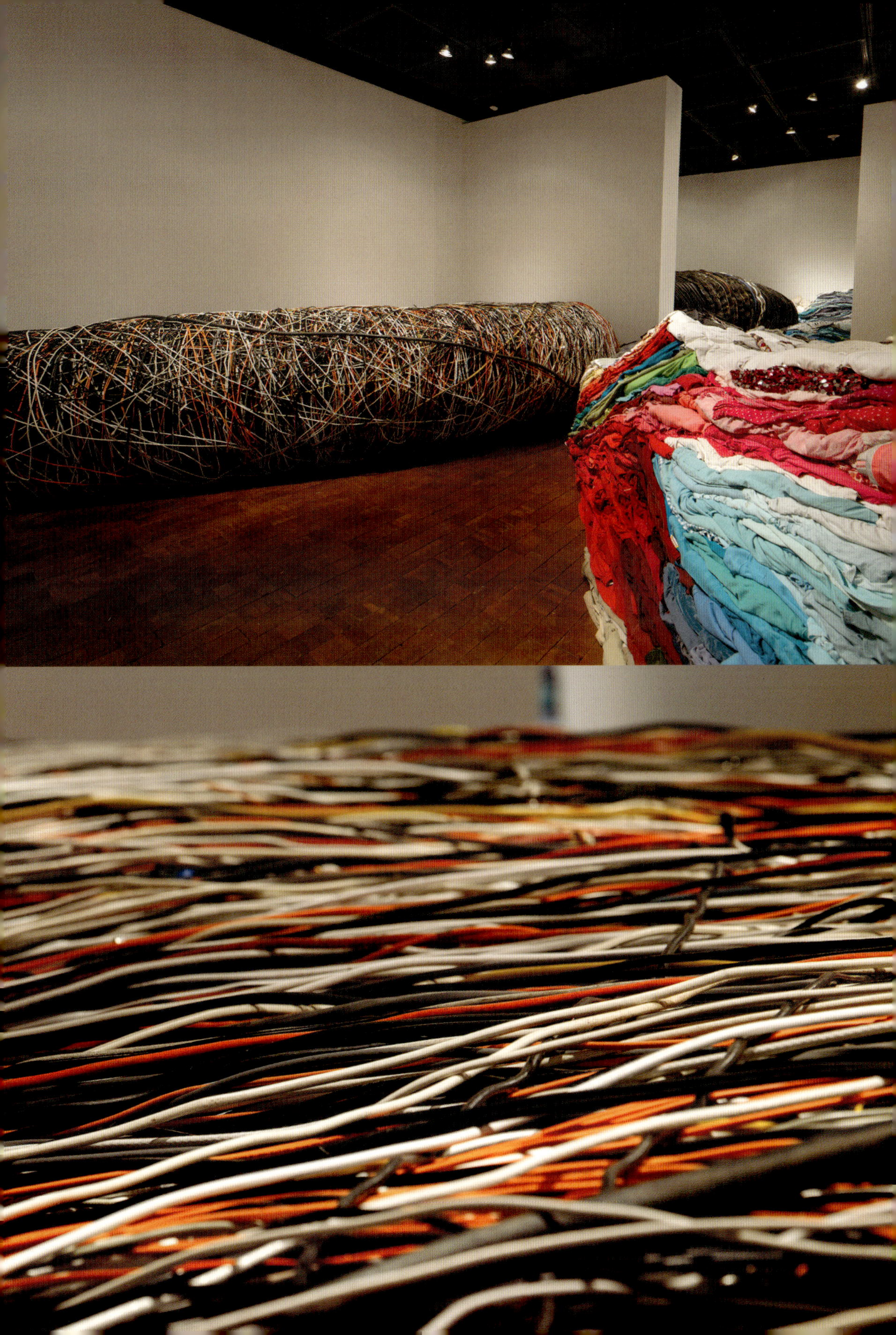

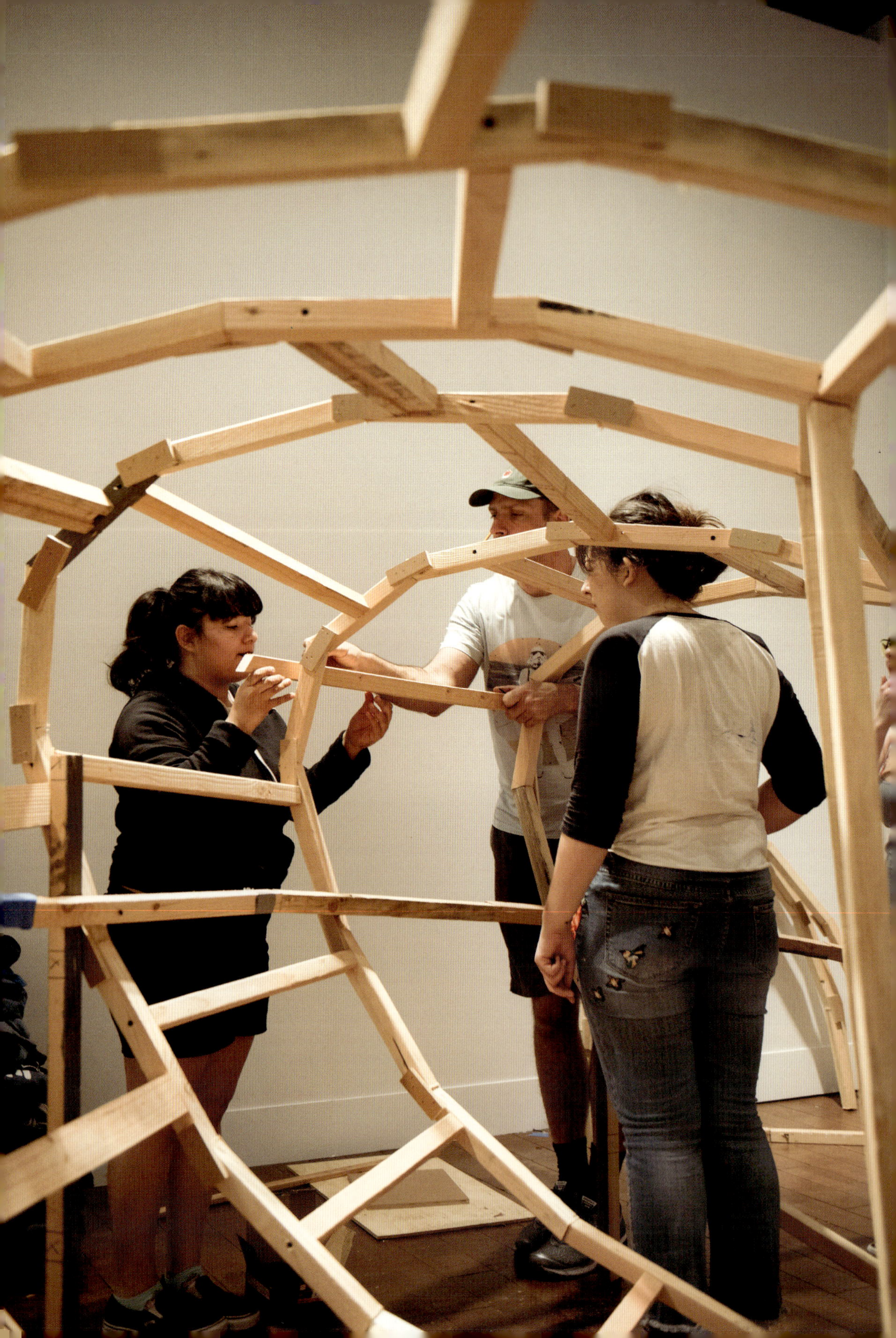

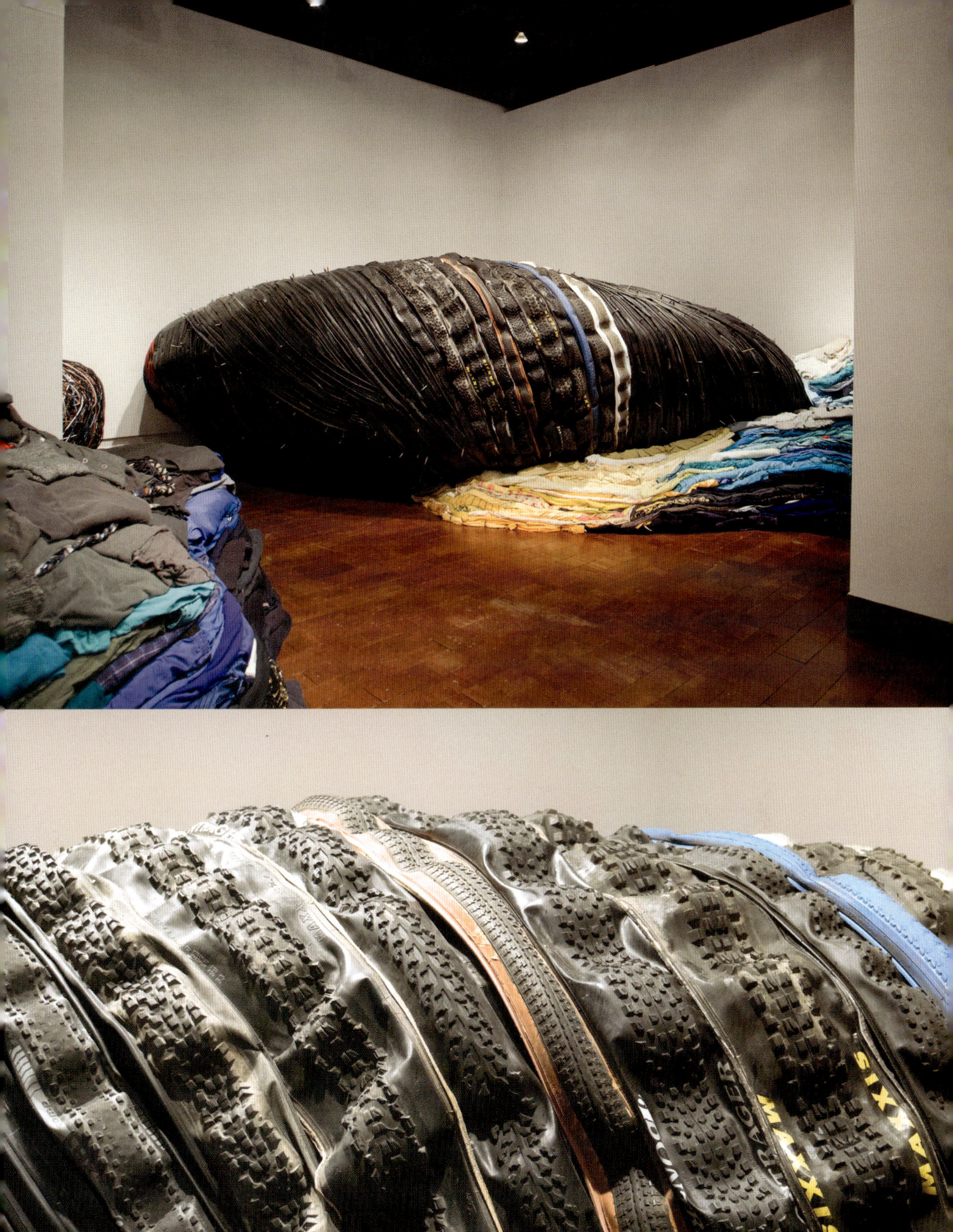

RECLAIMED LANDSCAPES

Jennifer Minasian

For decades Americans' dependence on manufactured goods has produced multibillion-dollar industries that form the basis of capitalism and corporate culture. Companies' pursuit of profit has promoted, through manipulative marketing, unsurpassed consumer greed and an addiction to purchasing cheap goods. Further, this addiction reinforces a detrimental cycle that associates the purchase of manufactured goods with the pursuit of happiness. As a consequence of making prosperity a commodity, the staggering number of buyer purchases and the subsequent waste have risen to a point of global concern.

While the United States has less than 5 percent of the global population, it accounts for 60 percent of the private consumption spending worldwide[1] and generates 258 million tons of waste per year, with only about 35 percent of the waste being recycled.[2] And the United States is the largest consumer market in the world,[3] with consumers spending $130.6 trillion per year on consumer goods.[4] These shocking statistics are studied not only by environmentalists, economists, and scientists, but by artists as well. Artists can offer unique insights into conspicuous consumption and can mirror the world around us with visceral images

---

[1] "The State of Consumption Today," State of the World 2011: Innovations that Nourish the Planet. Worldwatch Institute, 2011, www.worldwatch.org/node/810.

[2] "Advancing Sustainable Materials Management: 2014 Fact Sheet," Assessing Trends in Material Generation, Recycling, Composting, Combustion with Energy Recovery and Landfilling in the United States. Environmental Protection Agency, 2016. https://www.epa.gov/sites/production/files/2016-11/documents/2014_smmfactsheet_508.pdf.

[3] From www.data.worldbank.org list of the largest consumer markets in the world. The countries are sorted by their "household final consumption expenditure" (HFCE), which represents consumer spending in nominal terms. See https://en.wikipedia.org/wiki/List_of_largest_consumer_markets for an aggregated list of countries.

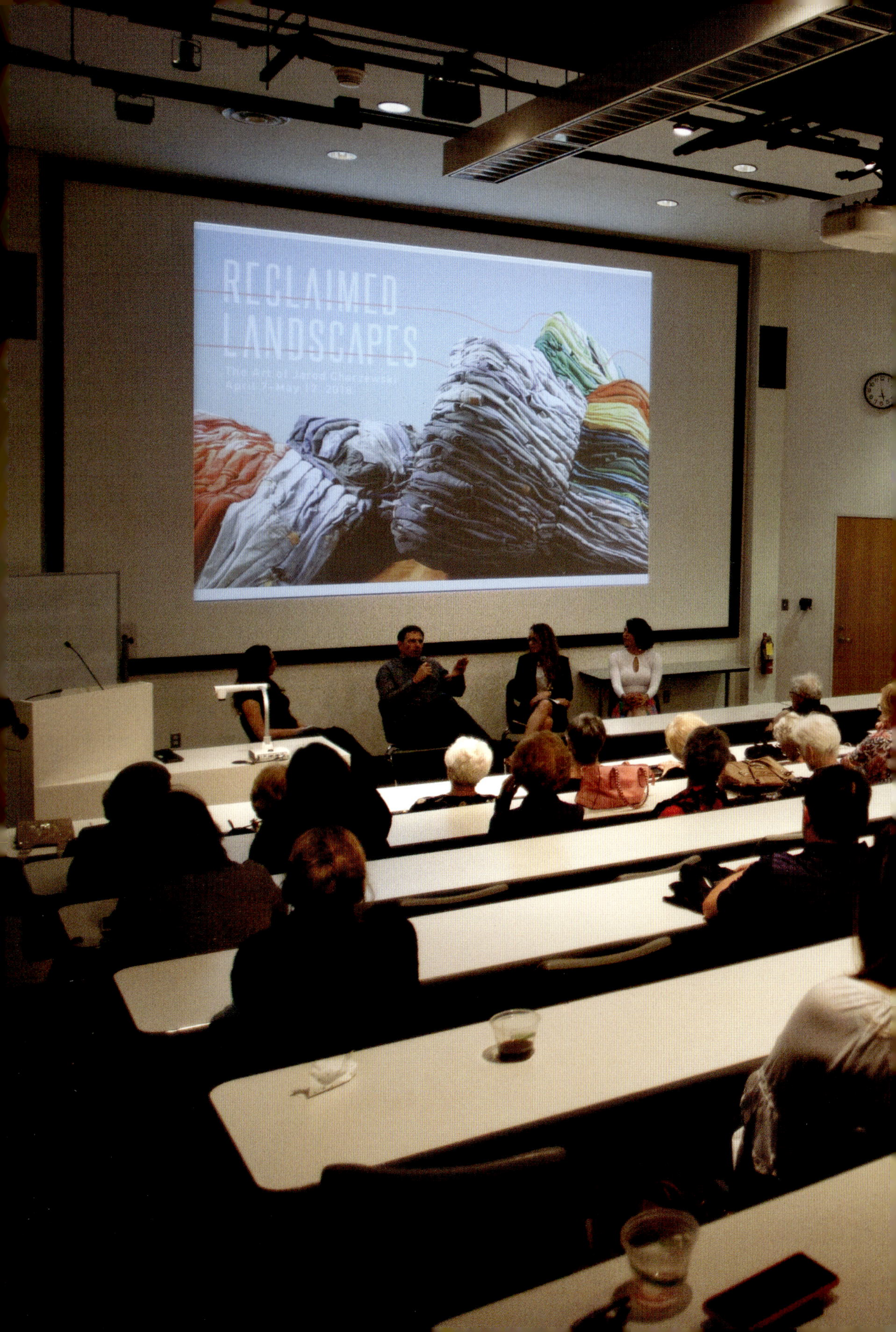
RECLAIMED
LANDSCAPES
The Art of Jarod Charzewski
April 7–May 17, 2018

and messages that offer a profound understanding of our situation. Artist Jarod Charzewski champions the idea that viewers begin to rethink their purchasing habits. By utilizing discarded materials for his monumental installations, he zeroes in on our consumption patterns and wasteful practices. By exploring his artwork, audiences may see the immediate and irreversible impacts these destructive and compulsive behaviors have on our environment and society.

Reclaimed Landscapes: The Art of Jarod Charzewski is a timely midcareer retrospective exhibition and site-specific installation exploring America's current relationship with consumerism, the fast-fashion industry, and our deeply rooted habits of purchasing disposable and cheap goods. As an artist and activist, Charzewski makes vivid installations that illustrate the results of our out-of-control behaviors toward purchasing. The exhibition is part of an ongoing conversation surrounding consumer culture, reminding individuals to reconsider their habitual actions and adopt alternatives that will lead to a sustainable future.

The Real Cost of Consumerism in America

Consumerism in America has become a pervasive cultural belief system. It has developed into an ideology that assumes that well-being and happiness depend heavily on the level of one's personal consumption, particularly on the rate and amount of purchased goods.[5] Erik Olen Wright, a prominent scholar analyzing the social impact of class in the United States, comments, "The idea is not simply that well-being depends upon a standard of living above some threshold, but that at the center of happiness is consumption and material possessions."[6] Many states in the U.S. are reframing the concept of well-being to include advanced initiatives in recycling and reuse. These trailblazing states, such as Vermont (ranked first), Oregon (ranked second), and Washington (ranked third) on "America's Greenest States" list,[7] all share a dedication to having a low carbon-footprint, or low carbon-dioxide emissions, in their cities, and now have high air-quality standards. They are also among the states to have the most "green" buildings per capita and have received the U.S. Green Building Council's benchmark certification.[8] These states set an example for other states to adopt their initiatives and promote the longevity of their ecosystems. Yet many states are slow to change, such as California, ranking number 14 on this list. And, unfortunately, when these initiatives are put forth as efforts for global change, they become even more difficult to implement.

Globalization is a worldwide process of interaction and integration involving people, companies, and governments.[9] With increased global interaction comes the growth of international trade, ideas,

---

4   Data from Evan Comen, "What Americans Spent in 2017," 17 Dec 2017. See 247wallst.com/special-report/2017/12/22/what-americans-spent-in-2017/

5   Robert C. Paehlke, *Democracy's Dilemma: Environment, Social Equity, and the Global Economy.* MIT Press, 2003.

6   Eric Olin Wright and Joel Rogers, *American Society: How It Really Works.* Norton, 2015: 363.

7   Brian Wingfield and Miriam Marcus, "America's Greenest States." *Forbes,* 17 Oct 2007."

8   Wingfield and Marcus, "America's Greenest States."

9   See Paehlke, *Democracy's Dilemma,* Chapter 1, opening paragraph, for an in-depth explanation of globalization.

and culture. Yet Robert C. Paehlke, in Democracy's Dilemma, showcases one of the most disturbing, though subtle, threats associated with globalization, which he calls "economism."[10] Paehlke defines this as the commercialization of everyday life, resulting in everything becoming a commodity—from what we wear to our cultural preferences. Everything we consume can be translated into an economic product created for financial gain. Advertising is central to perpetuating the mechanisms and values of consumer culture, convincing us that when we purchase a new car, the latest phone, or the latest styles in clothing we will not only be more satisfied consumers but happier individuals. The unfortunate downside of these manipulative marketing tactics is that consumers soon come to believe that last year's items are disposable and can be replaced. Once they are deemed no longer necessary, wanted, new, fashionable, or satisfactory for any reason, we discard the obsolete items into the trash and replace them with the newer versions, updates, alternatives, and options of the same use, in a continuous cycle.

The consequences of pursuing quantity over quality are not revealed in advertising. A commercial for the latest must-have electronic gadget is not juxtaposed with images of overfilled landfills; the trendy new clothing is not shown amidst smog-filled air; and efficient new household items (such as Teflon-coated cookware) are never shown with images of the congenital disabilities and cancer that result from polluted water.[11] Although these authentic images are not exposed in advertising due to strategic bypass, contemporary artists, including Charzewski, uncover the true stories behind false forms of advertising. Other artists who focus on social and environmental commentary in their practice include Ron English, who utilized "billboard hijacking"[12] to expose corporations that produce mass-consumed items and the real impacts of their products. Martin Basher, Josephine Meckseper, Gabriel Kuri, and Irina Korina are of the same philosophical mindset and thoroughly deconstruct controversial elements related to commerce. Basher and Meckseper use the physical construct of the commercial window display to underscore the role consumerism places in the concept of self within society, while Kuri and Korina compel viewers to reconsider their excessive spending, which is often used a way to circumvent the banality they sometimes associate with everyday life.

Jarod Charzewski's work allows people the opportunity to consider the lifespan of objects they purchase, as well as their relative importance. He challenges us to view consumer behaviors from a different perspective, stating, "We all buy things to live and function in society. Our economy depends on it. It must, however, be done responsibly. If we over purchase and consume,

---

[10] See Paehlke, *Democracy's Dilemma*, Chapter 1, p. 16, for an in-depth explanation of economism.

[11] According to a recent lawsuit, DuPont exposed hundreds of thousands of North Carolinians to water laden with toxic chemicals that have been linked to a wide range of diseases, public health, and environmental effects. The chemical GenX is used in its manufacturing process, and Nafion, a product which is a compound of Teflon and other fluoridated chemicals. Cohen Milstein, "Chemical Companies Accused of Poisoning Drinking Water with Known Toxins." Cohen Milstein, 24 Oct 2017, www.cohenmilstein. com/update/chemical-companies-accused-poisoning-drinking-water-known-toxins.

[12] Ron English is best known for "billboard hijacking," appropriating this mass-media platform for consumer messages to create his own subversive and political statements that were overlaid on these billboards. English utilizes these highly recognizable brands of mass-consumed items and juxtaposes them with political statements that expose the real impacts of these brands on society.

redemption is not as simple as donating or recycling the items. The problem is much, much bigger than that." This idea of responsible consumerism, or ethical consumerism, is characterized by favoring products that support altruism,[13] such as Starbucks encouraging people to bring in their own cups for a discount on coffee, or Tom's shoes that famously offers their "Buy One, Give One" initiative, or grocery stores encouraging people to bring in their own shopping bags to avoid using plastic bags. Artists such as Charzewski don't shame or guilt their viewers, but simply invite them to make simple changes that will lead them to become more mindful people when faced with a purchasing decision. The action of improving one thing a year, or other simple changes, brings us closer to a more sustainable future that, in the long term, is much more satisfying.

Art as an Agent for Change: Charzewski Compels Viewers To Reconsider Their Relationship with Objects

This connection between happiness and consumer behavior is compounded by the multitude of physical, emotional, and cultural reactions experienced when purchasing goods. Our compulsive and uncontrollable relationship with retail has led to an environmental crisis. It is overfilling our landfills, harming our environment, and creating disease in our citizens. In *Reclaimed Landscapes*, Charzewski explores this dilemma. Utilizing thousands of pounds of strategically folded and layered clothing, Charzewski presents his version of this fabricated and crowded reality. Mimicking compressed layers of soil and earth, the striations of bold color amongst seemingly endless textiles showcase America's cyclical obsession with purchasing and disposing of clothes, or more specifically, "fast fashion." Fast fashion is a term given to fashion retailers that quickly move their designs from the fashion debut to their stores, to capture current fashion trends.[14] This term also refers to companies that cheaply copy designs seen on the high-fashion/ couture runways and quickly feature these trendy items in their stores for a fraction of the price.[15] According to the Textile Council of Recycling, Americans create 25 billion pounds of textile waste annually, representing 5.2 percent of all the trash disposed of over the course of a year.[16] Another 3.8 billion tons of textiles are donated per year, but charities sell only about 20 percent of the textiles donated to them at their retail outlets.[17] This translates to the common misconception that, when the community donates clothes, all of them will go to those in need. In the Newsweek article "Fast Fashion Is Creating an Environmental Crisis," Pietra Rivoli, a professor of economics at Georgetown University, states, "People like to feel like they are doing something good, and the problem they

---

[13] See the Ethical Consumer's website for more information on the definition of an ethical consumer and how you can get involved in making businesses more sustainable through consumer pressure. https://www.ethicalconsumer.org/about-us/our-mission

[14] See Elizabeth Cline, Overdressed: The Shockingly High Cost of Cheap Fashion (Penguin, 2013), for an in-depth explanation of fast fashion.

[15] See Cline, Overdressed.

[16] See the Council for Textile Recycling's "The Facts About Textile Waste" infographic for more information. Also, see the 2010 United States Environmental Protection Agency, Municipal Solid Waste in the United States: 2009 Facts and Figures report (pages 36 and 57).

[17] From Alden Wicker, "Fast Fashion is Creating an Environmental Crisis," Newsweek, 1 Sep 2016, https://www.newsweek.com/2016/09/09/old-clothes-fashion-waste-crisis-494824.html.

run into in a country such as the U.S. is that we don't have people who need [clothes] on the scale at which we are producing." This means that in addition to textile-production waste, 760 million pounds of clothing end up in our landfills or sold to overseas buyers.

If someone donates clothes to Goodwill, a well-known retailer of donated items, and they do not sell in the retail store, Goodwill sends them to their outlets, but they can't sell everything. Michael Meyer, vice president of donated goods retail and marketing for Goodwill Industries International, states, "When it doesn't sell in the store, or online, or outlets, we have to do something with it."

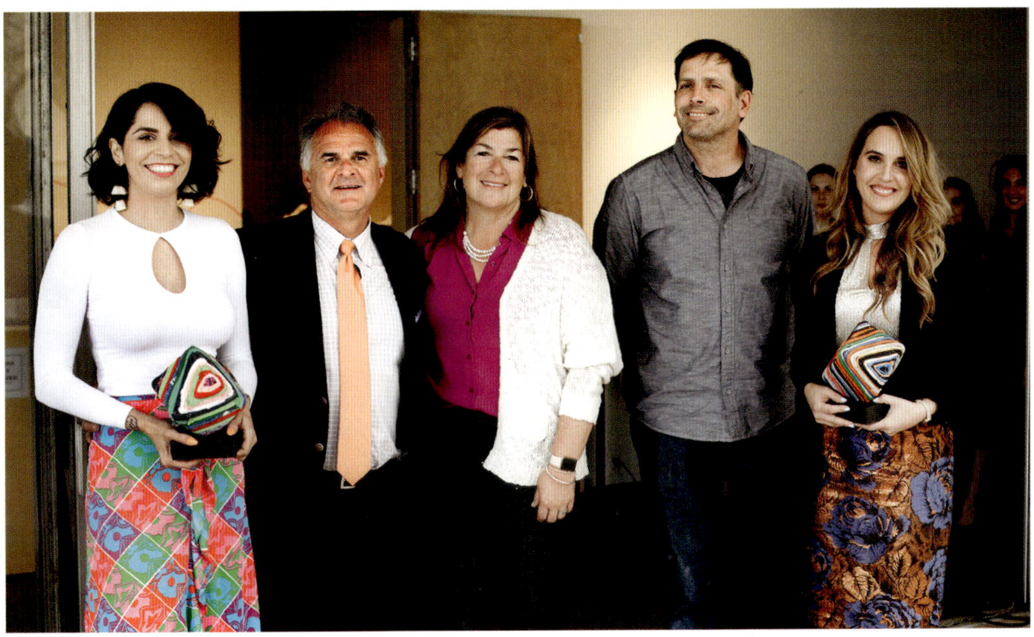

From left to right: Curator, Danielle Clark, *California State University, Fullerton's President* Framroze Virjee *with wife* Julie Virjee, *Artist* Jarod Charzewski, *and Curator,* Jennifer Minasian.

The result is that Goodwill—and others such as the Salvation Army and American Red Cross—must "bale up" the unwanted clothing into cubes weighing 2,000 pounds each and sell them to textile recyclers across the globe. Charzewski's installation for this exhibition utilized three of the these one-ton bundles of unsellable and unusable textiles that the Goodwill of Orange County generously donated to the project. Finding another use for this unusable material, Charzewski states that "What was unique about this installation was the inspiration behind the color scheme. I wanted the piece to emulate the distant mountains seen from the Fullerton campus. The many different greys, browns and greens on these hillsides and mountain tops is where the palette of colors originated." The idea of recreating a natural landscape using man-made items is not new for this artist. The first iteration of this installation was exhibited in 2008 at the Halsey Institute for

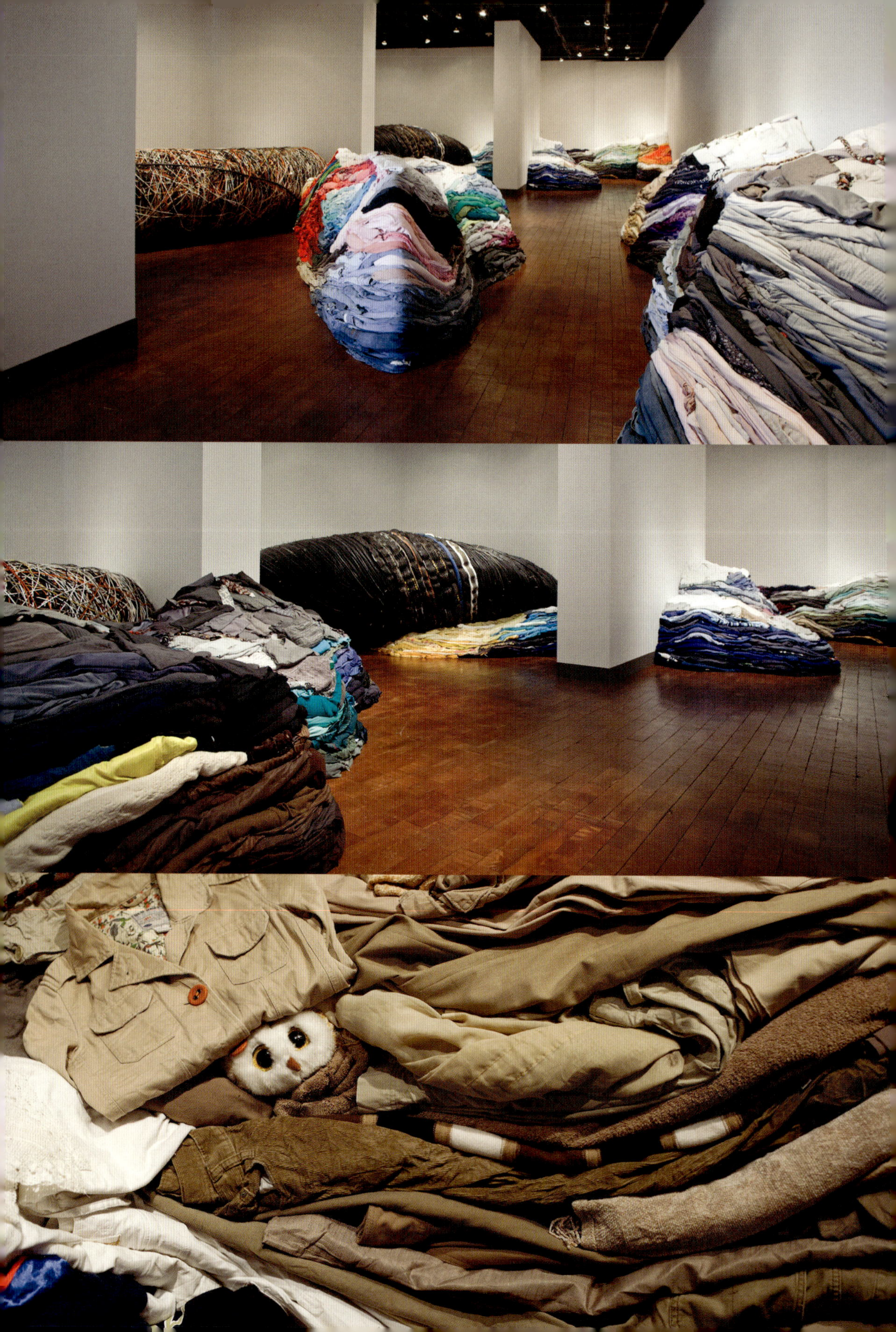

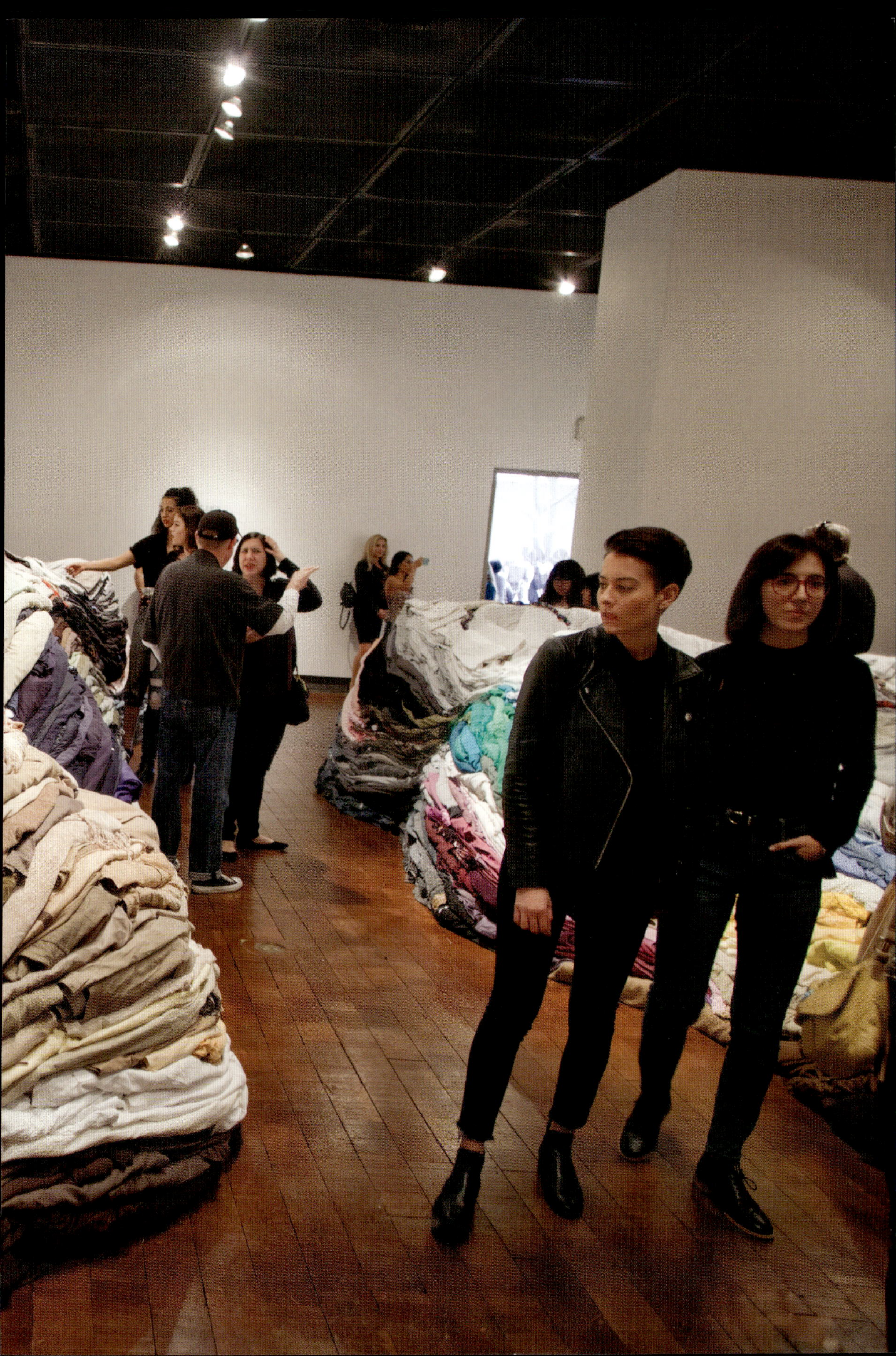

Contemporary Art in Charleston, South Carolina, where his utilization of donated materials from Goodwill began *(Figure 1)*.

Charzewski goes beyond our relationship with clothing, as the installation is composed of other commonly discarded and forgotten materials. One of the sculptures in the exhibition utilized electronic waste, also donated by the Goodwill in Orange County. The United States produces more e-waste annually than any other country, with 11.7 million tons of e-waste ending up in our landfills.[18] For this exhibition, 4,000 pounds of e-waste in the form of wires, cords, cables, chargers, and extensions cables were made into a large sculptural work. Charzewski first utilized e-waste as material in 2015 at his DuPont Hall Art Gallery (University of Mary Washington, Fredericksburg, VA) exhibition, where a large sculpture snaked through the space *(Figure 2)*. In his installation here at CSUF Begovich Gallery, Charzewski used e-waste to create an overwhelming, seemingly immovable mass that rose from the floor to emulate conditions that exist in our landfills today.

Another poignant installation in this exhibition was the use of 500 pounds of discarded bicycle tires and tubes, collected from Jax Bicycle Centers across Orange County. These materials were configured into a structure similar to the one Charzewski built in his 2016 *Soil* work *(Figure 3)*.

Each year, California drivers alone generate more than 40 million used automobile tires, many of which end up in landfills.[19] Although California started a recycling initiative for rubber in the early 2000s, a good portion of the state's excess tires are being sold to Australia, China, and Vietnam, where coal prices have increased and the tires are burned in factory furnaces as a cheaper option for fuel.[20] The practice of using such alternative fuel sources negatively affects our planet's air quality.[21] To illustrate the impact of this malpractice, Charzewski built a monumental structure with the bike tires that resembled a tidal wave ready to crash down on the viewer. Within this exhibition, Charzewski's three separate structures filled the gallery's spaces and collided with each other in a massive singular installation, creating a mass of byproducts to emphasize the harsh realities of our landfills, a powerful metaphor signifying our problematic relationship with consumerism. But the story does not end here. It continues with those of us who are ready for a change.

Charzewski Leading Us to a Sustainable Future

Charzewski's installation for *Reclaimed Landscapes* exemplifies our rampant consumption patterns and wasteful practices. Any changes to the status quo will require endorsement from many individuals, groups, and governments on a global scale. The damage committed thus far is irreparable and its impact will be far reaching for decades to come. At its core, change requires that we unite toward the common goal of sustainable living. Reaching this goal will depend

---

[18] Rick LeBlanc, "Here Is a Look at E-Waste Recycling Facts and Figures," *The Balance Small Business*, 15 March 2018. www.thebalancesmb.com/e-waste-recycling-facts-and-figures-2878189.

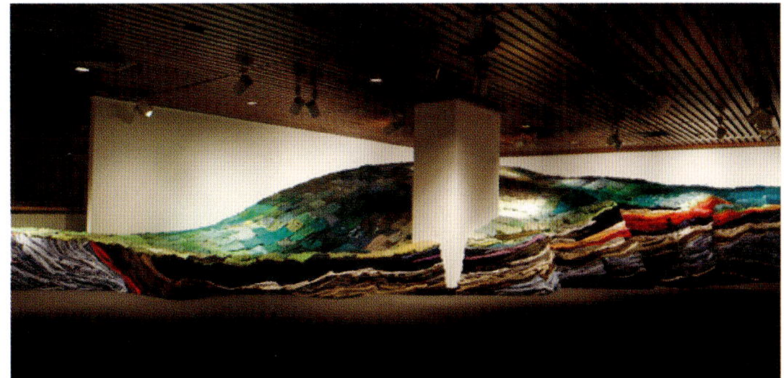

Figure 1

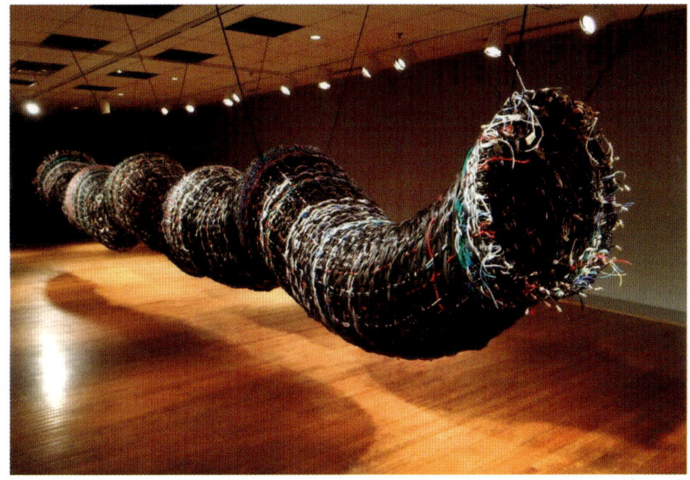

Figure 2

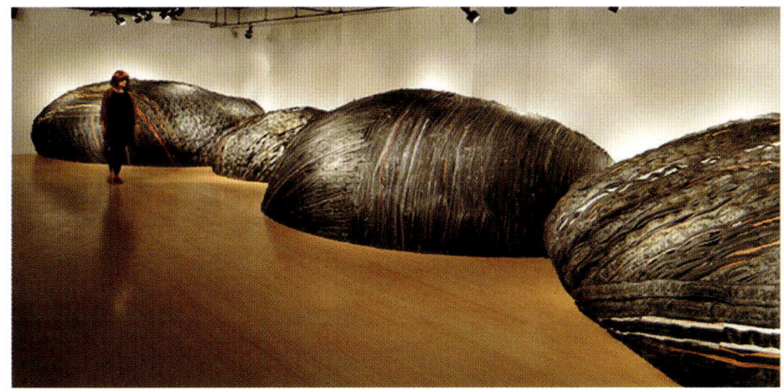

Figure 3

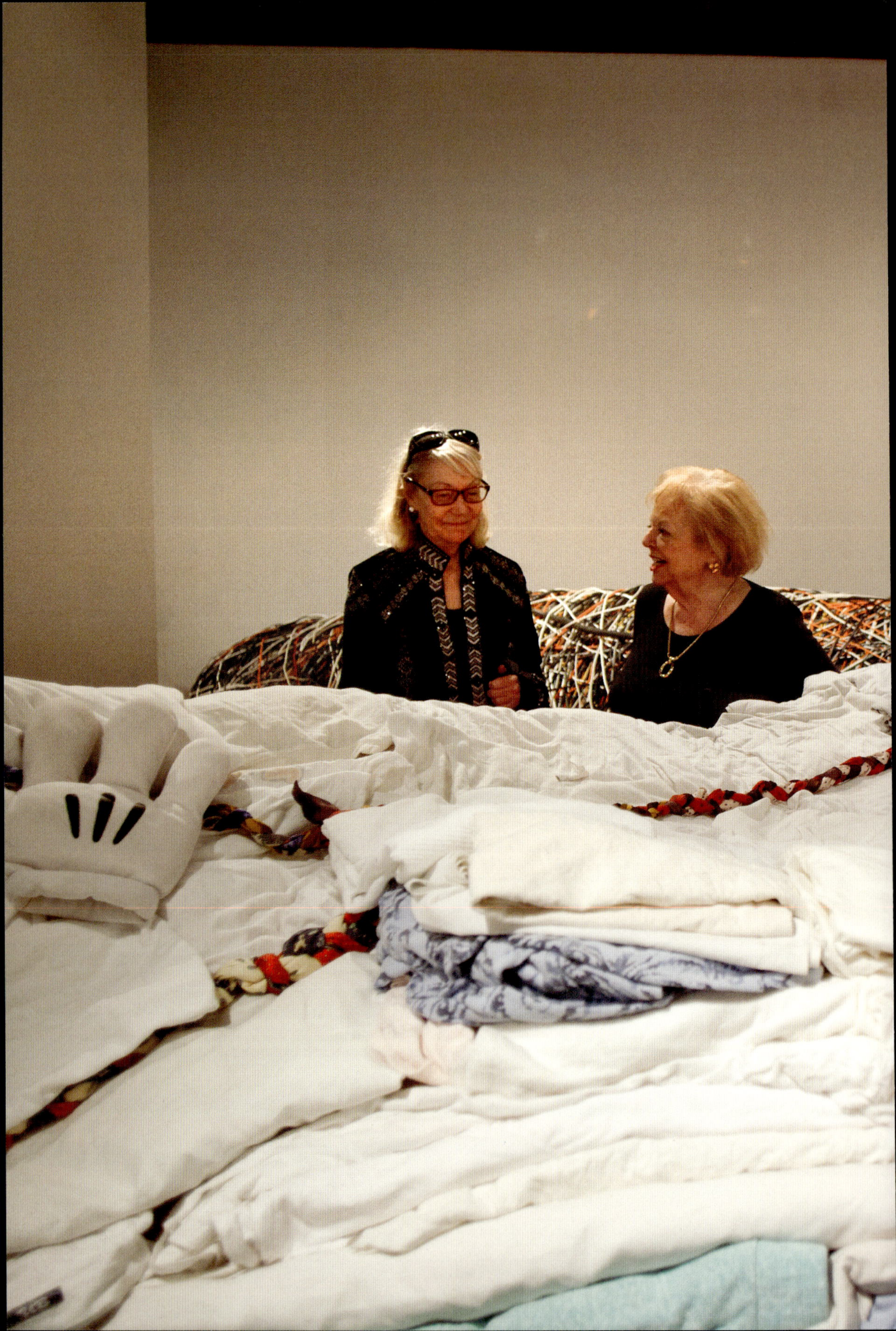

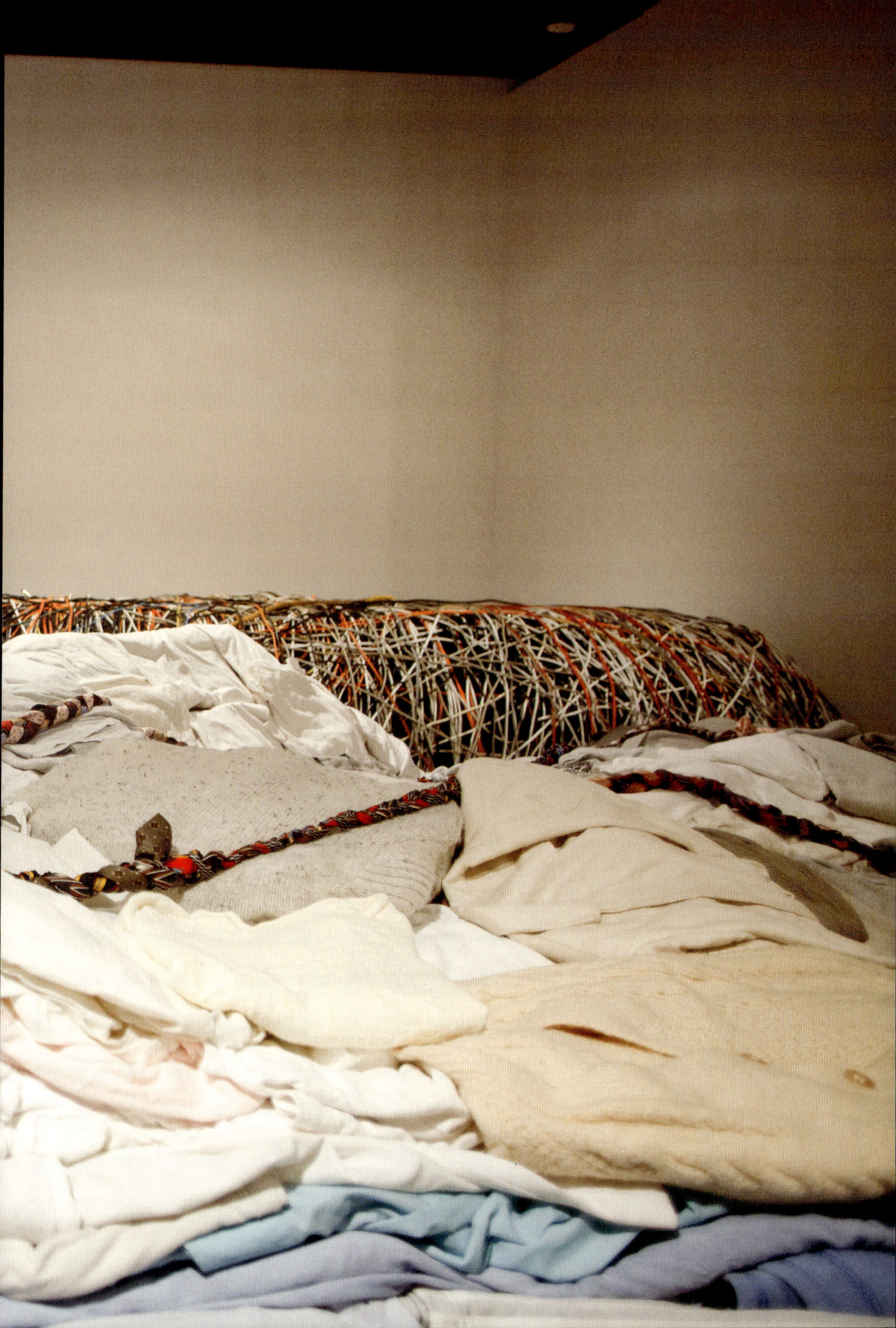

on our ability to connect with one another in ways that are mutually satisfying and personally comforting. A life-affirming community cooperation will be essential to this effort, which can become a cocreative human experience. The way we treat our land defines how we will progress in the future. The tenets of sustainable practice seek not just to protect our environment, but also encourage us to interact with the world around us.

Charzewski's life's work champions the idea that we can find solutions for ensuring a sustainable future by working together. When he was working with the community during the installation of *Reclaimed Landscapes*, he pointed out, "The same spirit of camaraderie was present in this exhibit as in other installs that required volunteers. It has become one of the most rewarding parts of this kind of work. It's fascinating to me to hear what the students have to say when they see the amount of clothing the piece demands. While they are organizing the clothes as well, the most interesting banter of jokes and memories emerges from the group. I like to just listen and take it in. One reason the piece is so appreciated is that people connect through clothing." California State University, Fullerton, had 100 volunteers who provided 500 volunteer hours to help install the entire exhibition. United by a shared goal, streams of individual action can result in a collective action that can usher in change for the environment.

Charzewski's art serves as both a warning and a testament, commenting on how alternative practices and products could radically improve our landscape. His separate structures came together to form a singular installation, a symbol of how separate entities can culminate together to produce something powerful and bring about social change. Many people came together to bring this exhibition to fruition, and I would like to thank everyone who worked on this project, including my cocurator, Danielle Clark. This exhibition itself and the conversations created by the themes it explored can shift the behaviors that contribute to the harsh realities of consumerism to an enlightened understanding of how to buy less, use less, and waste less. Charzewski's upcycled processes using discarded materials bring awareness to our consumer behaviors, advocating for more renewable ways of living and more mindful purchasing practices.

---

[19] From Zach St. George, "California's Old Tires Cross the Ocean and Come Back as Smog."
http://www.takepart.com/feature/2016/02/12/tire-recycling-california-smog

[20] From St. George.

[21] "Numerous studies have shown that pollution from China makes it across the Pacific Ocean, fouling California air. A 2015 study by NASA's Jet Propulsion Laboratory, published in Nature Geoscience, found that although the Western United States greatly reduced its pollutant emissions between 2005 and 2010, air quality remained the same because of a simultaneous increase in emissions in China." See St. George.

Works Cited

"Advancing Sustainable Materials Management: 2014 Fact Sheet." Assessing Trends in Material Generation, Recycling, Composting, Combustion with Energy Recovery and Landfilling in the United States. Environmental Protection Agency, 2016, https://www.epa.gov/sites/production/files/2016-11/documents/2014_smmfactsheet_508.pdf.

Cline, Elizabeth L. Overdressed: The Shockingly High Cost of Cheap Fashion. Portfolio/Penguin, 2013.

Comen, Evan. "What Americans Spent in 2017." 247wallst.com, 22 Dec 2017, 247wallst.com/special-report/2017/12/22/what-americans-spent-in-2017/.

Council for Textile Recycling. "The Facts About Textile Waste." Council for Textile Recycling, 2018, weardonaterecycle.org/about/issue.html.

"Ethical Consumerism." Wikipedia, Wikimedia Foundation, 7 Aug 2018, en.wikipedia.org/wiki/Ethical_consumerism.

"Fast Fashion." Wikipedia, Wikimedia Foundation, 21 Sep 2018, en.wikipedia.org/wiki/Fast_fashion.

George, Zach, California's Old Tires Cross the Ocean and Come Back as Smog, http://www.takepart.com/feature/2016/02/12/tire-recycling-california-smog

"Household final consumption expenditure (current US$) – Data," https://data.worldbank.org/indicator/NE.CON.PRVT.CD?year_high_desc=true

Laporte, John. "Topic: Municipal Solid Waste in the United States." Statista, 2018, www.statista.com/topics/2707/municipal-solid-waste-in-the-united-states/.

LeBlanc, Rick. "Here Is a Look at E-Waste Recycling Facts and Figures." The Balance Small Business, 15 Mar 2018, www.thebalancesmb.com/e-waste-recycling-facts-and-figures-2878189.

Milstein, Cohen. "Chemical Companies Accused of Poisoning Drinking Water with Known Toxins." Cohen Milstein, 24 Oct 2017, www.cohenmilstein.com/update/chemical-companies-accused-poisoning-drinking-water-known-toxins.

"Our Mission." Ethical Consumer, 3 Jun 2018, www.ethicalconsumer.org/about-us/our-mission.

Paehlke, Robert C. Democracy's Dilemma: Environment, Social Equity, and the Global Economy. MIT Press, 2003.

"The State of Consumption Today." State of the World 2011: Innovations that Nourish the Planet. Worldwatch Institute, 2011, www.worldwatch.org/node/810.

United States Environmental Protection Agency. Municipal Solid Waste in the United States: 2009 Facts and Figures. Washington DC, Office of Solid Waste, December 2010, Print. EPA530-R-10-012.

Wicker, Alden. "Fast Fashion Is Creating an Environmental Crisis." Newsweek, 1 Sep 2016, https://www.newsweek.com/2016/09/09/old-clothes-fashion-waste-crisis-494824.html.

Wingfield, Brian, and Miriam Marcus. "America's Greenest States." Forbes, Forbes Magazine, 19 Jul 2012, www.forbes.com/2007/10/16/environment-energy-vermont-biz-beltway-cx_bw_mm_1017greenstates.html#468d576c119d.

Wright, Erik Olin, and Joel Rogers. American Society: How It Really Works. Norton, 2015.

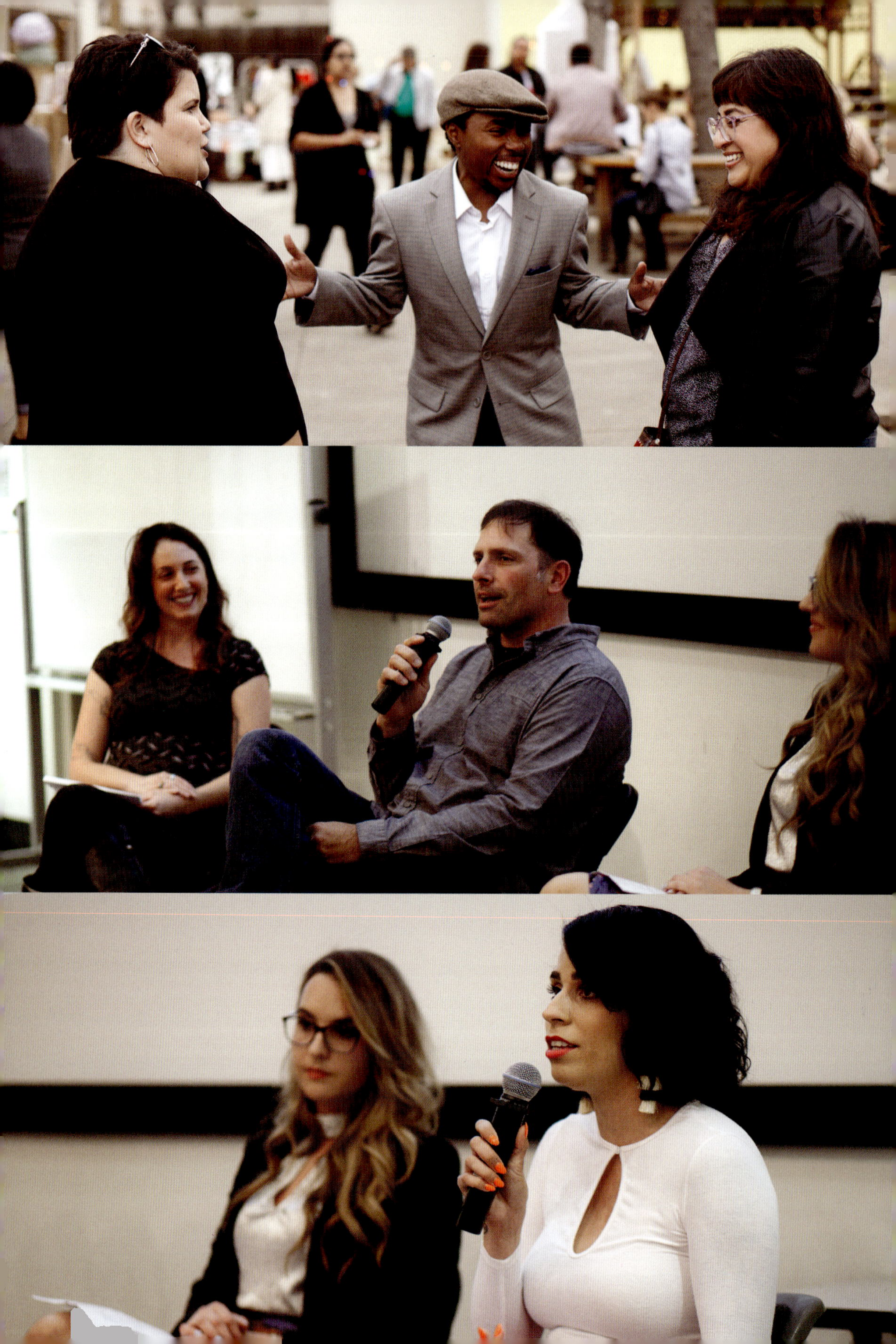

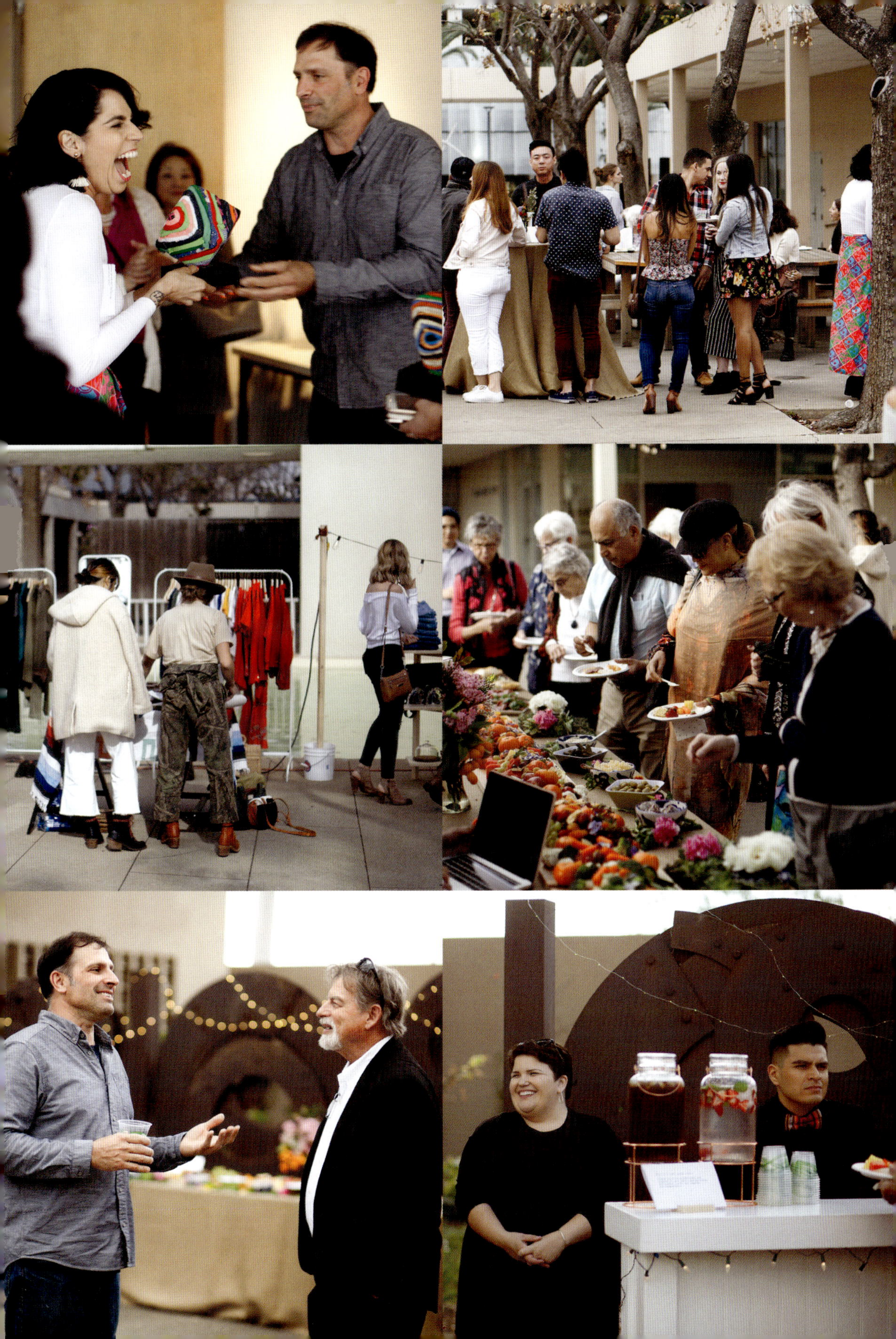

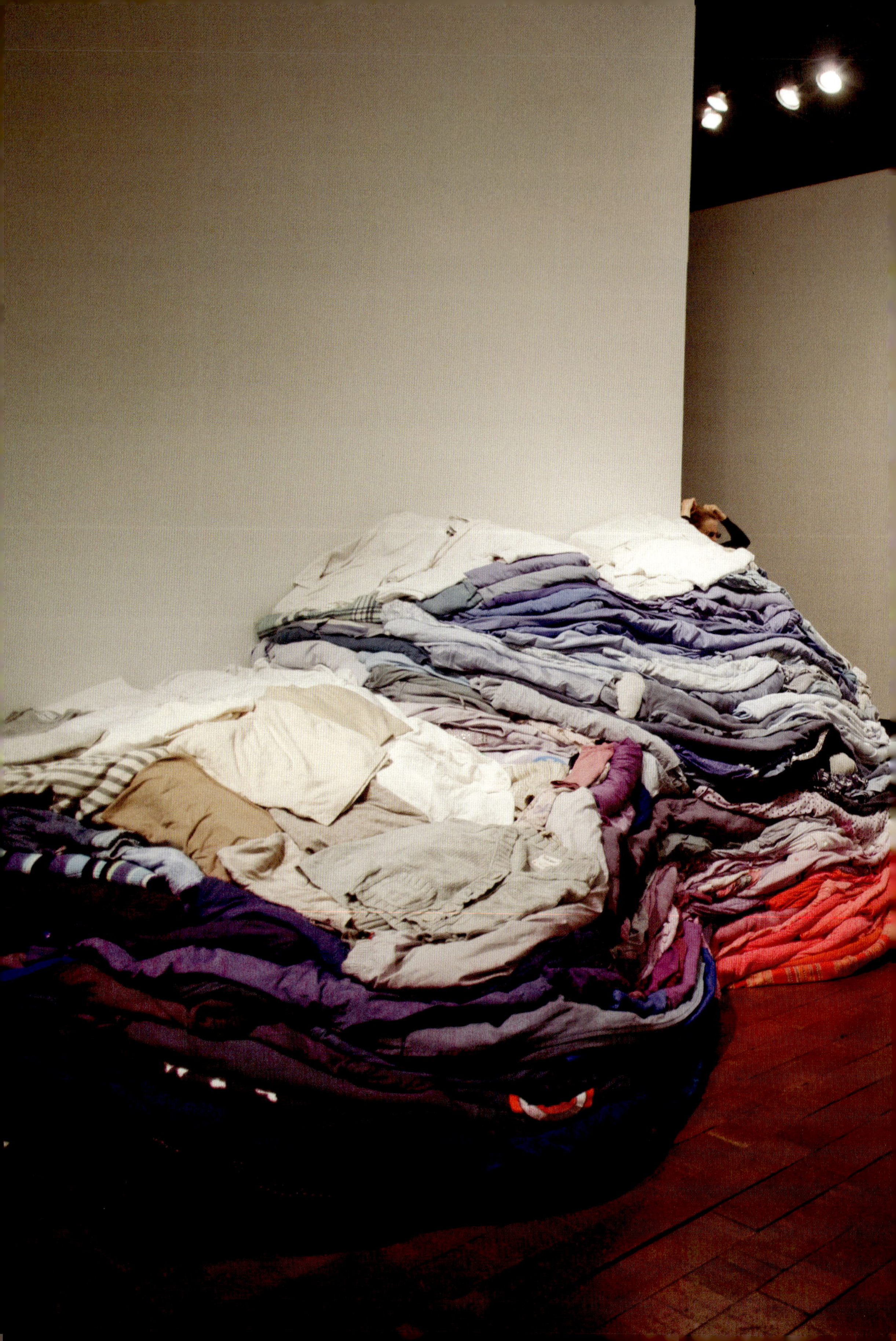

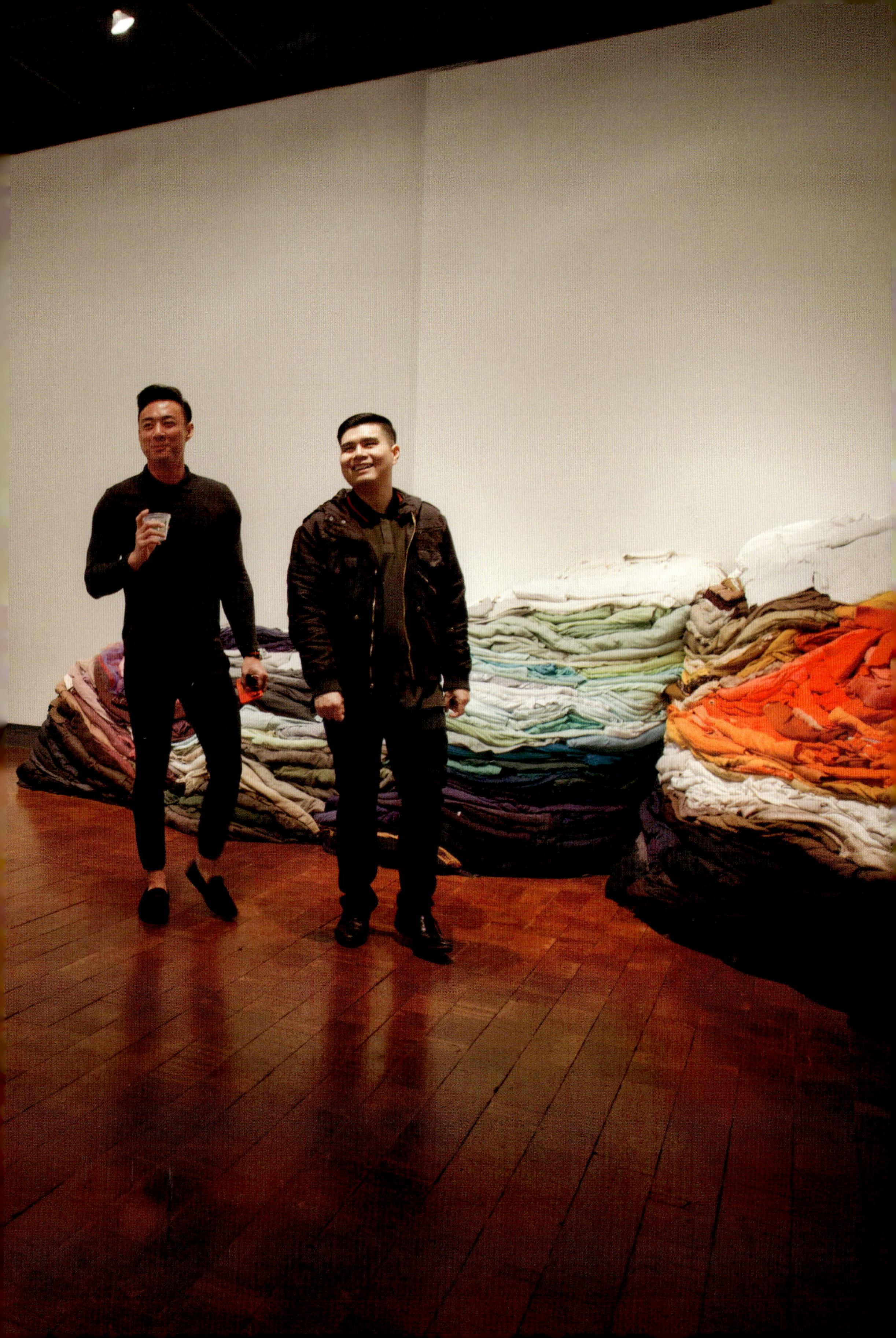

Jarod Charzewski's work engages with two categories unique to human societies: textiles and trash. He joins a list of artists who have chosen to employ one or the other in order to speak to issues of sustainability. For example, British climate physicist Ellie Highwood recently made headlines for crocheting striped "climate change blankets" as "a creative way to visualise trends in global mean temperature" *(n.p.)*. Highwood notes that her choice of textile product is symbolic in and of itself, insofar as "global warming is often explained as greenhouse gases acting like a blanket, trapping infrared radiation and keeping the Earth warm" *(n.p.).*[1] Meanwhile, other artists use trash as a medium—as seen, for example, in the 2010 documentary film *Waste Land*, which follows Brazilian artist Vik Muniz and a group of pickers from the world's largest landfill as they put their gleanings on display. Charzewski's *Reclaimed Landscapes* chimes with the aforementioned artistic developments but insists that we consider textiles and trash together, as uniquely connected.

And indeed, if textiles and trash are unique to human societies, stretching back to time immemorial, Charzewski's work intervenes in a more recent, and urgent, development: textiles, particularly clothing, have *become trash*, and at an extremely alarming rate. As I describe in more detail below, clothing production and consumption have skyrocketed in recent decades, requiring the expenditure of massive amounts of fossil fuels and water, while the usage cycles for clothing have contracted, leading to the mass disposal of garments in landfills. Charzewski's work thus speaks to the

---

[1] While Highwood's design consists of colored stripes, other makers prefer hexagonal patterns. See, for example, https://makezine.com/2017/10/18/crochet-climate-change-data-visualization-blanket/

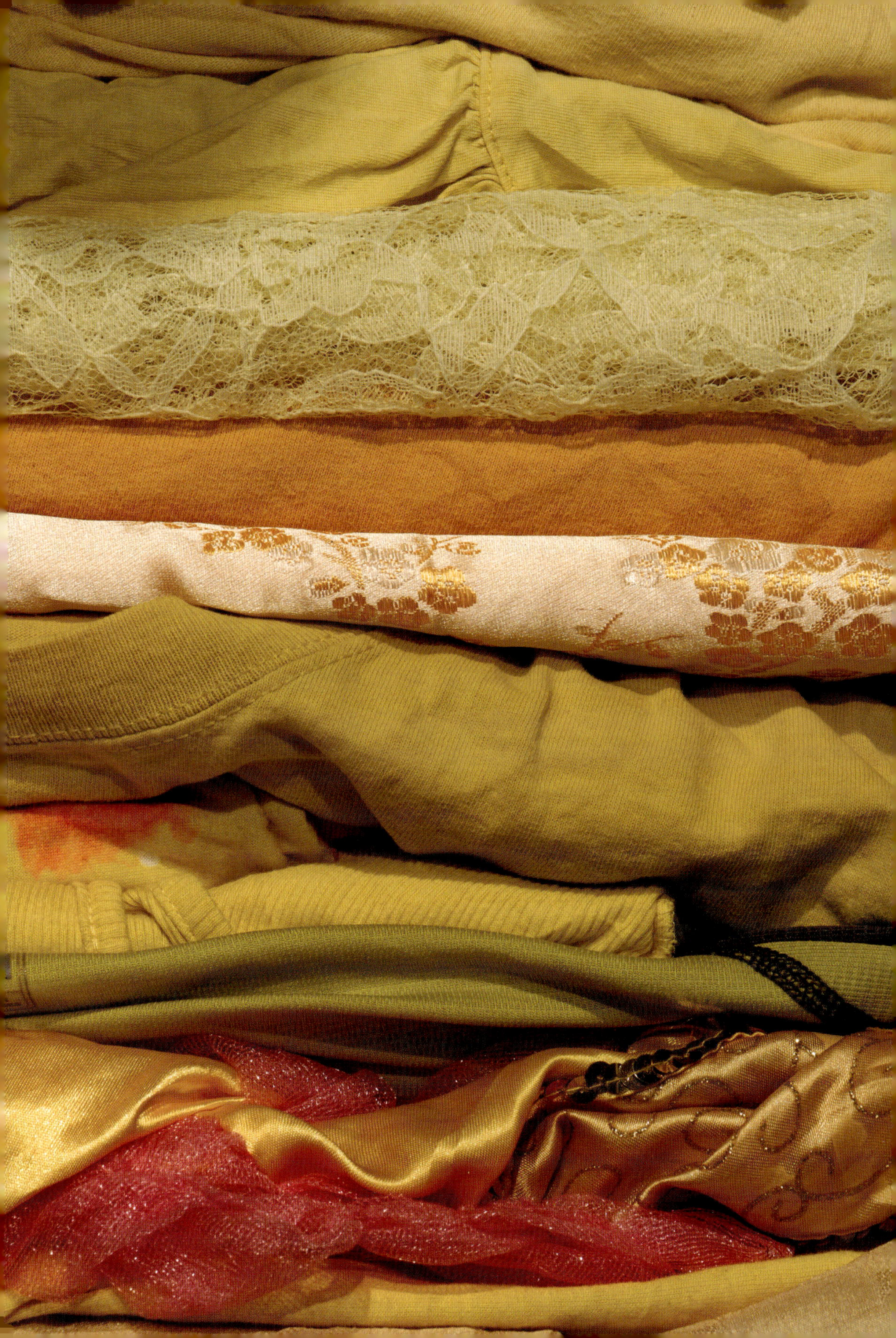

cultural truism that "[t]rash is considered unsightly. And so we are quick to conceal our trash" *(Mauch 5)*. And yet, as environmental historian Christof Mauch argues, "[w]aste…never disappears completely. What matters is how and where it reappears" *(6)*. While Mauch has negative reappearances in mind—for example, how the U.S. exports its electronic waste to developing nations—we might take his point a slightly different way: Charzewski's art makes specific types of trash reappear in the public consciousness.

In these senses, we must identify Charzewski as an artist of the Anthropocene: one who responds to a new era in which the human appetite for resources has changed the planet irrevocably, such that we have become part of the geological record. As journalist Andrew Revkin puts it, we have become "such a potent environmental influence that a signature of our doings…will be measurable in layered rock for millions of years to come" *(n.p.)*. I propose that we see the layers of clothing in *Reclaimed Landscapes* as an echo of this Anthropocene insight. But we must also note one major critique of the Anthropocene concept: it lumps all of humanity into one group, thereby invisibilizing social inequalities; it suggests only that "humans" in general are to blame for crises such as climate change, while ignoring the fact that the Global South consumes vastly fewer resources—from fossil fuels to, of course, clothing—than the Global North. Looking at Charzewski's work, then, necessarily means visualizing sustainability from two social vantage points: consumption and production. In what follows, I attempt to model this visualization.

Consuming Fast Fashion

The rate of textile production, especially that of clothing, has rapidly increased since World War II—perhaps not coincidentally, one of the dates proposed by scholars as the start of the Anthropocene. In her acclaimed book, *Overdressed: The Shockingly High Cost of High Fashion*, U.S. journalist Elizabeth Cline notes that world fiber use leapt from a total of 10 million tons in 1950 to 82 million tons by 2012 *(125)*. This new wave of clothing production brings with it a steep environmental toll, from the water used to make a given T-shirt or pair of jeans to the fuel spent to ship it to stores to the energy used to dry it in a home dryer. One Swedish analyst found that clothing purchases in her country "produce the fourth largest share of all carbon emissions for the country—after transportation, food, and housing" *(Hurst)*. But not only do we in the Global North buy exponentially more clothing than ever before, we also cast it off at higher rates. As Cline reports, "[e]very year, Americans throw away 12.7 million tons, or 68 pounds of textiles per person"; while an estimated "1.6 million tons of this waste could be recycled or reused," that still leaves many millions left over *(122)*. If these tons don't wind up in landfills, they're incinerated or shipped to developing nations—thus furthering their global footprint and exacerbating the "out of sight, out of mind" mentality.

One could argue that "fast fashion" consumption is largely rooted in the social realm—driven by a desire to always have new clothes or to look on-trend, or even by the social aspects of the act of shopping itself. But if its causes are social, it also has social solutions. One of these is the contemporary concept of the clothing swap. Whether designed as a party amongst friends or as a larger community event advertised through means such as social media, clothing swaps aim to make recycling fun and friendly. One citywide clothing swap, advertised on Meetup.com, exhorts followers to "swap instead of shop" and promises food and drink at every gathering (*"Berlin Clothing Swap"*). And in May 2017, students at Fullerton College organized a clothing swap with a more explicitly politicized message: "to demonstrate the power of community in subverting the exploitation central to the 'fast-fashion' industry, we call on the students of FCC to participate in a free clothes-swap!" The Facebook event description also promised, "ALL SIZES & GENDERS WELCOME!"

Producing Fast Fashion

The message of the Fullerton College event alludes to the other element of social sustainability when it comes to the problems with fast fashion: production. Wealthy countries like the U.S. now outsource 97% of their garment production to developing countries, according to the 2015 fast fashion documentary *The True Cost*. The average price tag on such garments has dropped but, as the documentary explains, the "true cost" can be found in the low wages and lack of labor protections for workers in those countries. Deadly fires, building collapses, and human trafficking are just some of the horrors associated with the industry. In 2013, for example, 1,127 people died in Bangladesh when a garment factory caved in *(Yardley)*. Meanwhile, just down the road in Los Angeles, the Garment Workers Center recently reported that that 85% of garment factories in the city had committed wage violations *("Drop That Sweatshop Pledge")*.

Thus, "sustainability" in the fashion industry, understood from a social justice standpoint, would mean greater protection for workers—including safe working conditions, fair wages, whistleblower protection, affordable childcare, and other good practices. It would also mean greater visibility— for, again, it's not just the waste of fast fashion that we've invisibilized, it's also the humans who make it in the first place. As U.S. journalist Kelsey Timmerman puts it in his best-selling long-form investigation, *Where Am I Wearing? A Global Tour to the Countries, Factories, and People That Make Our Clothes*, "[a]s far as most consumers are concerned, clothes come from the store. Consumers don't see the chain of transportation and manufacturing that comes before they take [an item of clothing] off the rack" *(3)*. In an effort to combat that invisibilization, *Where Am I Wearing?* zeroes in on a handful of individual garment workers in Bangladesh, Cambodia, and China.

We must note, of course, that humans, both consumers and producers, are absent from *Reclaimed Landscapes*. Indeed, the human presence that comes to mind for most viewers is likely that of the artist, as we ponder the vision and labor required to reshape these cheaply—possibly unjustly—made, castoff materials into something well designed, beautiful, and (relatively) lasting. But perhaps therein we recognize the distinction between their first life and this one. And perhaps, in the irony inherent in that transformation, we recognize the long-lasting tolls, both social and environmental, of supposedly fast fashion.

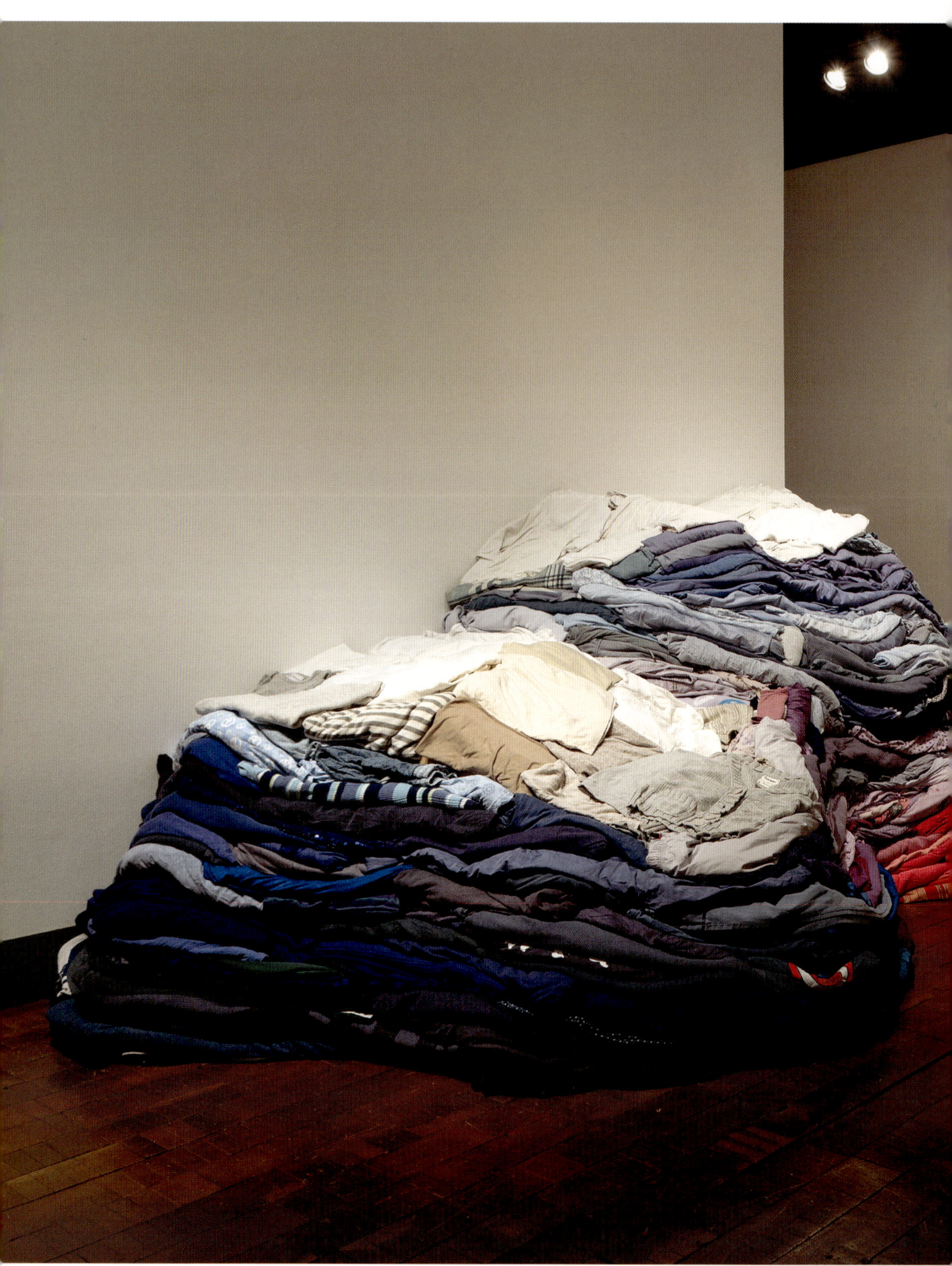

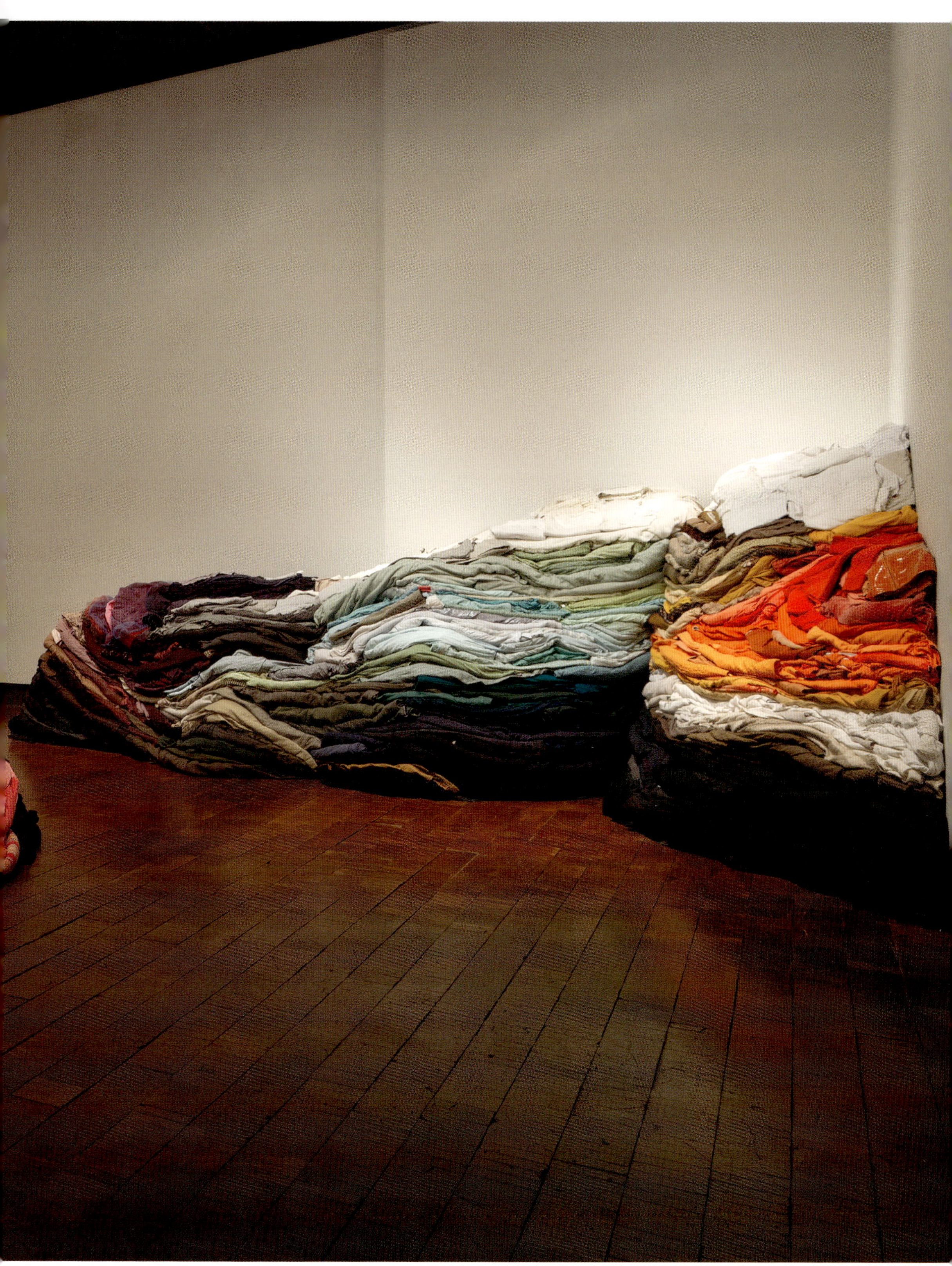

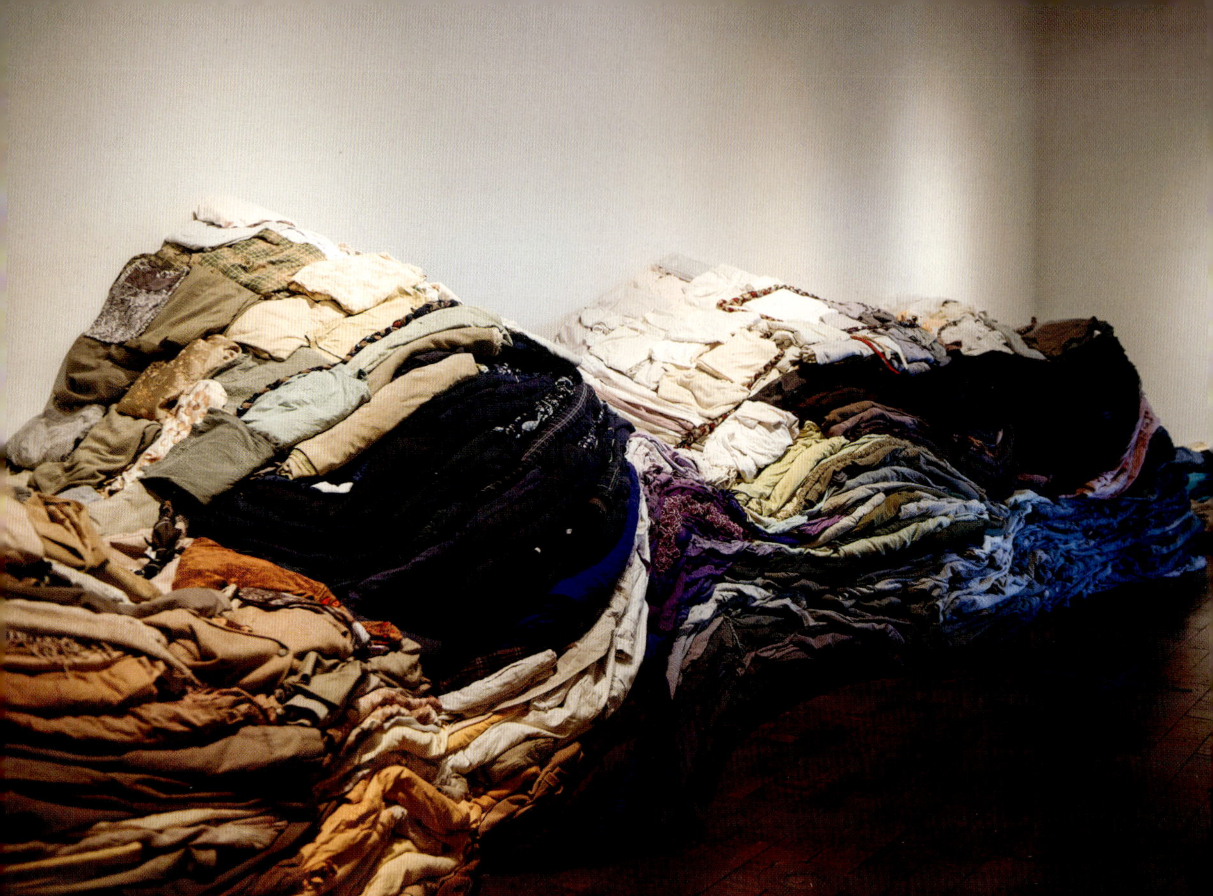

Works Cited

"Berlin Clothing Swap." Meetup.com. N.d. https://www.meetup.com/BerlinClothingSwap/

Cline, Elizabeth. Overdressed: The Shockingly High Cost of Cheap Fashion. New York: Penguin, 2012.

"Drop That Sweatshop Pledge." Garment Worker Center. 2017. http://garmentworkercenter.org/drop-that-sweatshop-pledge/

Highwood, Ellie. "#climatechangecrochet — The global warming blanket."
https://elliehighwood.com/2017/06/12/climatechangecrochet-the-global-warming-blanket/

Hurst, Nathan. "What's the Environmental Footprint of a T-Shirt?" 12 Apr 2017. Smithsonian Magazine.
https://www.smithsonianmag.com/innovation/whats-environmental-footprint-t-shirt-180962885/

Mauch, Christof. "Introduction." In "Out of Sight, Out of Mind: The Politics and Culture of Waste." RCC Perspectives: Transformations in Environment and Society 2016, no. 1.
http://www.environmentandsociety.org/perspectives/2016/1/out-sight-out-mind-politics-and-culture-waste

Revkin, Andrew C. "An Anthropocene Journey." 8 Nov 2016. Dot Earth: New York Times Blog.
https://dotearth.blogs.nytimes.com/2016/11/08/an-anthropocene-journey/?_r=0

The True Cost. Dir. Andrew Morgan. Los Angeles: Life is My Movie Entertainment, 2015.

Timmerman, Kelsey. Where Am I Wearing: A Global Tour to Countries, Factories, and People That Make Our Clothes. Wiley, 2012.

Waste Land. Documentary film featuring artist Vic Muniz. 99 min. 2010.

Yardley, Jim. "Report on Deadly Factory Collapse in Bangladesh Finds Widespread Blame." 22 May 2013. The New York Times.
http://www.nytimes.com/2013/05/23/world/asia/report-on-bangladesh-building-collapse-finds-widespread-blame.html

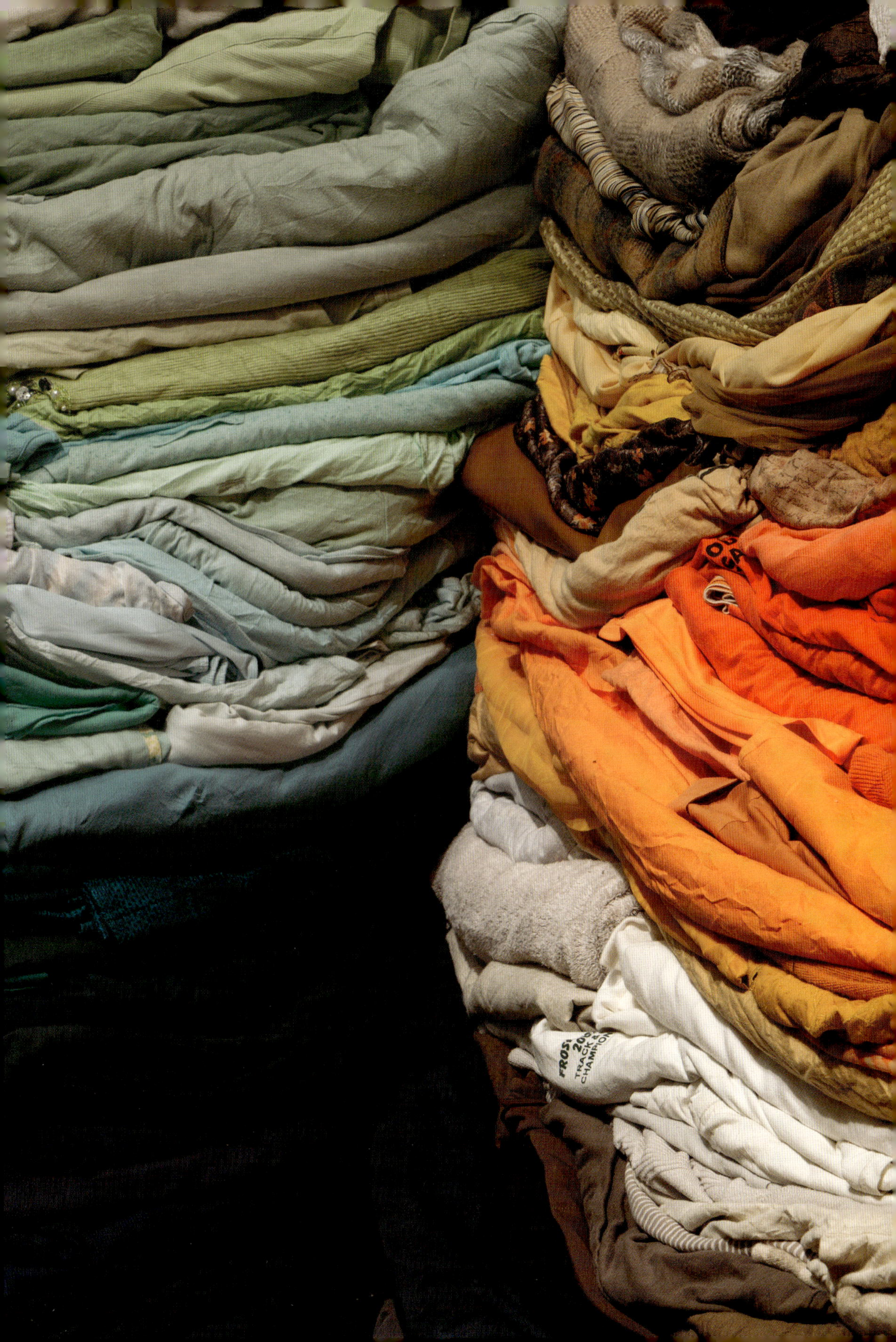

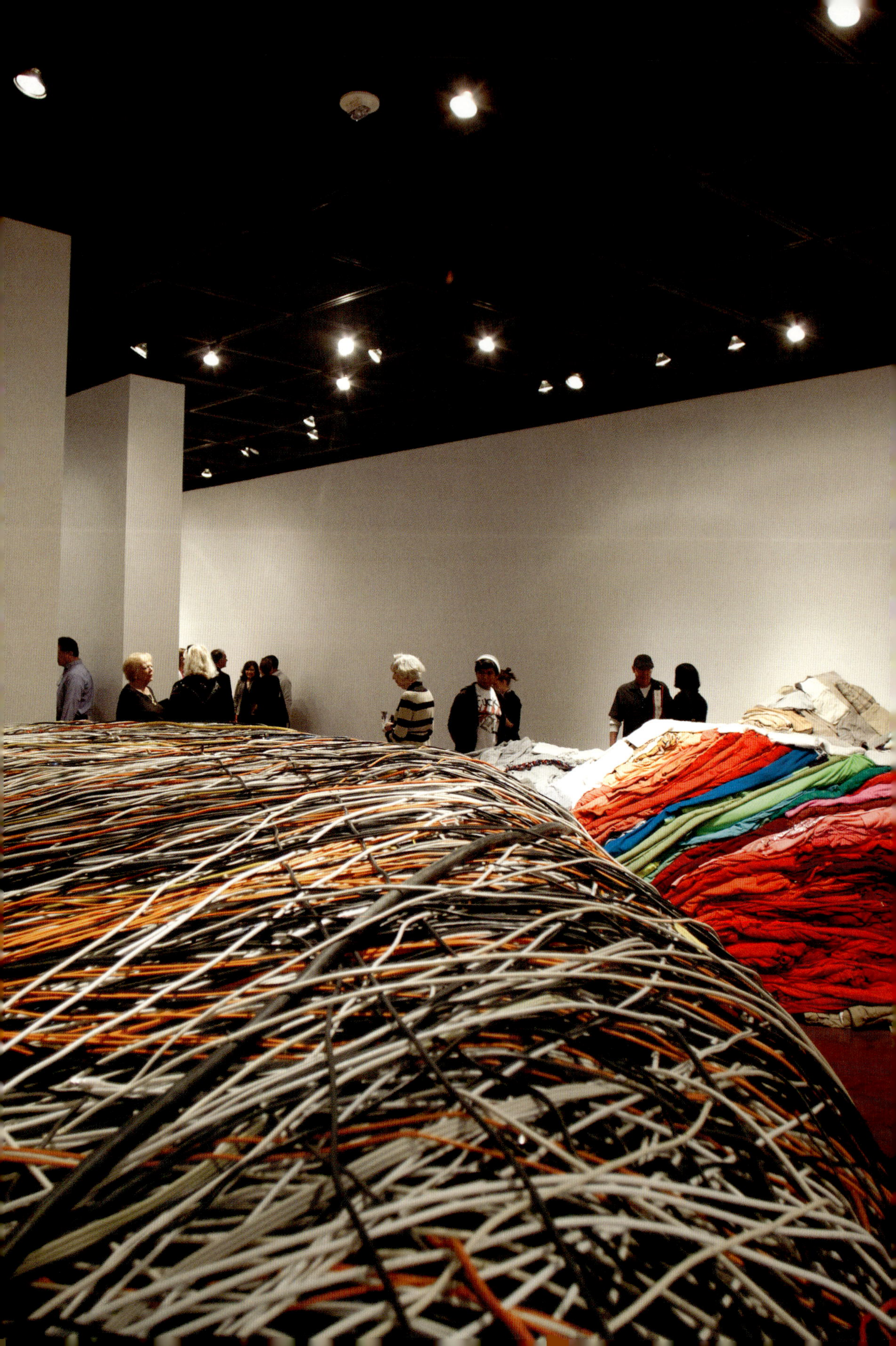

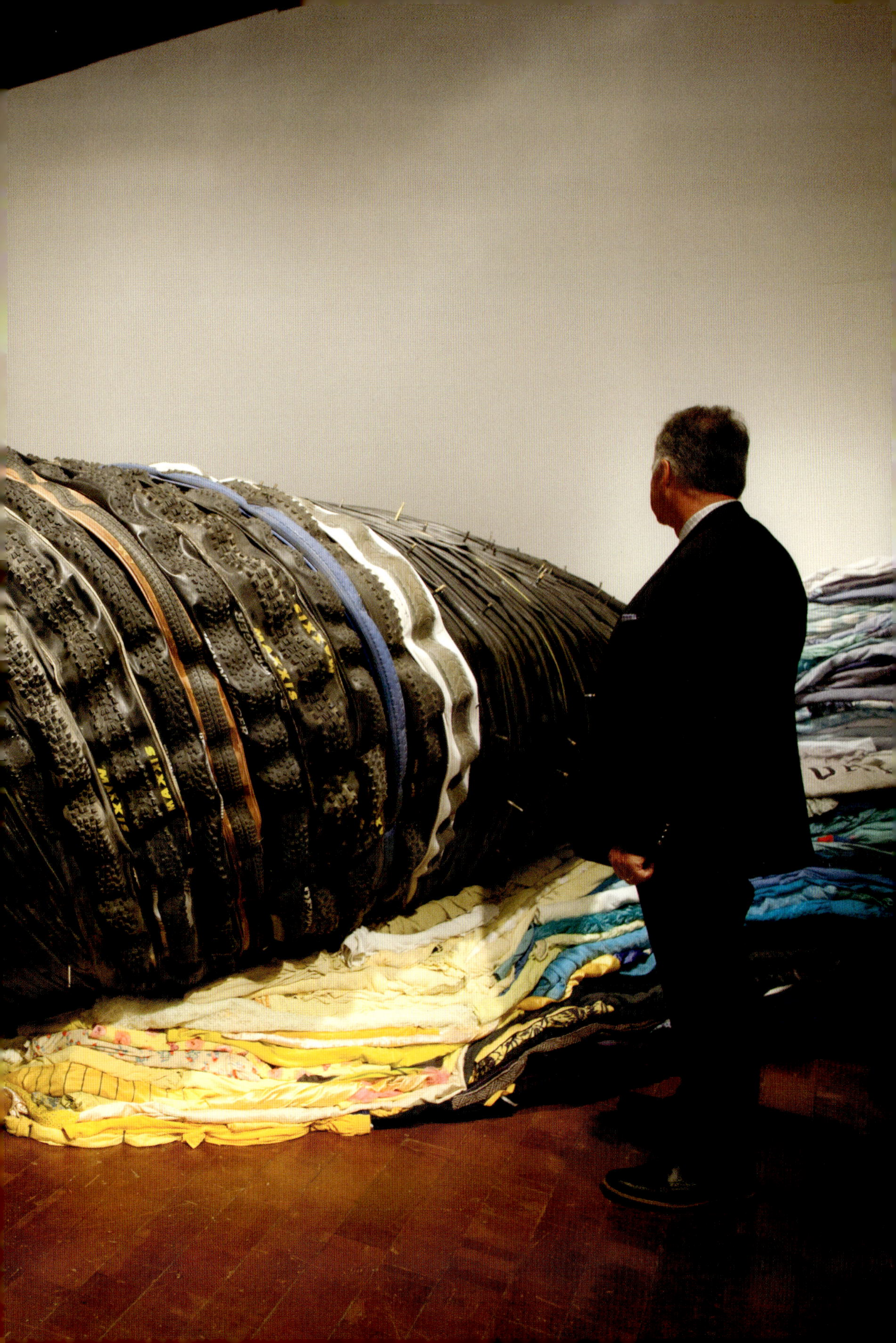

BRINGING SUSTAINABILITY INTO FOCUS

Dr. John Bock

The Development of the Sustainability Concept

Most people reading this catalogue probably believe "sustainability" is important and use the concept in their daily lives—in their purchasing decisions, water use, and energy consumption. Perhaps you eat a certain kind of diet and carefully separate trash and recycle and compost. Maybe your coffee is free-trade and your clothes are organic cotton and made by adequately paid workers in a safe environment. Yet, because "sustainability" is also a vague notion, it is sometimes challenging to understand the full complexity underlying the term. Most current interpretations of the word date from the UN Brundtland Commission Report *(1987)*, which reflected concerns of the international development community, and defined sustainable development as "meet[ing] the needs of the present without compromising the ability of future generations to meet their own needs." The Report was the culmination of three years of discussion, meetings, and conferences including hundreds of participants from around the world. Incorporating the perspectives from intellectual currents that had been building since the end of the Second World War, the members of the commission reached a definition of "sustainability" that is both holistic and a compromise.

Environmental awareness had been growing over concerns about air and water pollution; in the United States, what had been a countercultural movement of authors, naturalists, artists, and activists led to, among other things, the establishment of the Environmental Protection Agency in 1970 by President Richard Nixon. Economists recognized

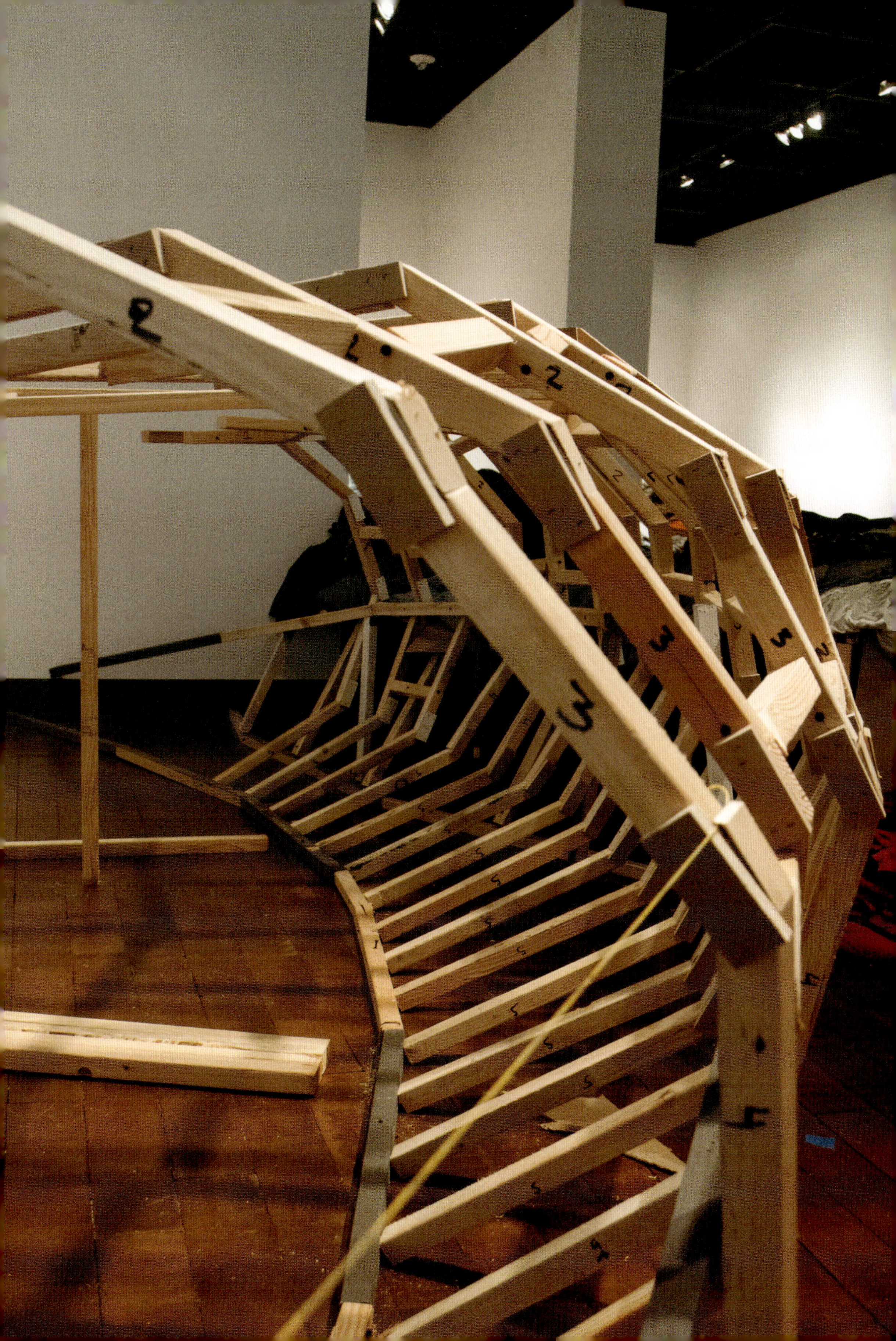

that economic and environmental impacts had an inextricable link. Other participants emphasized the differential effects of development due to poverty, gender, social class, and location, and the resulting definition was an attempt to represent the perceived balance between economic benefits and environmental costs. Perhaps the vagueness of this concept was an inevitable outcome of accommodating strong competing interests, but as a result, "sustainability" remains a miasma for many.

Representations of Sustainability

Understanding the historical context of the Brundtland Report provides essential insight to the ways in which "sustainability" is viewed today. Although the Report brought an expansive approach to the concept, the disparate schools of thought and approaches remained. As an oversimplification, these fall into two areas. The first is represented by The World Bank and other international financial institutions, who prioritized economic development over environmental protection. Economists working with The World Bank developed the Environmentally Sustainable Development (ESD) Triangle, which saw Economy, Ecology, and Equity as intrinsically linked *(Serageldin)*. The "Three E's" became known as the triple bottom line, meaning that rather than focusing on economic gains, development must achieve the maximum possible in all three areas; this level may result in lower economic gains than if environmental and social impacts were not addressed *(Serageldin, Goodland, and Daly)*. The corporate world has seized on this, emphasizing "sustainability" and "social responsibility," and many businesses have committed substantial resources to these areas *(Vitell)*. The payoffs to these investments lie not only in economic efficiency *(Hawken, Lovins, and Lovins)*, but also in consumer marketing, and corporations have regularly been accused of "greenwashing," or claiming to employ ostensibly sustainable practices that do not result in actual gains in sustainability *(Nyilasy, Gangadharbatla, and Paladino)*.

The second school of thought on sustainability is the domain of the global environmental movement, represented by organizations such as the International Union for the Conservation of Nature (IUCN). These groups emphasized development that conserved natural resources and biological diversity while improving the lives of those living with poverty. Building on the triangle approach, in 2005 the IUCN committed to a representation of sustainable development as three overlapping circles, which were labelled "Social," "Environmental," and "Economic." *(Adams)*. Sustainable development would occur in the area where the three overlapped. It is this formulation that is most prevalent today *(Figure 1)*, yet these concepts have proven difficult to operationalize, and there is an abundance of scholarly and other literature aimed at providing a concrete process *(Gibson, Hassan, and Tansey)*.

Perceptions of Sustainability

The vagueness in conceptualization and terminology means that the term "sustainability" still remains enigmatic. In general, there have been two disparate approaches to understanding perceptions of sustainability, one consisting of national and international surveys conducted by academic researchers and the other a variety of methods utilized by consumer marketing professionals. In the United States, a series of nationally representative studies between 2004 and 2011 showed that environmental concern is ranked as a serious issue

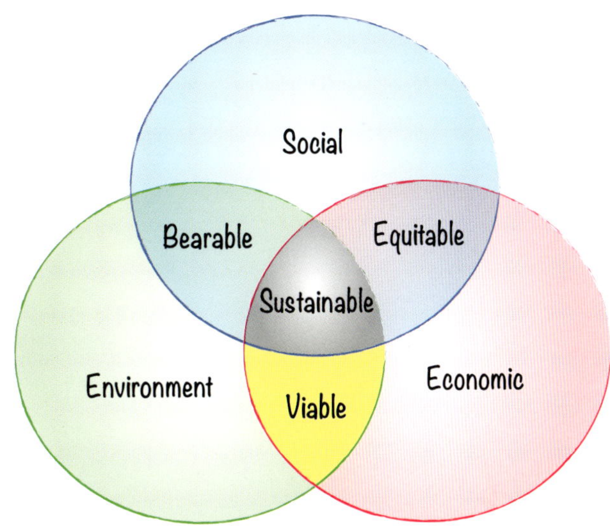

Figure 1. Venn diagram representation of sustainability.
https://commons.wikimedia.org/wiki/File:Sustainable_development.svg

by a majority of respondents, but when the other elements of sustainability such as social equity and economic costs are incorporated, the level of concern is significantly lower *(Lieu, Vedlitz, and Shi)*. In each wave of the survey, younger people expressed increasingly lower levels of concern. Global studies have shown a similar pattern *(Jorgensen and Givens; Marquart-Pyatt)*, with the United States falling in the middle of the industrialized countries in environmental concern. The responses of the United States' sample reflect a lack of understanding of trade-offs between economic development and environmental protection. A majority of respondents said that the environment must be protected no matter what it takes (54 percent), a large majority agreed that economic development is important to protect the environment (80 percent), about half (48 percent) were willing to pay higher prices for goods to protect the environment, but far fewer were ready to accept a reduction in standard of living to protect the environment (36 percent) *(Franzen and Vogl)*. A study, commissioned by the Rainforest Alliance, of 2000 consumers in China, India, Brazil, the United Kingdom, and the United States that focused on "sustainability" as a marketing tool, found that more than 65 percent of respondents equated "sustainable" with environmentally friendly, that younger respondents were more likely to consider sustainability as a positive attribute when making a purchase, but older respondents were more likely to equate sustainability with preservation for future generations *(Kho, Buzzback)*. In the United States sample, 80 percent of respondents reported seeing the word "sustainability" occasionally to very often. Of those familiar with the term, 80 percent indicated it was important in purchasing products, but only 45 percent associated "ethics" with "sustainability" *(Buzzback)*.

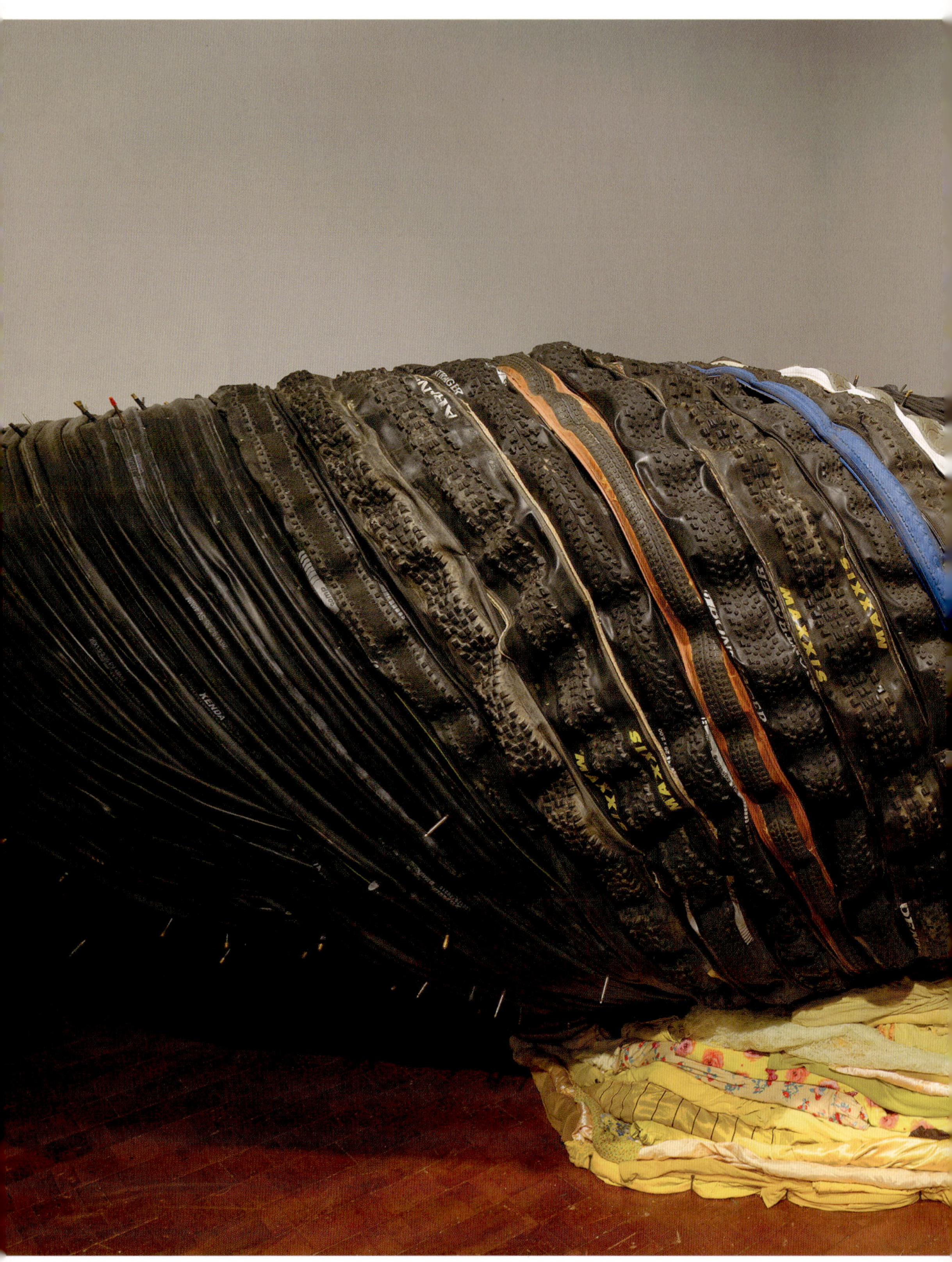

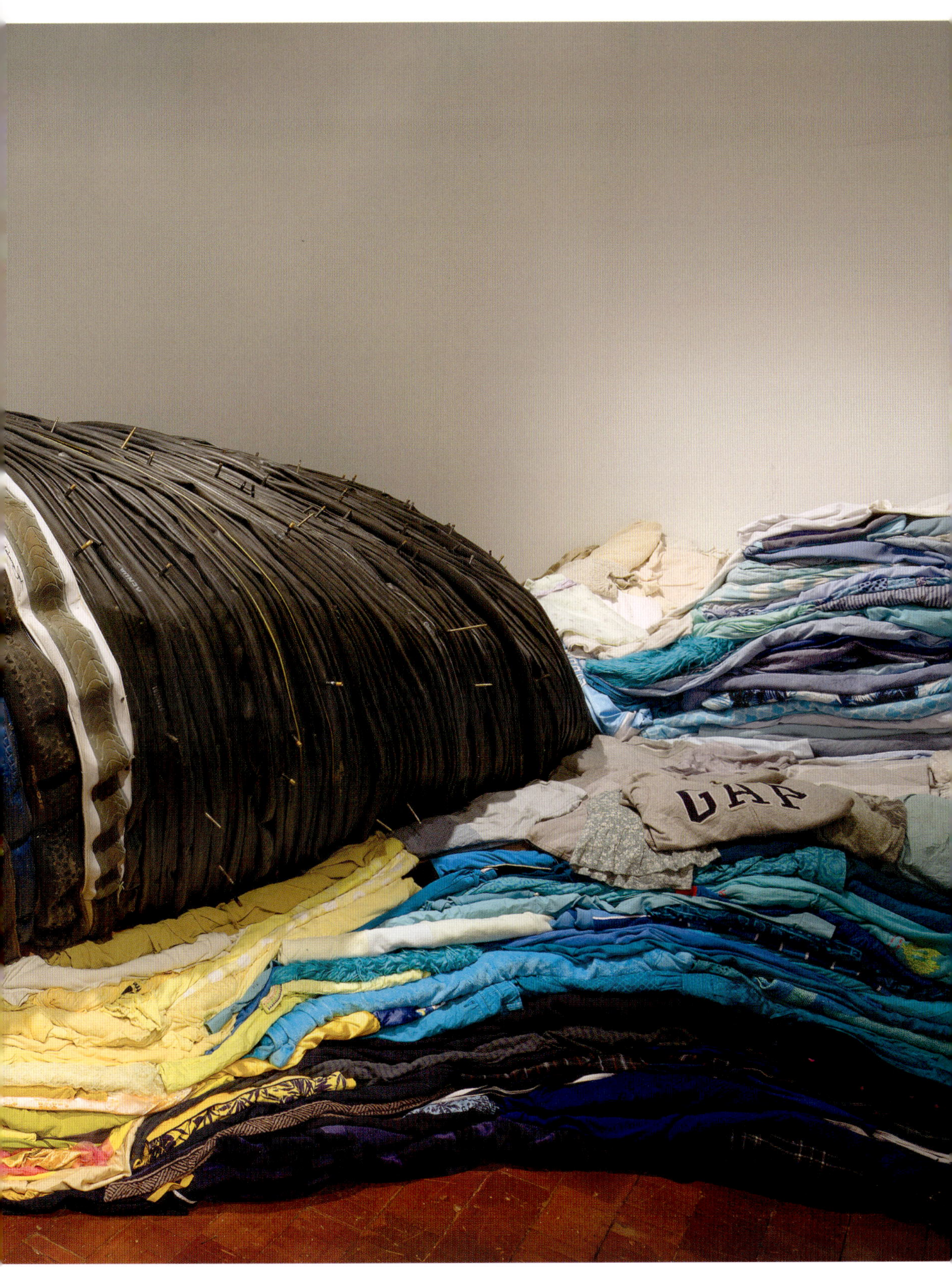

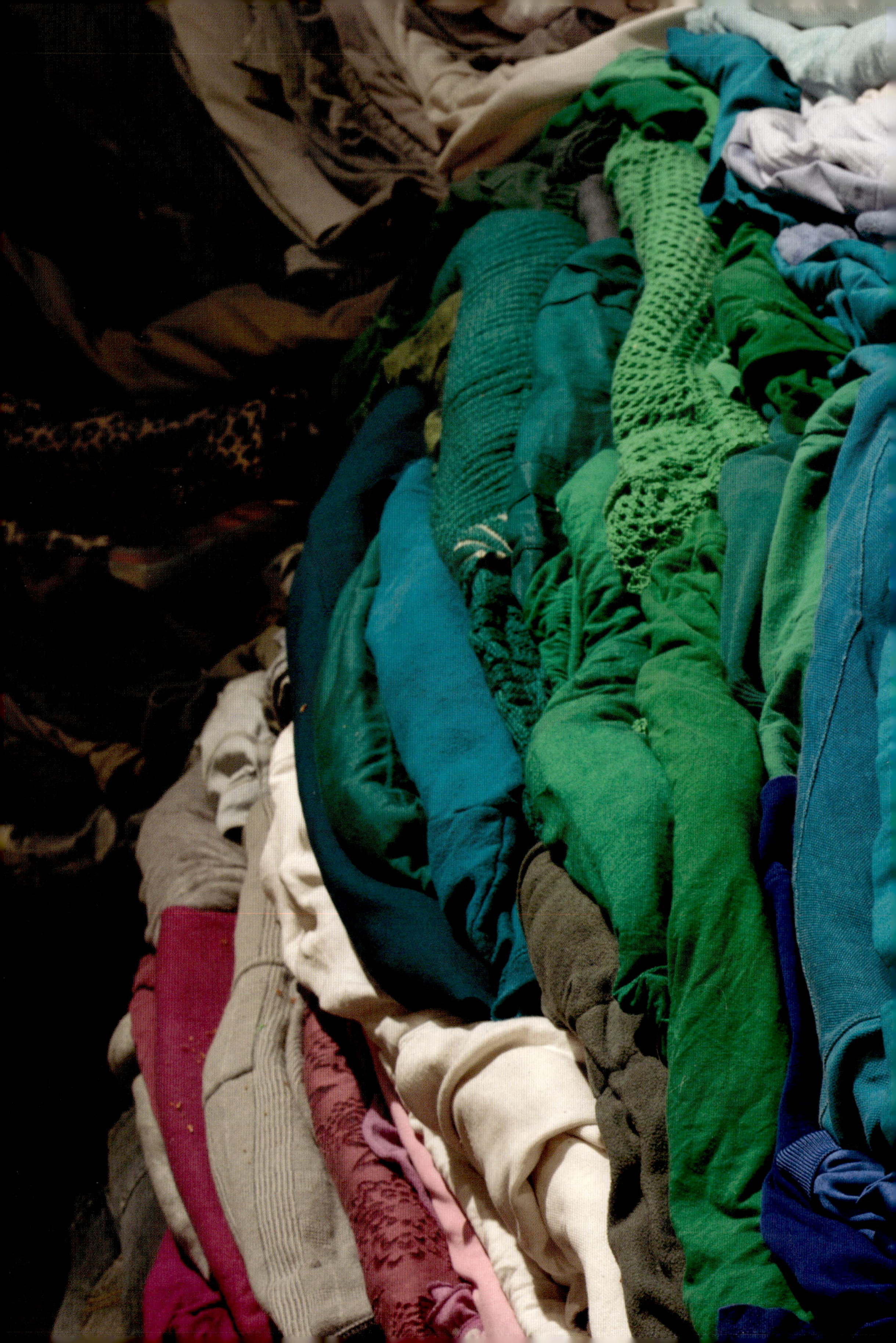

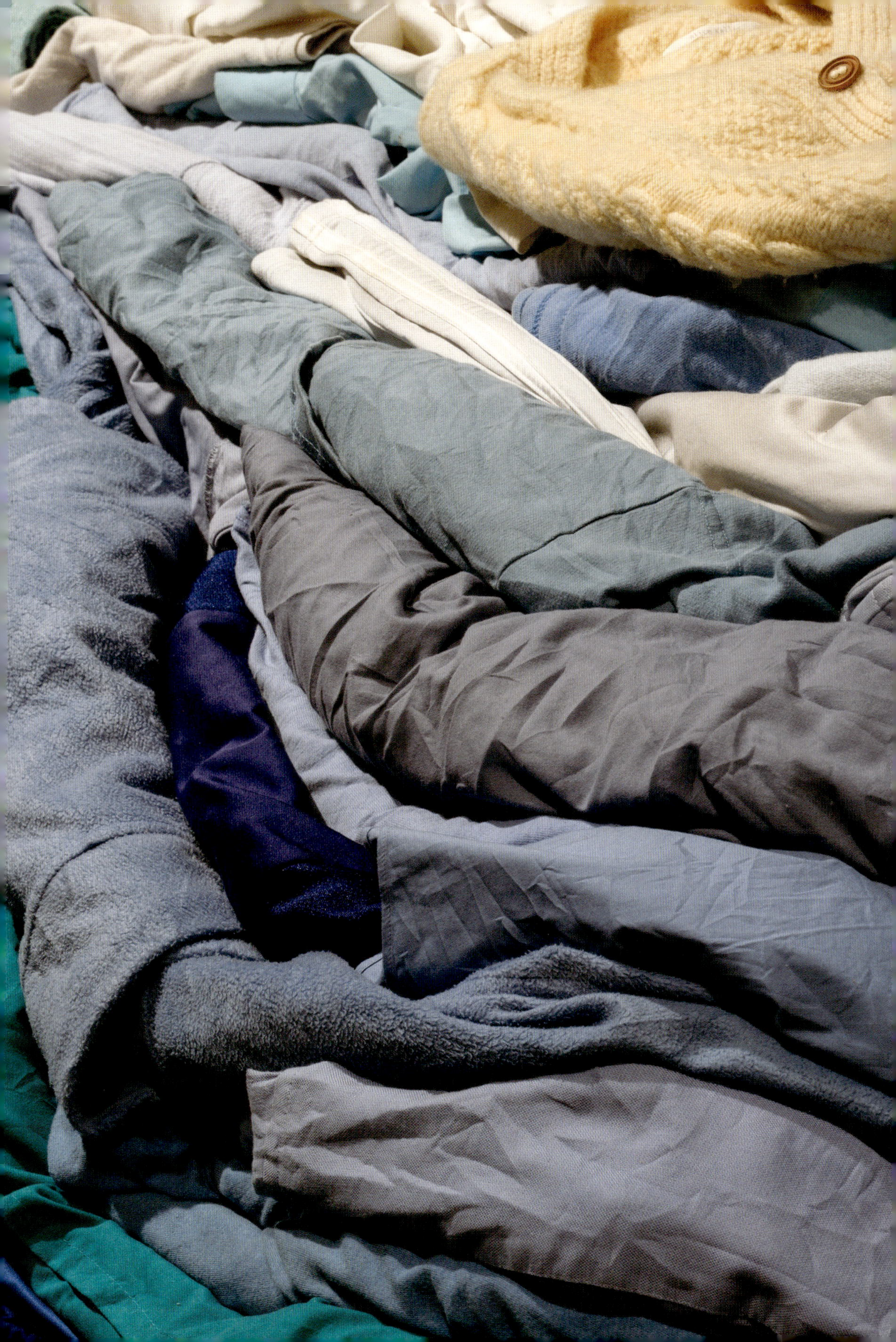

Toward a Deeper Understanding of Time and Place

From these studies, we see that around the world, as well as in the United States, a large percentage of adults believe the environment is a concern, but they have an imperfect understanding of the other elements of sustainability. And we also see that a large percentage of individuals do not see environmental concern as important. Some of this may be due to misperceptions of science, or the belief that there will be technological innovation that will ameliorate environmental damage *(Liu, Vedlitz, and Shi)*. An additional factor may be the short-sighted nature of our experiences in both time and distance. The conundrum of balancing immediate actions against long-term consequences has been a serious focus of study across disciplines, including economics *(Bisin and Verdier)*, political science *(Oded and Özak)*, psychology *(Wang, Reiger, and Hens)*, sociology *(Breen. van de Werfhorst, and Meier Jæger)*, anthropology *(Winterhalder, Lu, and Tucker)*, biology *(Hayden)*, philosophy *(Gardner)*, and religious studies *(Brousselle and Lessard)*. Changes in the local environment can have immediate impact, so preference for thinking in the short term is reinforced. Local environments are detectable using one's senses, while those occurring far away can only be known through information about distant conditions, either through technology or from information sharing. For most of human history, people generally interacted with few others; estimates range from 30 *(Lieberman)* to around 300 *(Barnard, Shelley, and Killworth)*. Most widely cited is "Dunbar's number" of about 150 social interactants *(Dunbar)*. In addition, archaeological evidence indicates that for most of human history people rarely traded or moved farther than about a 200-kilometer radius, and often much less. Around 10,000 years ago, worldwide non-anthropogenic climate change caused many areas to become wetter and warmer, and agriculture arose on several continents. Among many other changes, the rise of agriculture led to increased population size, more intensive extraction of resources, increasingly compact environmental impact, and massively higher levels of interaction, both within local communities and across large distances as a result of trade and war *(Kuhn, Reichlin, and Clark)*. These agriculture-based complex societies brought new levels of power differentials and access to resources based on gender, class, geographic origin, and wealth *(Bowles, Smith, and Borgerhoff Mulder)*, and these characteristics have continued to intensify as a result of technological innovation, industrialization, and globalization, to the present day.

What Can I Do To Promote Sustainability?

Throughout prehistory, and into the present, people have had significant impacts on the environment. That impact today is both more intense and global in scope, but this historic process does not lead to an inevitable outcome. The mutually interactive and reinforcing relationship of technology and globalization is an agent under our control. It is not necessarily intuitive to think that a simple act of buying an item of clothing, eating a hamburger, taking an airline flight, or flushing the toilet will have an effect sometime in the future, and perhaps on distant people and places. Yet, today each of us can use more than our senses to understand the ways in which our

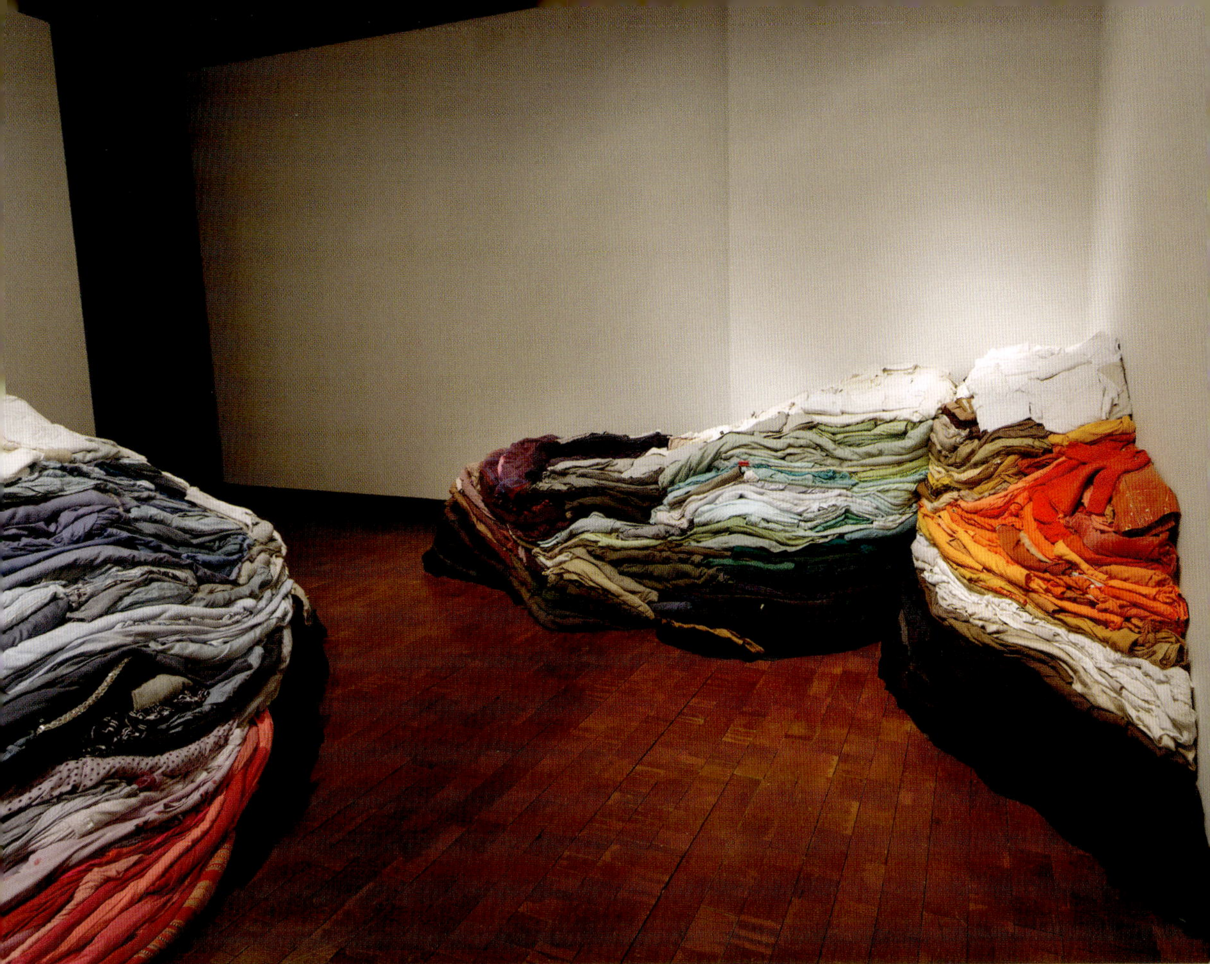

consumer choices and standard of living can make it more or less likely that future generations can meet their needs. We vote with our dollars. Chocolate, sugar, coffee, and palm oil are a few products where making purchase choices based on their sourcing has an identifiable effect on both the environment and the quality of life for those who produce the commodities. By virtue of living in the United States—no matter what your life choices are— your ecological footprint, or the effects of your resource consumption and waste, is eight times that of an average resident of sub-Saharan Africa *(Collins and Flynn)*. It is easy for us to think that "the people over there" should do something about population growth or environmental impacts. We as a country are less than 5 percent of the global population but use over 20 percent of the resources *(Hoekstra and Wiedmann)*. We each have the ability to promote sustainability in two ways. The first is through accessing information ourselves. We now live in a small world, where through technology we can obtain news but also communicate directly with people everywhere. By understanding our choices and behaviors in larger context of time and place, we can act in a sustainable fashion. Second, it is essential to engage with the social, economic, and political spheres to promote policy and practices that are rooted in sustainability. Technology and globalization have expanded our choices, and how we move forward is up to us. We need to be careful consumers not only of products and resources, but also of information.

Works Cited

Adams, William M. "The future of sustainability: Re-thinking environment and development in the twenty-first century." Report of the IUCN Renowned Thinkers Meeting. Vol. 29. 2006.

Bernard, H. Russell, Gene Ann Shelley, and Peter Killworth. "How much of a network does the GSS and RSW dredge up." *Social Networks* 9.1 (1987): 49-61

Bisin, Alberto, and Thierry Verdier. "The economics of cultural transmission and the dynamics of preferences." *Journal of Economic Theory 97.2* (2001): 298-319.

Bowles, Samuel, Eric Alden Smith, and Monique Borgerhoff Mulder. "The emergence and persistence of inequality in premodern societies: introduction to the special section." *Current Anthropology* 51.1 (2010): 7-17.

Breen, Richard, Herman G. van de Werfhorst, and Mads Meier Jæger. "Deciding under doubt: A theory of risk aversion, time discounting preferences, and educational decision-making." *European Sociological Review* 30.2 (2014): 258-270.

Brousselle, Astrid, and Chantale Lessard. "Economic evaluation to inform health care decision-making: promise, pitfalls and a proposal for an alternative path." *Social Science & Medicine* 72.6 (2011): 832-839.

Brundtland, Gro Harlem. Report of the World Commission on Environment and Development: "Our Common Future." United Nations, 1987.

Buzzback.com. "Making the Consumer + Sustainability Connection." Webinar, 2014. https://www.youtube.com/watch?v=IRmfQVMs7mE.

Collins, Andrea, and Andrew Flynn. The ecological Footprint: New Developments in Policy and Practice. Edward Elgar Publishing, 2015.

Dunbar, Robin IM. "Neocortex size as a constraint on group size in primates." Journal of Human Evolution 22.6 (1992): 469-493.

Franzen, Axel, and Dominikus Vogl. "Two decades of measuring environmental attitudes: A comparative analysis of 33 countries." *Global Environmental Change* 23.5 (2013): 1001-1008.

Gardiner, Stephen M. *A perfect moral storm: The Ethical Tragedy of Climate Change.* Oxford University Press, 2011.

Gibson, Bob, Selma Hassan, and James Tansey. *Sustainability Assessment: Criteria and Processes.* Routledge, 2013.

Hawken, Paul, Amory B. Lovins, and L. Hunter Lovins. *Natural Capitalism: The Next Industrial Revolution.* Routledge, 2013.

Hoekstra, Arjen Y., and Thomas O. Wiedmann. "Humanity's unsustainable environmental footprint." Science 344.6188 (2014): 1114-1117.

Jorgenson, Andrew K., and Jennifer E. Givens. "Economic globalization and environmental concern: A multilevel analysis of individuals within 37 nations." Environment and Behavior 46.7 (2014): 848-871.

Kho, Jennifer. "Open thread: what does 'sustainable' mean to you?: The Guardian, 3 February 2014. https://www.theguardian.com/sustainable-business/sustainable-green-meaning-consumer-open-thread.

Kuhn, Steven L., David A. Raichlen, and Amy E. Clark. "What moves us? How mobility and movement are at the center of human evolution." *Evolutionary Anthropology: Issues, News, and Reviews* 25.3 (2016): 86-97.

Lieberman, Philip. *The unpredictable species: What makes humans unique.*Princeton University Press, 2013.

Liu, Xinsheng, Arnold Vedlitz, and Liu Shi. "Examining the determinants of public environmental concern: Evidence from national public surveys." *Environmental Science & Policy* 39 (2014): 77-94.

Marquart-Pyatt, Sandra T. "Environmental trust: A cross-region and cross-country study." *Society & Natural Resources* 29.9 (2016): 1032-1048.

Nyilasy, Gergely, Harsha Gangadharbatla, and Angela Paladino. "Perceived greenwashing: The interactive effects of green advertising and corporate environmental performance on consumer reactions." *Journal of Business Ethics* 125.4 (2014): 693-707.

Oded, Galor and Ömer Özak. "The agricultural origins of time preference." *American Economic Review* 106.10 (2016): 3064-3103.

Serageldin, Ismail. "Sustainability and the wealth of nations: First steps in an ongoing journey." *Environmentally Sustainable Development*, 3. World Bank, 1995.

Serageldin, Ismail, Robert Goodland, and Herman Daly. "The concept of sustainability." Taking Nature into Account—A Report to the Club of Rome. New York: Springer-Verlag, Inc., 1995: 99-123.

Vitell, Scott J. "A case for consumer social responsibility (CnSR): Including a selected review of consumer ethics/social responsibility research." *Journal of Business Ethics* 130.4 (2015): 767-774.

Wang, Mei, Marc Oliver Rieger, and Thorsten Hens. "How time preferences differ: Evidence from 53 countries." Journal of Economic Psychology 52 (2016): 115-135.

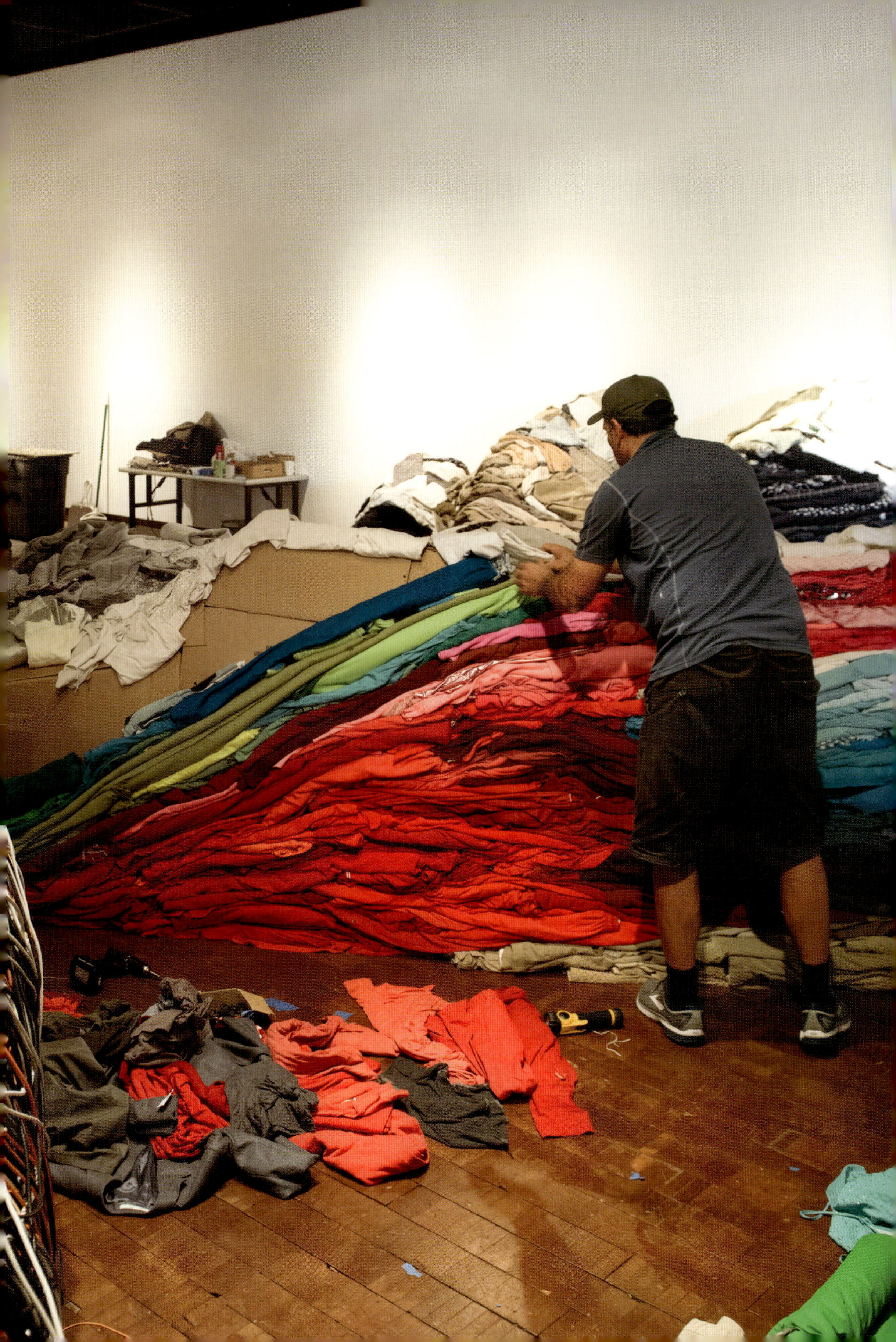

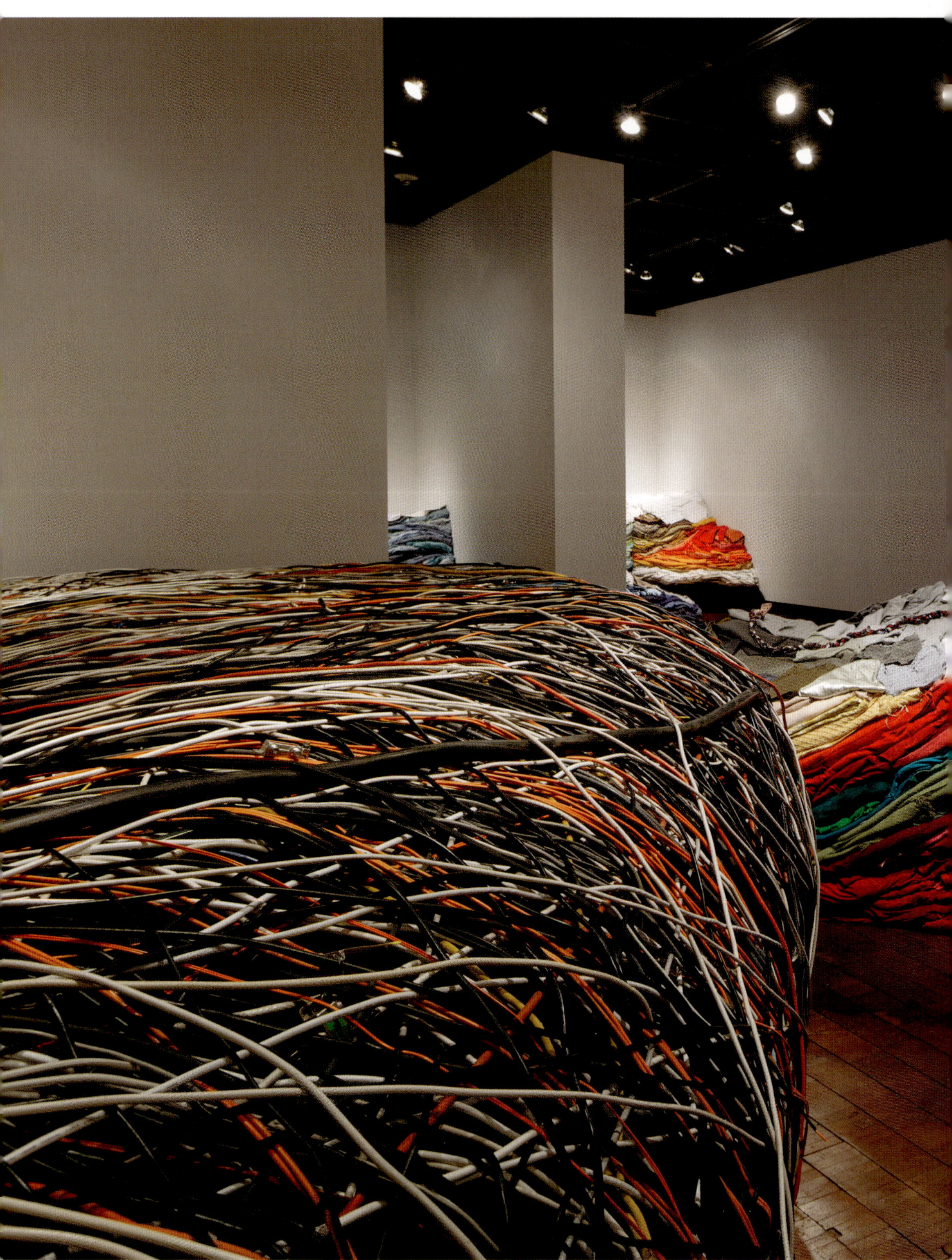

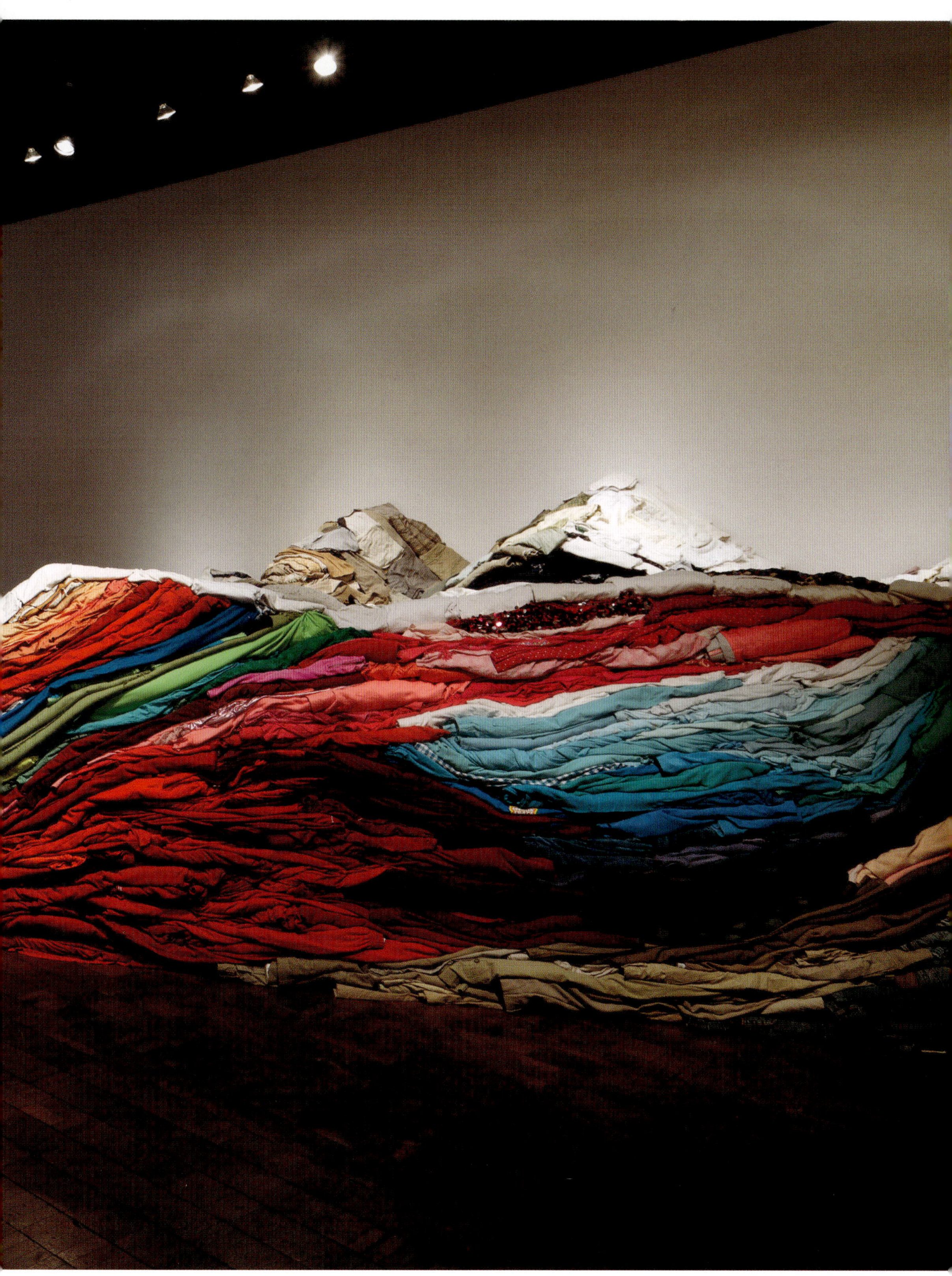

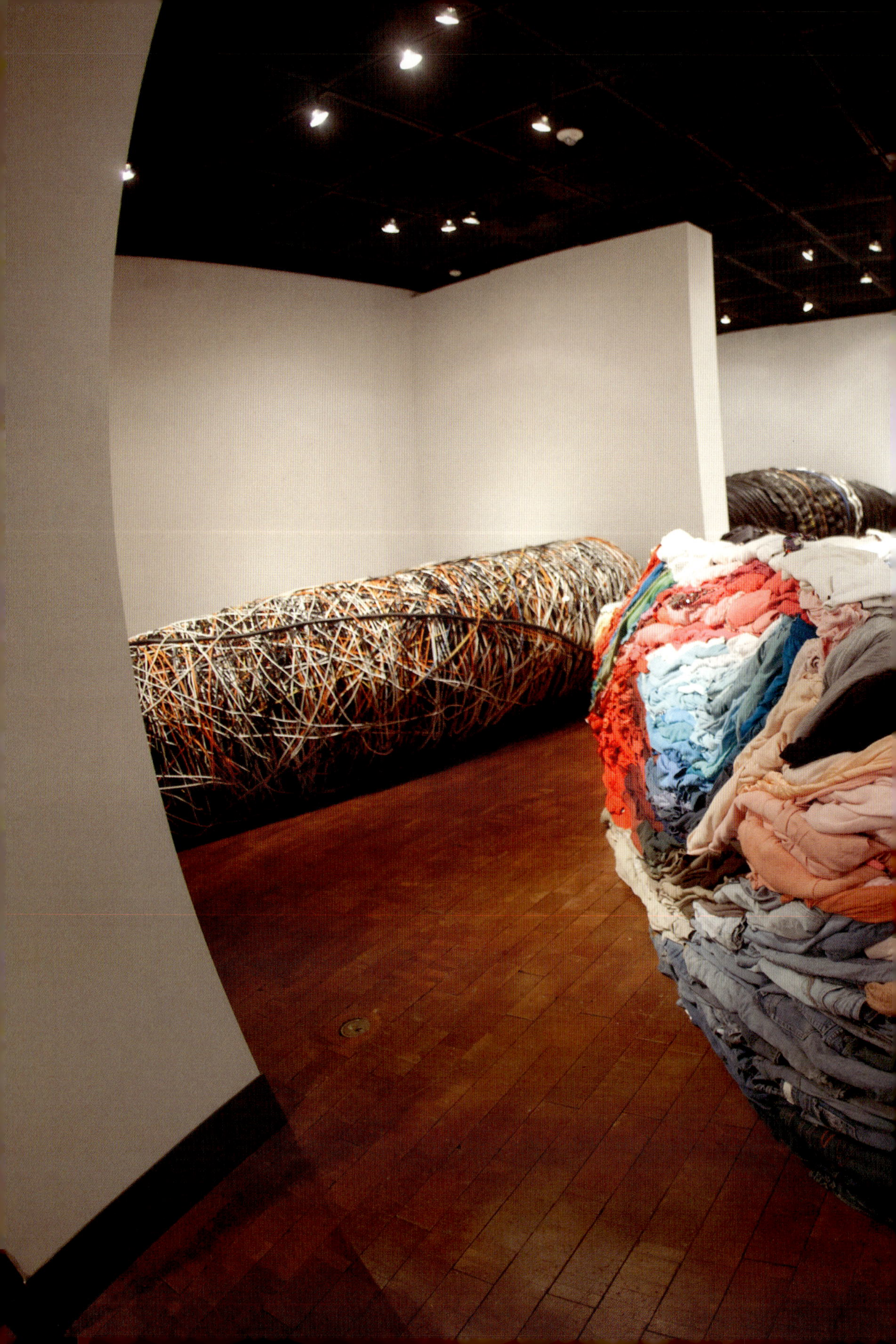

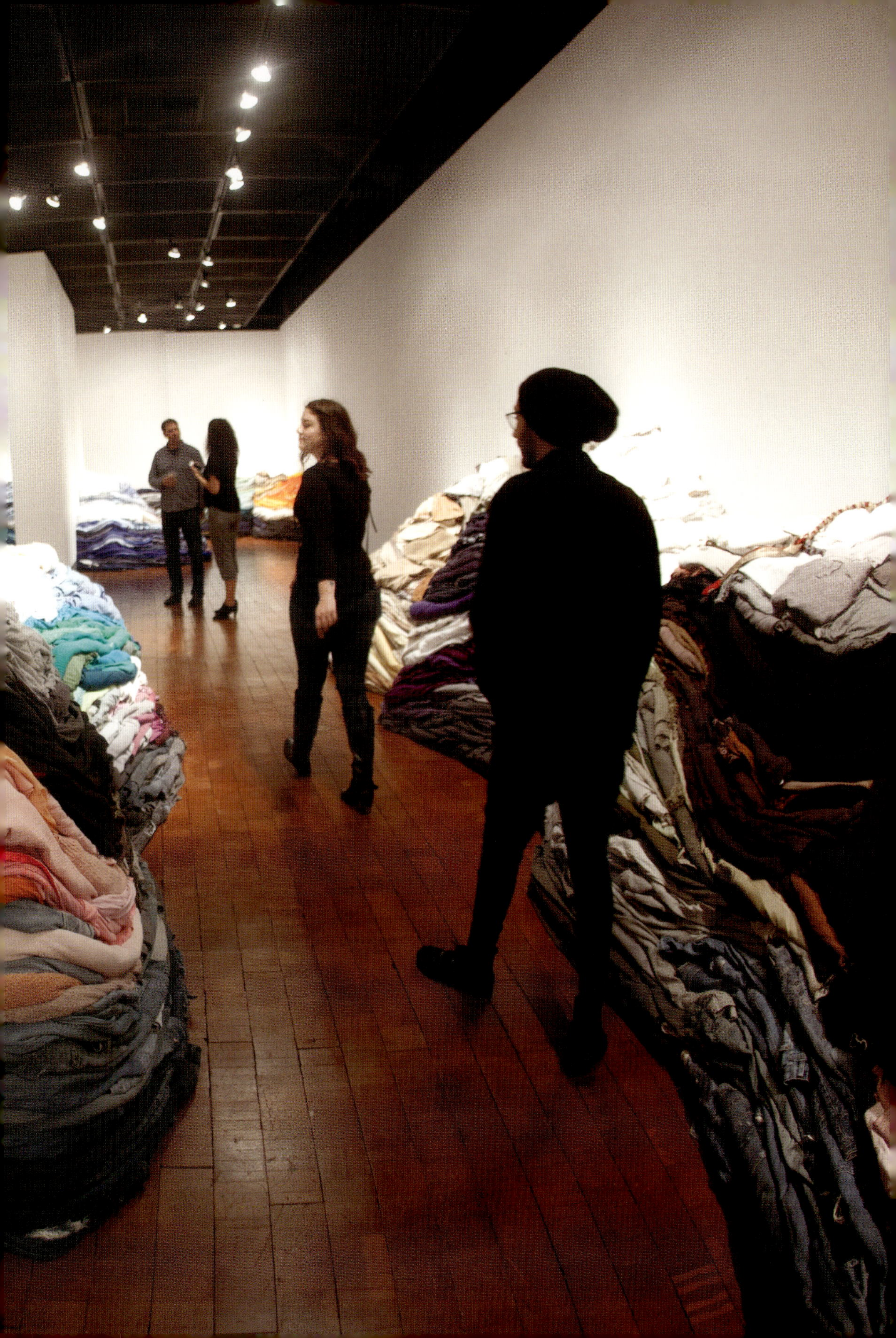

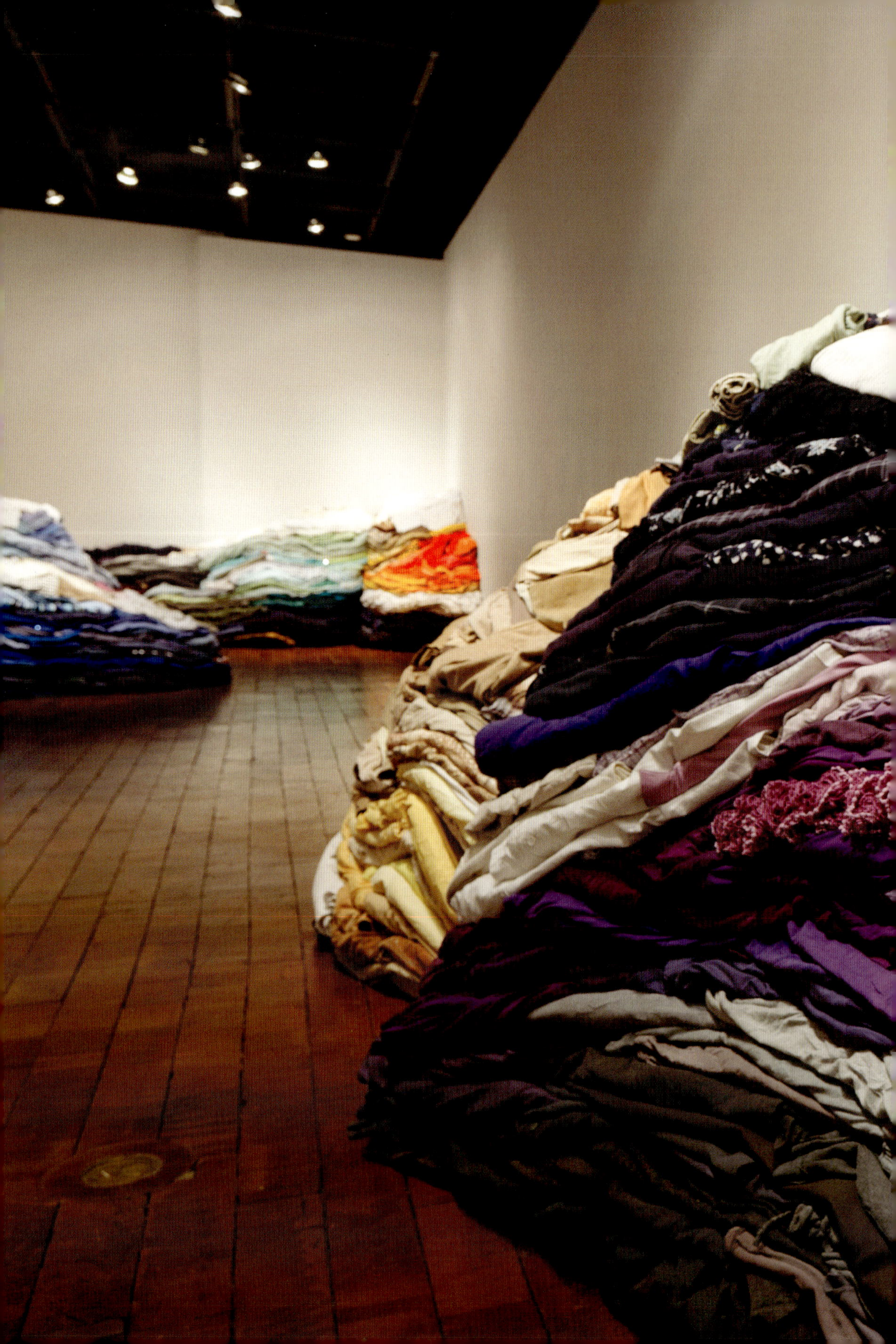

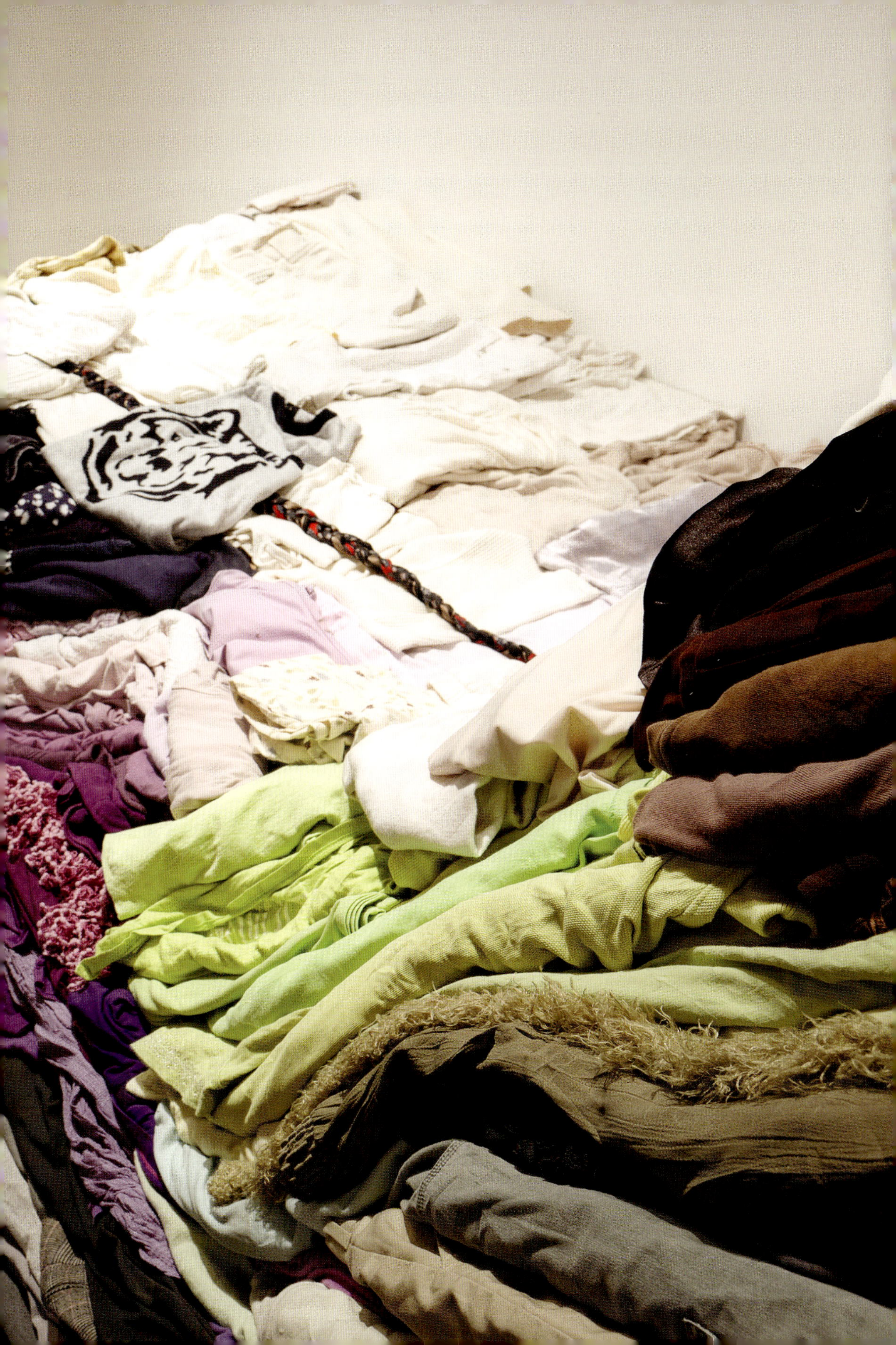

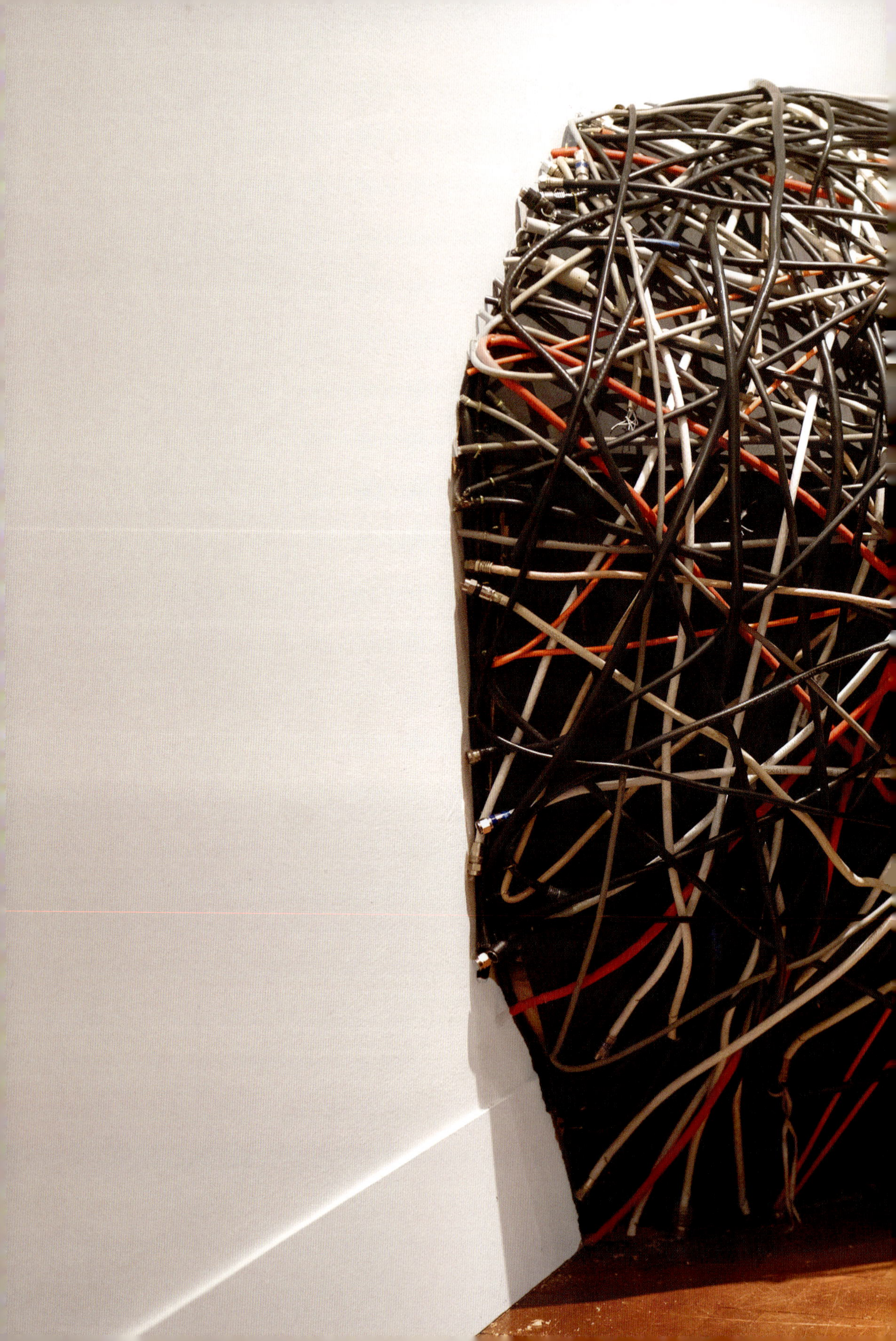

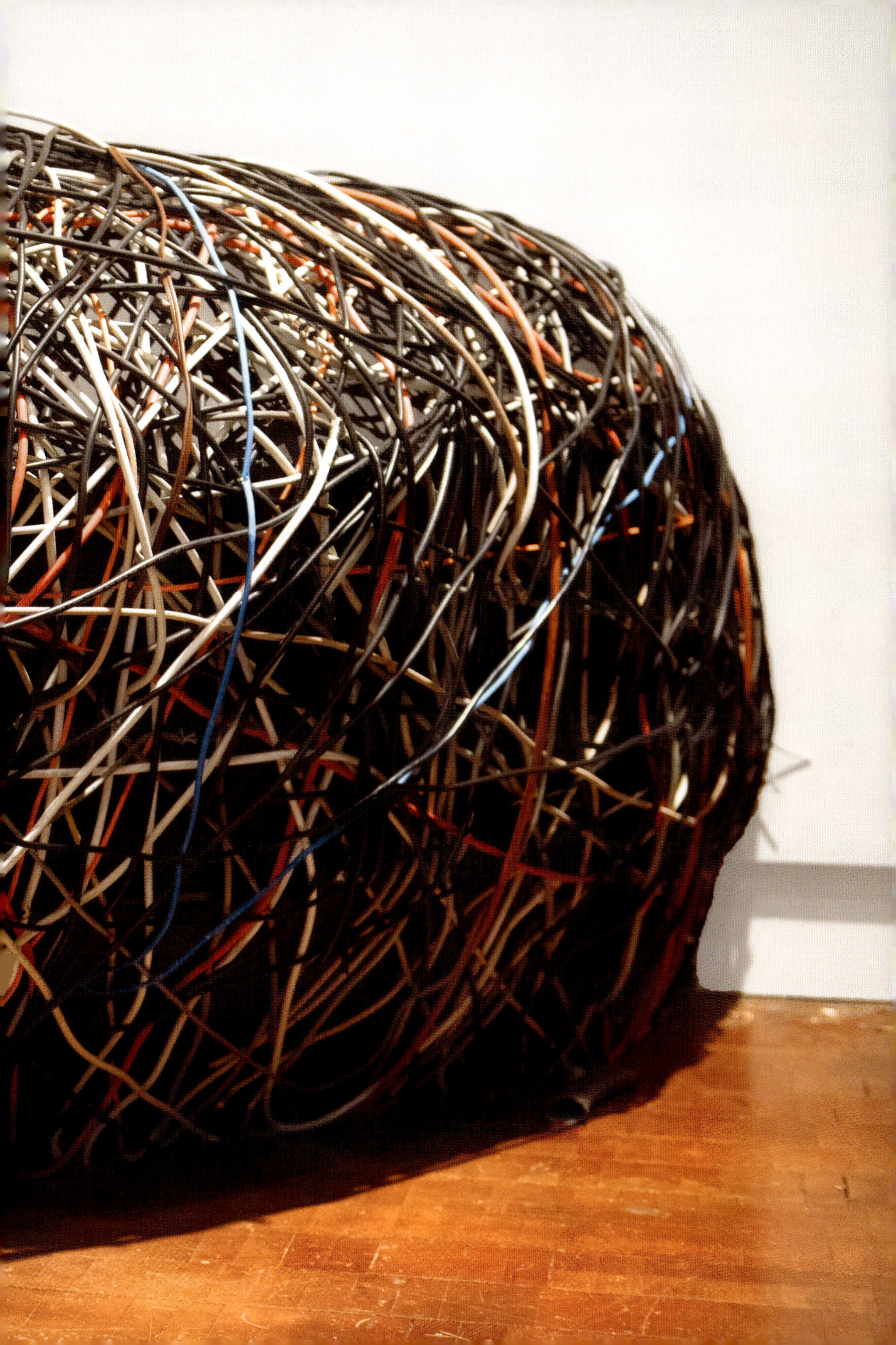

MICROFIBERS, UNFASHIONABLE FOR THE ENVIRONMENT

Joseph DeMarco

People have paid little attention to the overall material sustainability of clothing. Since there is a lack of universal environmentally conscious behavior, different people tend to focus on different aspects of environmental issues. People rarely think of the environmental impacts of fashion. This essay attempts to define some of the environmental impacts of the fast-fashion industry and to provide some suggestions about ways in which consumers can alleviate some of the issues summarized throughout this essay. Sustainability in the fast-fashion industry relates not only to the entire supply chain, from production to storefront, but also to consumer behavior—especially post-purchase *(Kohtala 2014)*. Related to Jarod Charzewski's artistic interpretations that mimic landfills and landscapes, the fast-fashion industry is the source of many related environmental issues, such as microfiber pollution, the focus of this essay.

According to the US Environmental Protection Agency (EPA), in 2014 the U.S. generated 16 million tons of textile and clothing waste, 64.5 percent of which was sent to landfills with only 16.2 percent recycled *(US EPA 2016)*. Additionally, clothing brands now offer more new clothing collections per year than ever before, and the number of garments produced annually has doubled since 2000 *(Remy et al. 2016)*. This tremendous growth in the market and an increase in shifting production overseas have led to a similar growth in environmental problems, many of which remain unnoticed. Today, these businesses produce lower quality items that last a shorter period of time, generally referred to as fast fashion—a problematic industry. Rather than regarding clothes as valuable, long-term assets, consumers now view garments as low-cost, disposable items.

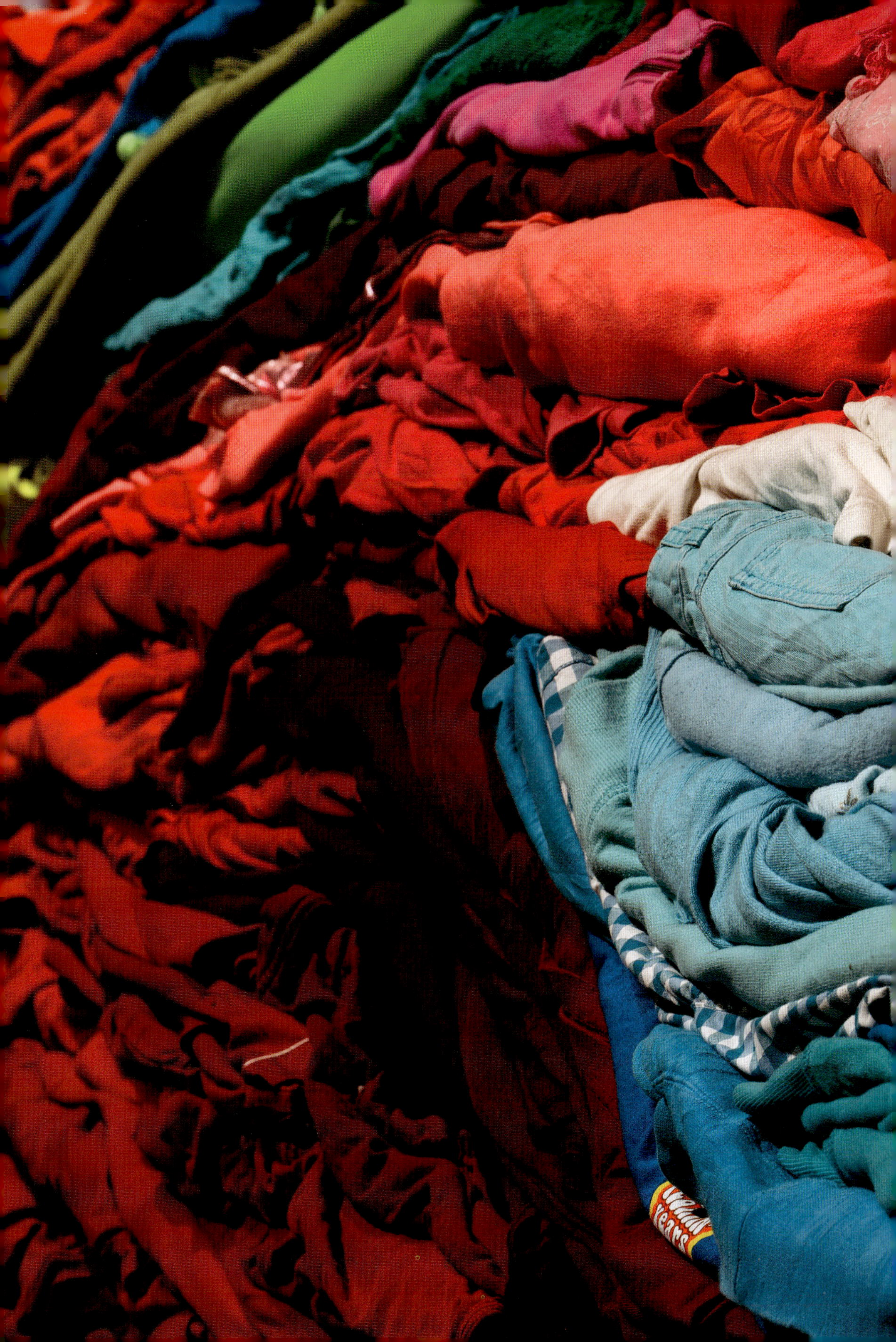

In the case of one well-known brand, H&M, research has revealed that more than one-half of the total greenhouse gases generated in production and distribution of products is released during transportation from production facilities to retail stores—determined by tracking garments' environmental impact from factory to landfill *(Shen 2014)*. Also, since 60 percent of clothes are made from petroleum-based synthetic fibers, compared to just 25 percent from cotton, most garments contain anthropogenic material *(LENZING Corp 2016)*. For the fast-fashion industry, anthropogenic material means clothing fiber that is derived from fossil fuels and turned into plastic fibers, such as polyester and nylon. This anthropogenic material is mass produced and mass consumed. Further, in the future, these synthetic fibers are expected to increase their market share due to decreasing arable land for growing natural raw materials and to a lack of other viable alternatives *(Qin 2014)*. The mass-production model of fast fashion, and the resultant trend of overconsumption affects manufacturers, retailers, people, and the environment alike *(Kim et al. 2013; Hernandez et al. 2017)*.

Although the way materials are sourced, produced, and disposed of are serious factors in the environmental impact, scientists have undertaken more and more research about the impact of consumer care. For citizens, sustainable consumption is more than just sustainability in purchasing. The way people use, reuse, and discard clothing after they leave the store is vitally important. For example, over the course of a garment's life cycle, washing 1 kilogram (2.2 pounds) of clothing emits 11 kilograms of greenhouse gases *(Remy et al. 2016)*. Another area of scientific investigation related to consumer care is quantifying how many microfibers enter water bodies during washing. Although it is well known that washing clothes keeps them clean and smelling good, recent research is finding that effluent, or discharge from washing machines, contains hundreds of thousands of synthetic and natural fibers (think cotton, polyester, and nylon) that shed from garments after each and every wash *(Bergmann et al. 2016; Bruce et al. 2016; Hartline et al. 2016; Cesa et al. 2017; Mintenig et al. 2017)*.

Microfibers are just one of many impacts fast fashion has on the environment. Many publications in reputable scientific journals show that microplastics—specifically microfibers—cause problems in aquatic foods destined for human consumption *(Browne et al. 2011; Ivar do Sol et al. 2014; Koelmans et al. 2014; Bergmann et al. 2015; Bruce et al. 2016; Hermabessiere et al. 2017)*. Moreover, in one study that sampled organisms destined for human consumption off the coast of San Francisco, CA, one-quarter of individual fish had anthropogenic debris in their intestinal tract and one-third of individual shellfish were contaminated with anthropogenic debris *(Rochman et al. 2015)*. Of the organisms that contained anthropogenic debris, microfibers constituted 80 percent of debris, as shown in *(Figure 1) (Rochman et al. 2015)*.

These microfibers travel to wastewater treatment plants, where a multistep process attempts to remove contaminants from the water before it is discharged into nearby water bodies. While wastewater treatment plants remove as much as 99 percent of microplastics during the filtration

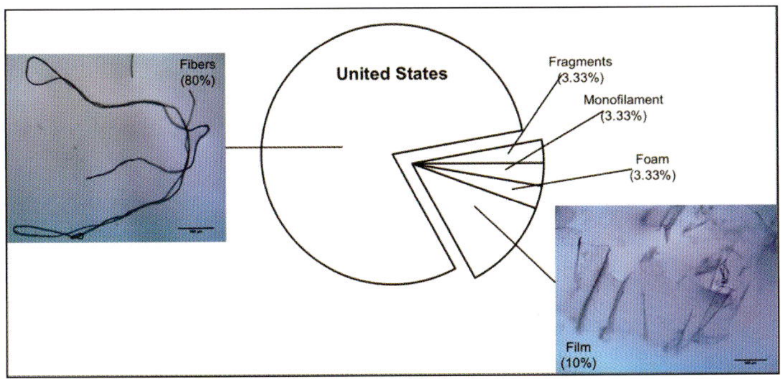

Figure 1: Anthropogenic debris in fish meant to be sold for human consumption in the United States, 80 percent of which were observed to be clothing-derived microfibers (Rochman et al. 2015).

process, the sheer amount of water they process daily means that billions of microscopic plastic pieces are being leeched into the aquatic environment each day *(Michielssen et al. 2014; Mintenig et al. 2017; Talvitie et al. 2017)*. The microfiber pieces that are effectively removed by these plants end up in sludge, which is either incinerated or used as agricultural soil. In other words, by washing synthetic clothing, microfibers leech into the aquatic and terrestrial environments.

Overall, the impacts of microplastics on wildlife are not well understood at this time. Scientists are concerned that organisms ingesting plastic debris are at risk from exposure to other chemicals, too, because microfibers act like sponges for certain environmental contaminants and cause endocrine disruption that creates hormonal imbalances *(Wright et al. 2013)*. Hormonal imbalances can cause cancerous tumors, birth defects, and other developmental disorders. Other problems with microfibers include their being biodegradable only on extremely long time scales and their ability to bioaccumulate in organisms *(Koelmans et al. 2016; Cesa et al. 2017)*. Bioaccumulation happens when organisms intake substances at rates that are faster than they can be metabolized and excreted, meaning that microfibers end up in the organisms' tissues and organs. While a range of environmental problems are related to the fast-fashion industry, the effects of microfibers in washing machine effluent are lacking in scientific literature and overlooked by society.

Although the extent to which these particles affect organisms is still being determined, it is clear parts of the fast-fashion supply chain. A relatively small number of wastewater treatment plants have been studied in terms of their microfiber filtration efficiency, but scientists are expanding their knowledge by quantifying these sources of oceanic plastic. It is estimated that, between 1950 and 2015, humanity generated 4.9 billion metric tons of plastic waste *(Geyer et al. 2017)*—equivalent to the mass of more than 19,000 Empire State Buildings. Of this number, 12 percent originated from petroleum-based fibers *(Geyer et al. 2017)*. However, this number is likely a low estimate since research about microfiber pollution has just begun. It is unknown exactly how many microfiber particles are in the ocean *(Teuten et al. 2009; Wright et al. 2013; Setälä et al. 2014; Hermabessiere et al. 2017)*. Regardless, microfibers threaten the environment in many ways.

Unfortunately, buying ethical garments is complicated because natural fiber production is also extremely detrimental to the environment. For example, in the High Plains of Texas, there are 1.2

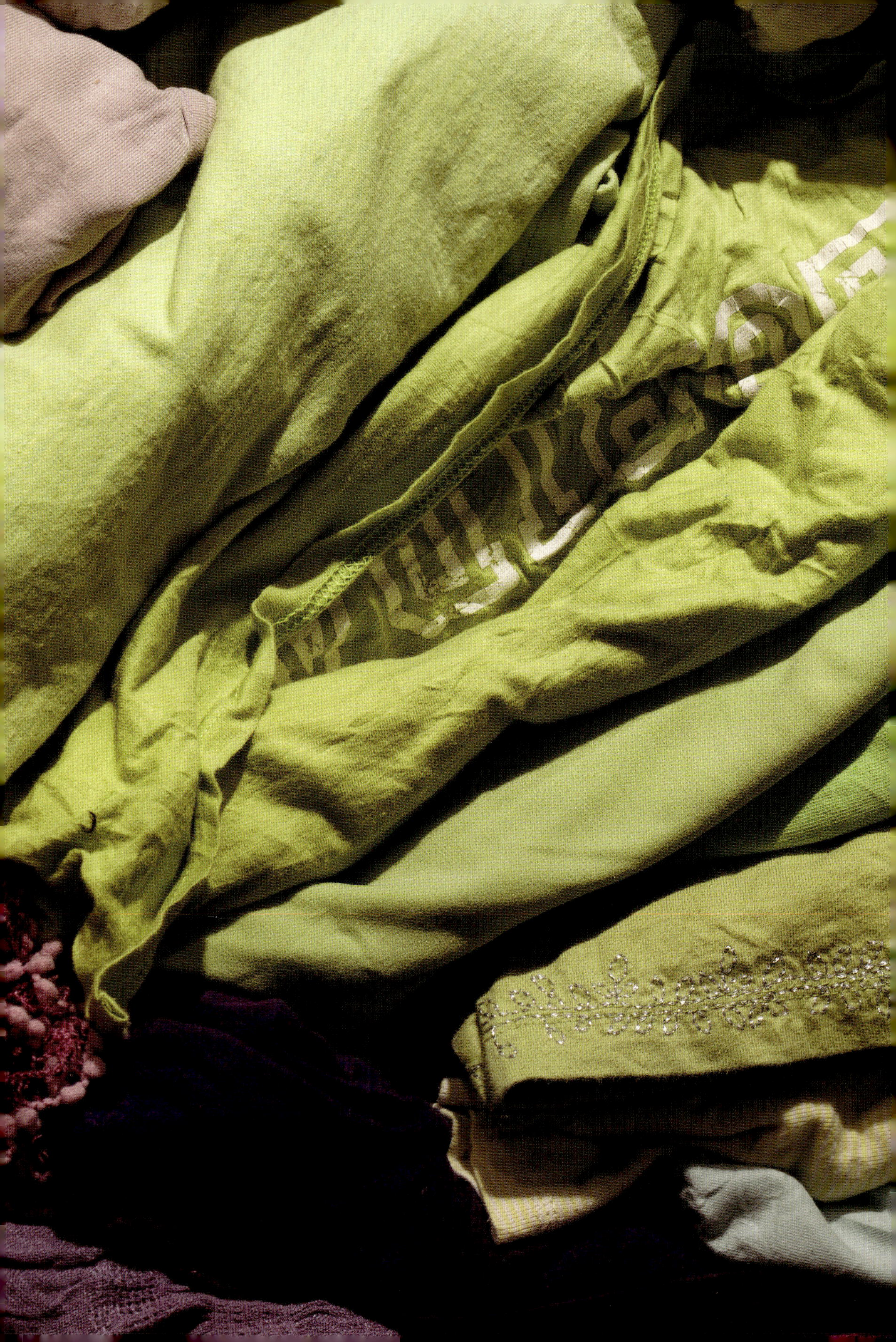

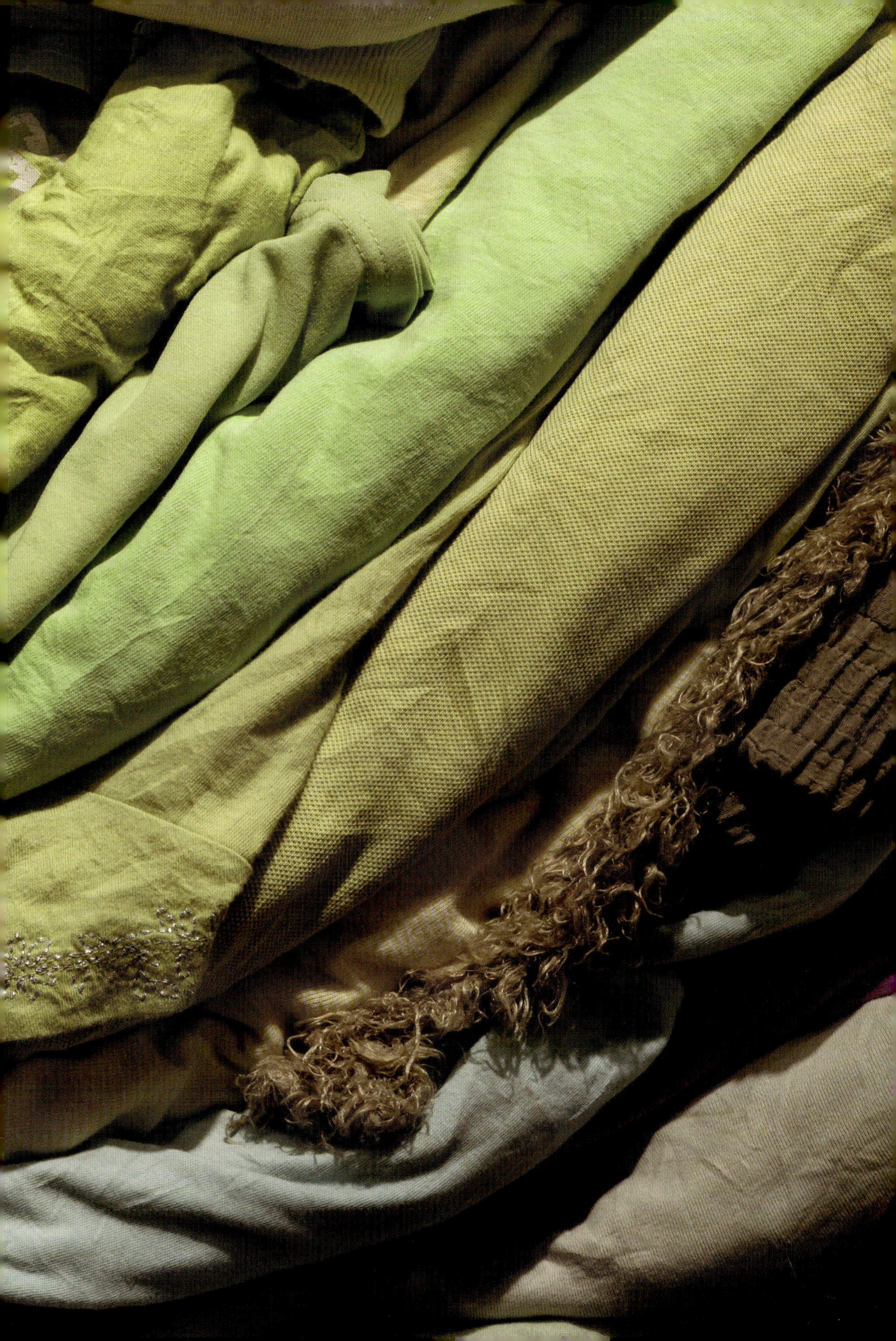

million hectares of cotton farmland, the majority of which are resource-intensive. To grow cotton, farmers must use huge quantities of water and pesticides *(Crane 2016)*. Plus, post-harvest, copious amounts of aqueous sodium hydroxide are used to dissolve cotton's outer waxy layer so dyes can penetrate it *(Karthik and Gopalakrishnan 2014)*. Bleach is also used, to yield better coloration. At the end of these products' lifecycles, recycling is difficult due to the presence of dyes and other materials—not to mention that clothes usually consist of fiber blends, making separation and reuse even harder. Therefore, despite cotton being natural, it has some severe environmental consequences itself. So, although it is clear to see that a product incorporating environmentally safe or recycled materials can be considered a good product, this is only part of the equation. Clothing manufacturers also have to consider the costs of production, manufacturing, distribution, usage, and ultimately disposal *(Karthik and Gopalakrishnan 2014)*.

We need collective action to change the system, and collective action is the best way to attempt to tackle this problem. Transformative solutions will require the fast-fashion industry itself to change. Collective action refers to collaboration between government officials, industry professionals, and citizens, among other stakeholders. The environmental impact of microfibers is a pervasive problem that will be difficult to legislate and fix. Both source reduction and cleanup strategies are crucial—these efforts need to be informed by the best available science and technology. Although relatively few comprehensive solutions have been proposed, some of the options include mass-producing filters to catch microfibers in washing machines; developing a dryer sheet of sorts that attracts and captures microfibers; and developing alternative materials to create garments from in the first place. For example, if recycling technologies improve in clothing production, it is estimated that air pollution released during production can be reduced by as much as 85 percent *(Karthik and Gopalakrishnan 2014)*. In the short term, countries need to begin strategizing how to create effective laws and regulations that include enforceable ways to hold companies and consumers accountable for microfiber pollution.

Works Cited

Bergmann, M, Gutow, L, and M Klages (2015). Sources and Pathways of Microplastics to Habitats. In *Marine Anthropogenic Litter* (pp. 229–244). Springer. https://doi.org/10.1007/978-3-319-16510-3

Browne, MA, Crump, P, Niven, SJ, Teuten, E, Tonkin, A, Galloway, T, and R Thompson (2011). Accumulation of Microplastic on Shorelines Worldwide: Sources and Sinks. *Environ. Sci. Technol*, 45, 9175–9179. https://doi.org/10.1021/es201811s

Bruce, N, Hartline, N, Karba, S, Ruff, B, and S Sonar (2016). Microfiber pollution and the apparel industry. Retrieved from http://brenmicroplastics.weebly.com/uploads/5/1/7/0/51702815/bren-patagonia_final_report.pdf

Cesa, FS, Turra, A, and J Baruque-Ramos (2017). Synthetic fibers as microplastics in the marine environment: A review from textile perspective with a focus on domestic washings. *Science of the Total Environment*, 598, 1116–1129. https://doi.org/10.1016/j.scitotenv.2017.04.172

Crane, D (2016). The puzzle of the ethical fashion consumer: Implications for the future of the fashion system. *International Journal of Fashion Studies*, 3(2), 249–265. https://doi.org/10.1386/infs.3.2.249_1

Geyer R, Jambeck JR, and KL Law (2017). Production, use, and fate of all plastics ever made. *Science Advances*, 3(7), e1700782. https://doi.org/10.1126/sciadv.1700782

Hartline NL, Bruce NJ, Karba SN, Ruff EO, Sonar SU, and PA Holden (2016). Microfiber Masses Recovered from Conventional Machine Washing of New or Aged Garments. *Environmental Science & Technology*, 50, 11532–11538. https://doi.org/10.1021/acs.est.6b03045

Hermabessiere L, Dehaut A, Paul-Pont I, Lacroix C, Jezequel R, Soudant P, and G Duflos (2017). Occurrence and effects of plastic additives on marine environments and organisms: A review. *Chemosphere*, 182, 781–793. https://doi.org/10.1016/j.chemosphere.2017.05.096

Hernandez E, Nowack B, and DM Mitrano (2017). Polyester Textiles as a Source of Microplastics from Households: A Mechanistic Study to Understand Microfiber Release During Washing. *Environmental Science & Technology*, 51, 7036–7046. https://doi.org/10.1021/acs.est.7b01750

Ivar do Sol J, and MF Costa (2014). The present and future of microplastic pollution in the marine environment. *Environmental Pollution*, 185, 352–364. https://doi.org/10.1016/j.envpol.2013.10.036

Karthik T, and D Gopalakrishnan (2014). Environmental Analysis of Textile Value Chain: An Overview. In S. S. Muthu (Ed.), *Roadmap to Sustainable Textiles and Clothing Environmental and Social Aspects of Textiles and Clothing Supply Chain* (pp. 153–188). Springer.

Kim H, Jung Choo H, and N Yoon (2013). The motivational drivers of fast fashion avoidance. *Journal of Fashion Marketing and Management: An International Journal*, 17(2), 243–260. https://doi.org/10.1108/JFMM-10-2011-0070

Koelmans AA, Besseling E, and EM Foekema (2014). Leaching of plastic additives to marine organisms. *Environmental Pollution*, 187, 49–54. https://doi.org/10.1016/j.envpol.2013.12.013

Koelmans AA, Bakir A, Burton GA, and CR Janssen (2016). Microplastic as a Vector for Chemicals in the Aquatic Environment: Critical Review and Model-Supported Reinterpretation of Empirical Studies. *Environmental Science & Technology*, 50, 3315–3326. https://doi.org/10.1021/acs.est.5b06069

Kohtala C (2014). Addressing sustainability in research on distributed production: an integrated literature review. *Journal of Cleaner Production*, 1–15. https://doi.org/10.1016/j.jclepro.2014.09.039

LENZING Corporation (2016). Global fiber market. Retrieved September 15, 2017, from http://www.lenzing.com/en/investors/equity-story/global-fiber-market.html

Michielssen MR, Michielssen ER, Ni J, and MB Duhaime (2014). Fate of microplastics and other small anthropogenic litter (SAL) in wastewater treatment plants depends on unit processes employed. *Environmental Science: Water Research & Technology*, (2), 1064–1073. https://doi.org/10.1039/c6ew00207b

Mintenig SM, Int-Veen I, Loder MGJ, Primpke S, and G Gerdts (2017). Identification of microplastic in effluents of waste water treatment plants using focal plane array-based micro-Fourier-transform infrared imaging. *Water Research*, 108, 365–372. https://doi.org/10.1016/j.watres.2016.11.015

Qin Y (2014). Global Fibres Overview. In *Synthetic Fibres Raw Materials Committee Meeting*. Pattaya, Thailand: Tecnon OrbiChem. Retrieved from http://www.orbichem.com/userfiles/APIC 2014/APIC2014_Yang_Qin.pdf

Remy N, Speelman E, and S Swartz (2016). Style that's sustainable: A new fast-fashion formula. McKinsey & Company. Retrieved from http://www.mckinsey.com/business-functions/sustainability-and-resource-productivity/our-insights/style-thats-sustainable-a-new-fast-fashion-formula?cid=sustainability-eml-alt-mip-mck-oth-1610

Rochman CM, Tahir A, Williams SL, Baxa DV, Lam R, Miller JT, Teh F-C, Werorilangi S, and SJ Teh (2015). Anthropogenic debris in seafood: Plastic debris and fibers from textiles in fish and bivalves sold for human consumption. Scientific Reports. 5: 14340. https://doi.org/10.1038/srep14340

Setälä O, Fleming-Lehtinen V, and M Lehtiniemi (2014). Ingestion and transfer of microplastics in the planktonic food web. *Environmental Pollution*, 185, 77–83. https://doi.org/10.1016/j.envpol.2013.10.013

Shen B (2014). Sustainable Fashion Supply Chain: Lessons from H&M. *Sustainability*, 6(12), 6236–6249. https://doi.org/10.3390/su6096236

Talvitie J, Mikola A, Setälä O, Heinonen M, and A Koistinen (2017). How well is microlitter purified from wastewater? A detailed study on the stepwise removal of microlitter in a tertiary level wastewater treatment plant. *Water Research*, 109, 164–172. https://doi.org/10.1016/j.watres.2016.11.046

Teuten, EL, Saquing JM, Knappe DRU, Barlaz MA, Jonsson S, Björn, A, Rowland SJ, Thompson RC, Galloway TS, Yamashita R, Ochi D, Watanuki Y, Moore C, Viet PH, Tana TS, Prudente M, Ogata Y, Hirai H, Iwasa S, Mizukawa K, Hagino K, Imamura A, Saha N, and H Takada (2009). Transport and release of chemicals from plastics to the environment and to wildlife. *Philosophical Transactions of the Royal Society* B, 364, 2027–2045. https://doi.org/10.1098/rstb.2008.0284

Wright SL, Thompson RC, and TS Galloway (2013). The physical impacts of microplastics on marine organisms: A review. *Environmental Pollution*, 178, 483–492. https://doi.org/10.1016/j.envpol.2013.02.031

United States Environmental Protection Agency. Advancing Sustainable Materials Management: 2014 Fact Sheet; *Office of Land and Emergency Management*, United States Environmental Protection Agency: Washington, DC, USA, 2016.

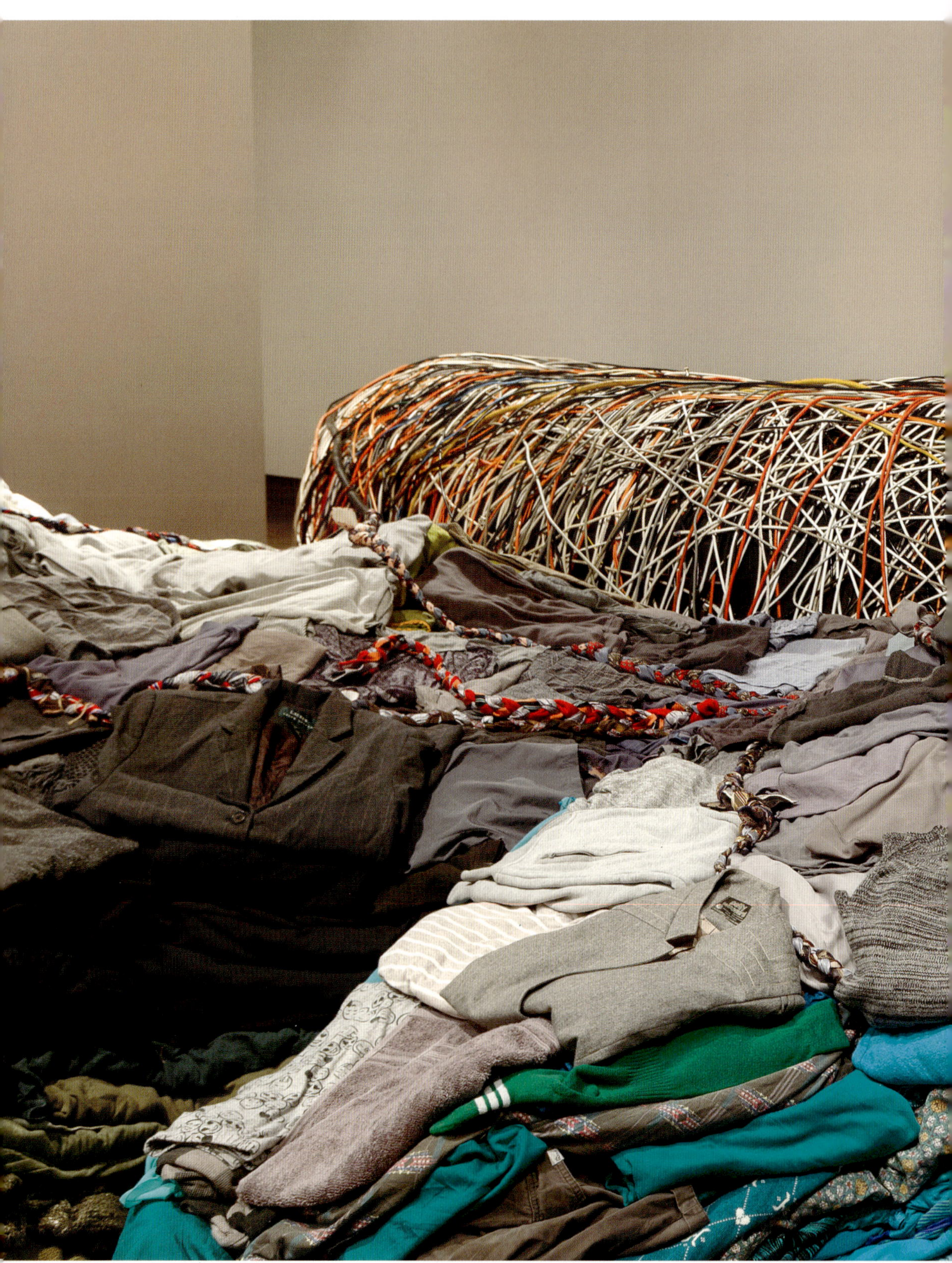

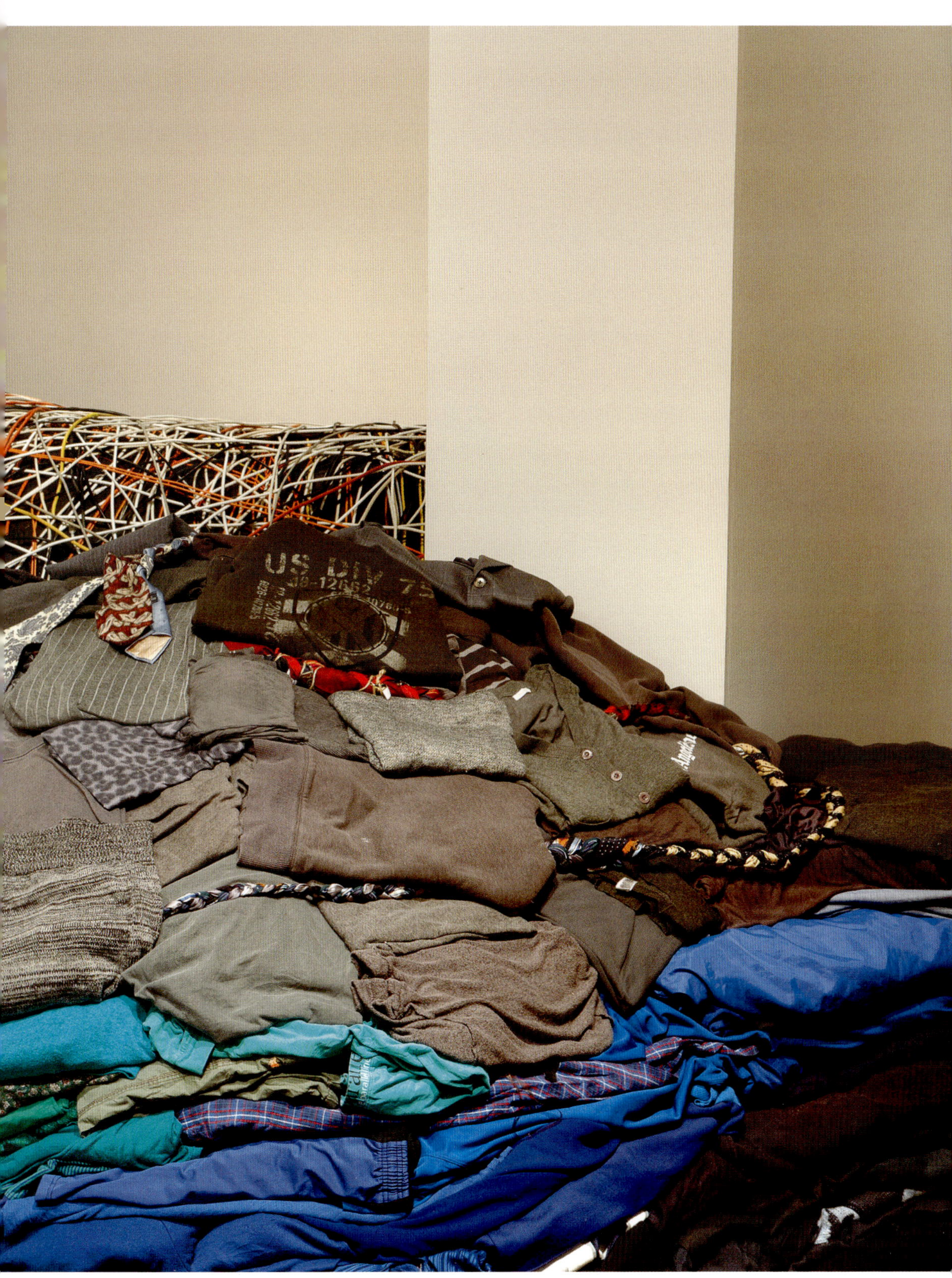

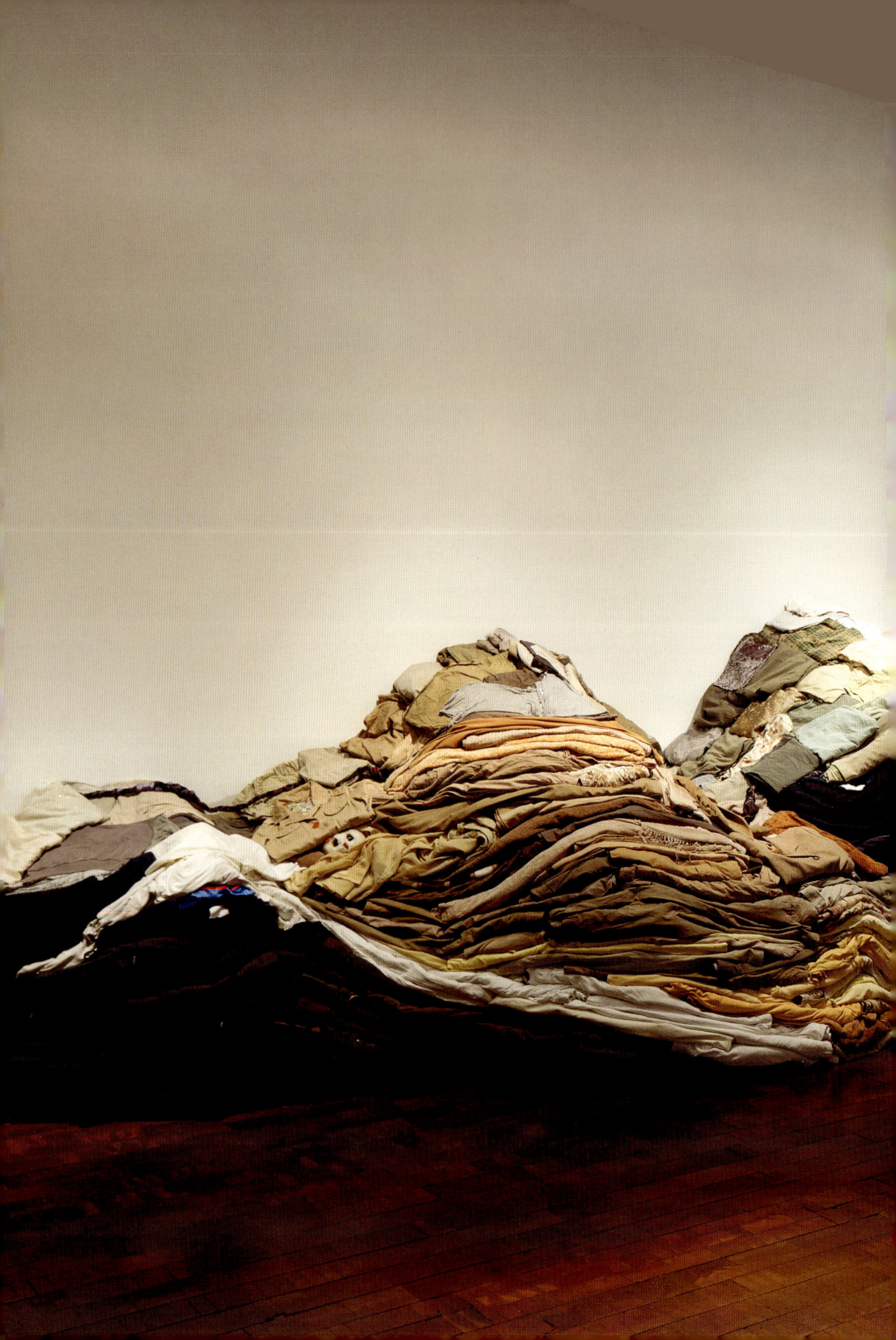

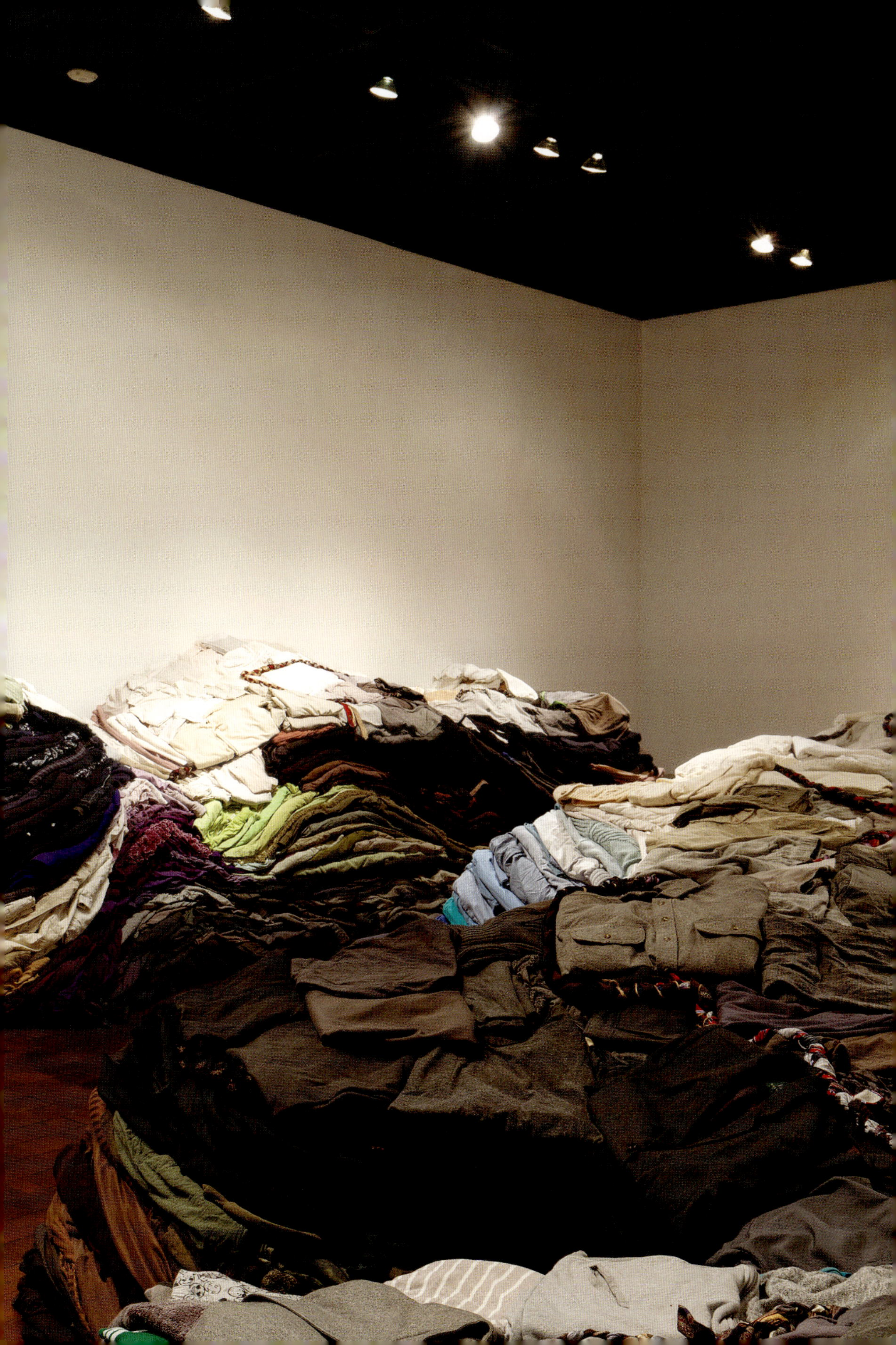

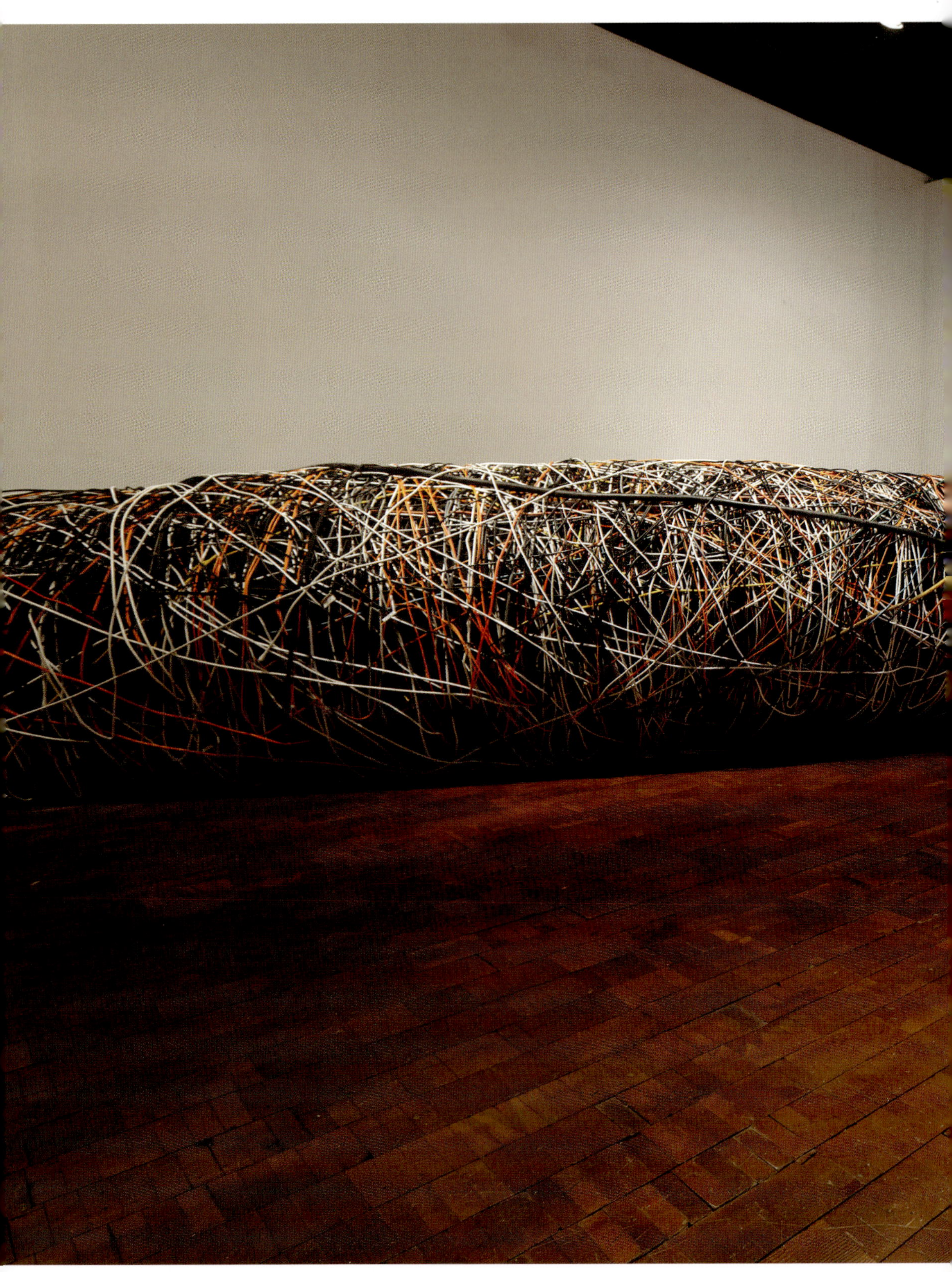

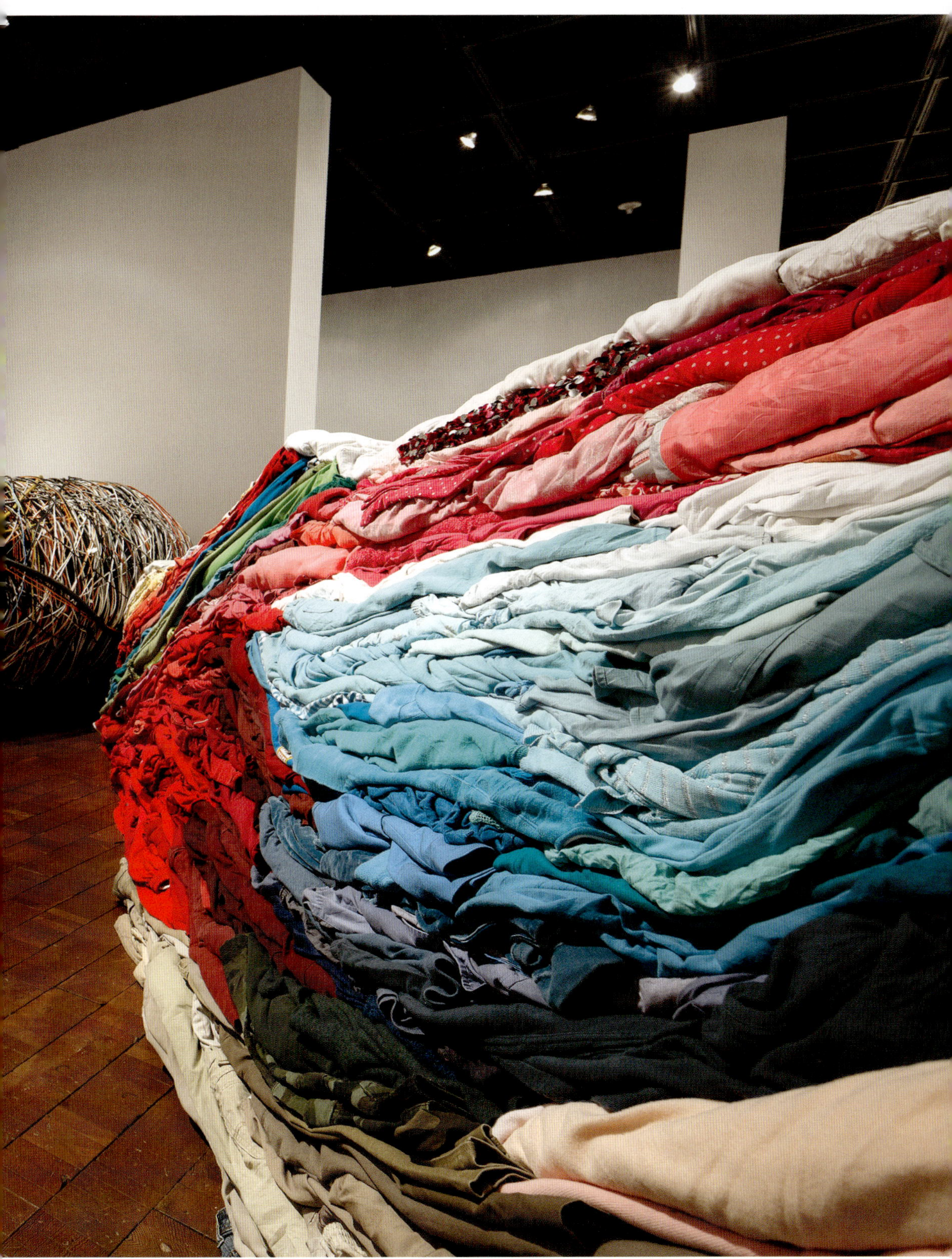

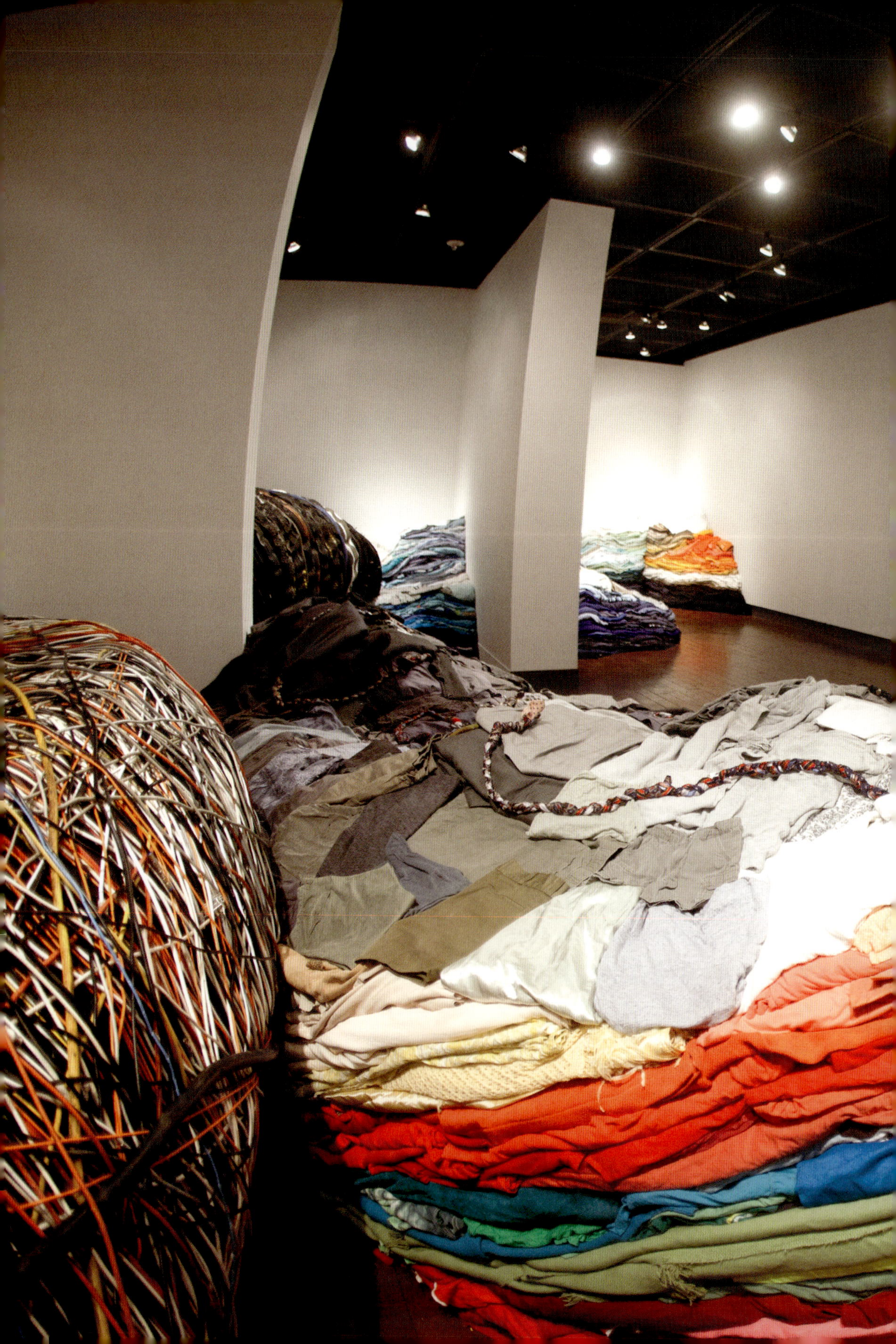

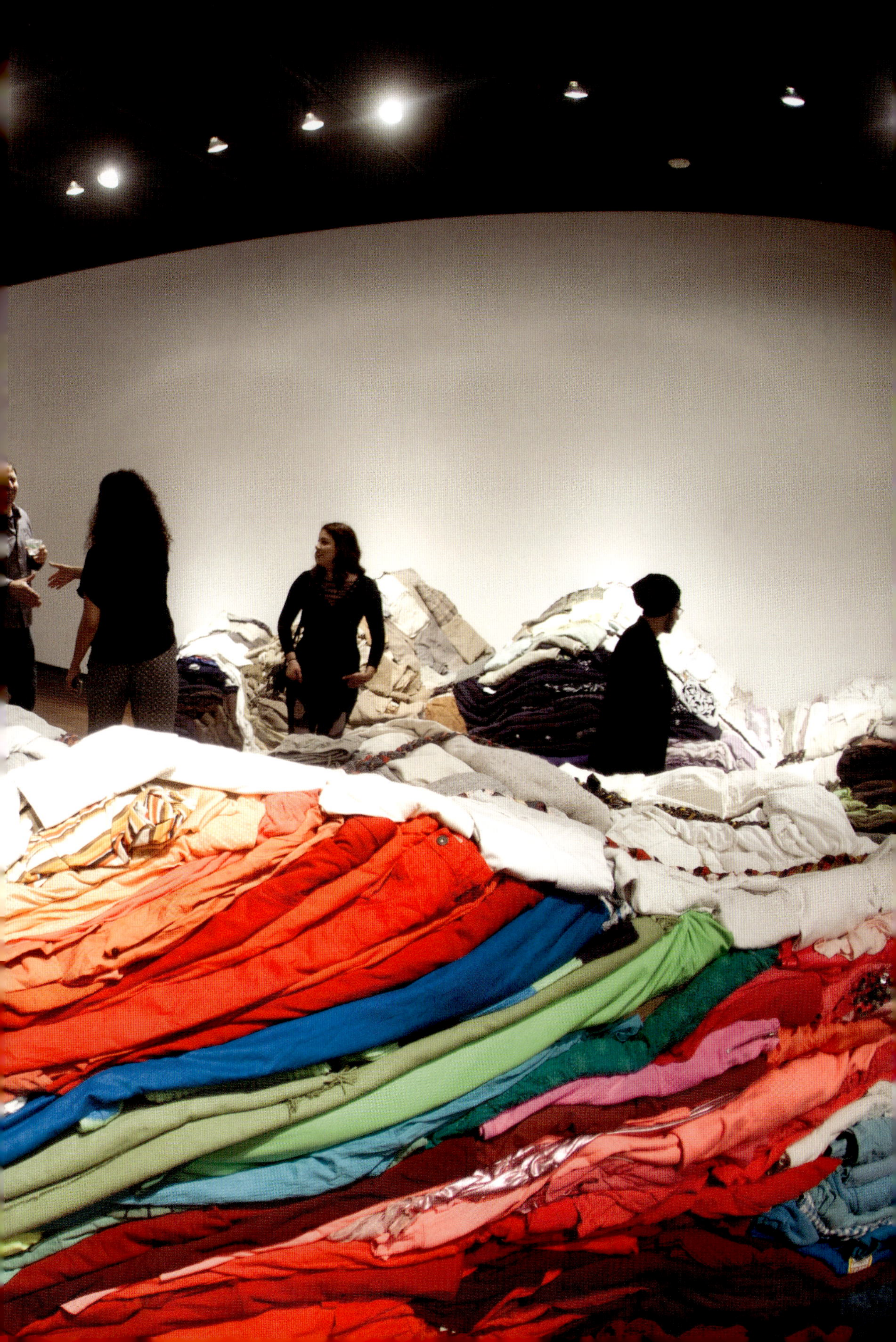

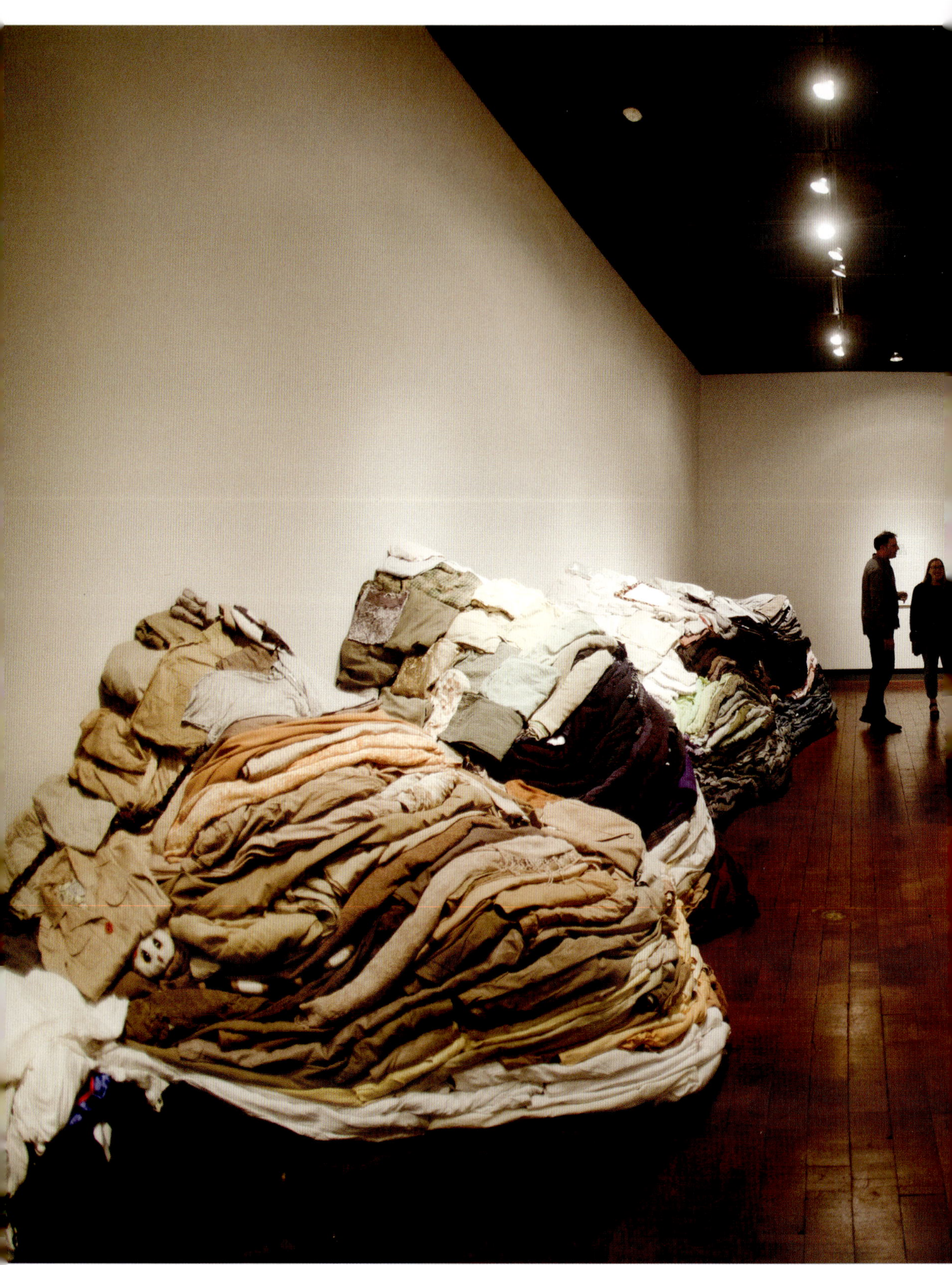

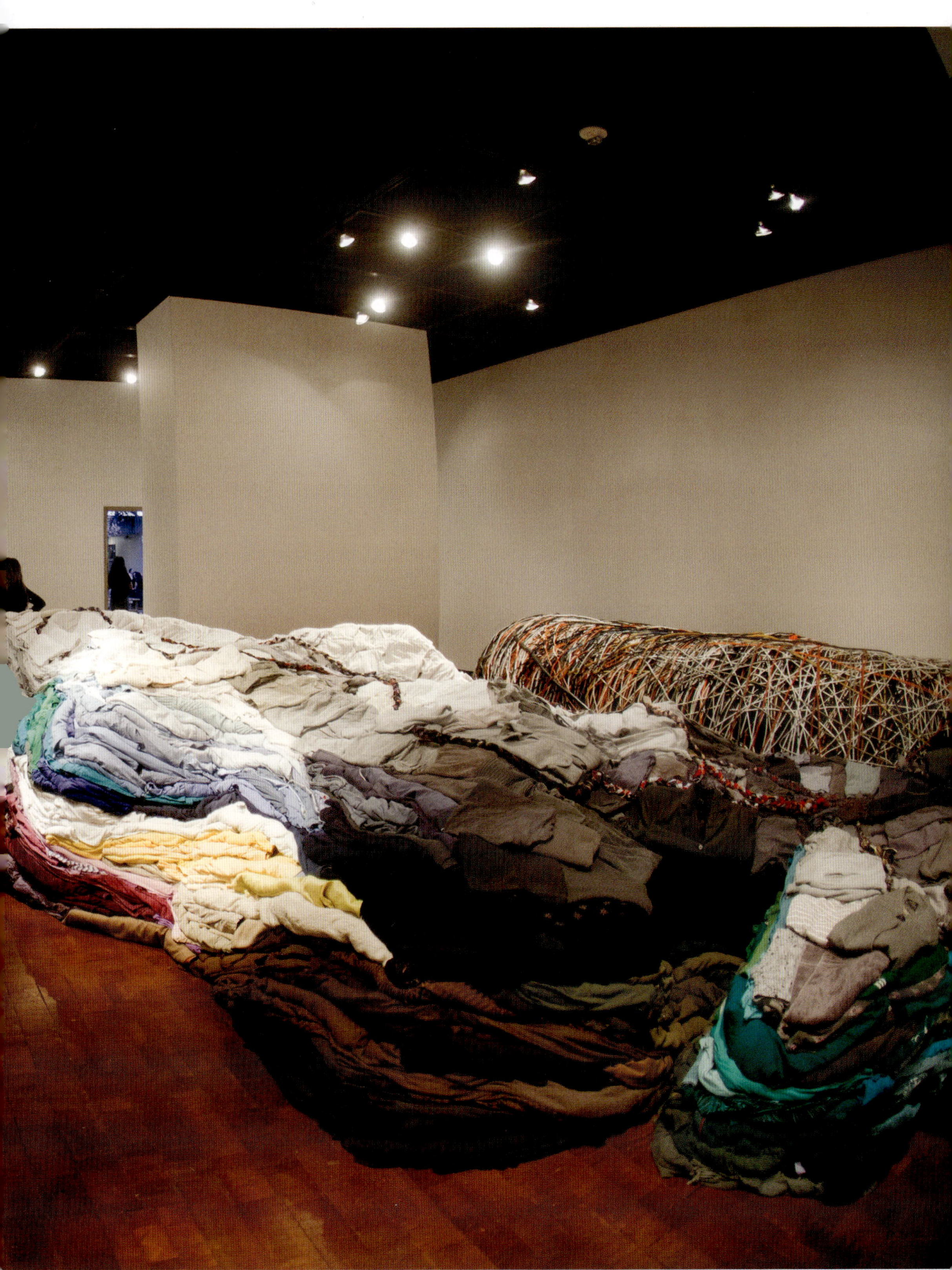

ETHICAL PRACTICES FOR A FASHION REVOLUTION

Tory Romero

The imbalance between fashion and health is affecting nearly every society in the world. The health of the earth, thus your health, is at major risk due to issues linked to mass production and consumption of clothing. This essay will highlight these issues and offer solutions and suggestions for a more conscious consumerism that can lead to institutional change as well.

Mass clothing consumption habits have degraded our planet, with negative effects in many regions as a consequence of the growth, extraction, and manipulation of materials destined to become fashion apparel; and after our clothes are no longer wanted, they become garbage. In 2014 alone, the third most populous country on earth, the United States, generated approximately 16.2 million tons of textile "garbage" *(EPA 8)*.

Textile manufacturing produces toxic chemicals that pollute the air, soil, and water. Additionally, when inexpensive clothing is created, it likely comes at the expense of degraded health for textile workers who risk unsafe conditions and cannot live on the wages they receive. The fashion industry workforce is often female-dominated and labor intensive (and also openly employs children), and the wages these workers are paid are alarmingly low *(ILO 25)*. For example, a monthly wage for a clothing industry worker in Sri Lanka is as low as $66 a month *(Luebker 1)*. Clothing companies that allow the exploitation of workers and the environment aren't concerned about this unfair treatment, as long as consumers keep their demand high and continue buying. Consumption and production aren't slowing, so these injustices will continue unless change by all cultures is supported. Understanding that people who purchase, create, or dispose of fashion at unsustainable rates are

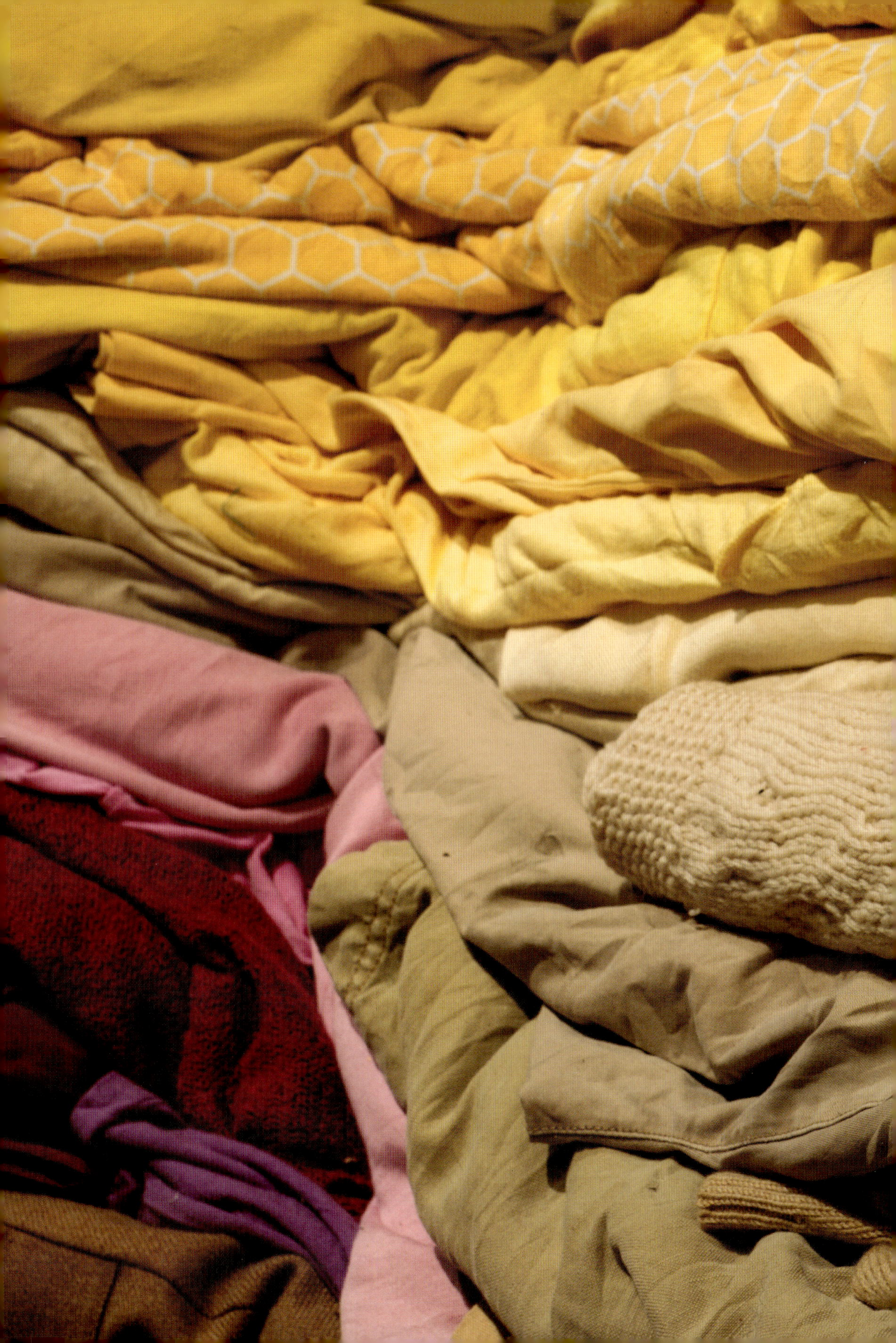

contributing to these ecological injustices may inspire consumers to make conscious decisions to work toward ending exploitive, unjust, and unsustainable practices related to the apparel industry.

For some consumers, clothing is simply a necessity; yet many, more-affluent buyers seek an added value, especially when their feelings become involved—fashions can boost confidence, show personal expression, denote cultural appreciation, and even represent cherished memories. Buying to fill an emotional need often leads to overpurchasing, with an excess of garments being produced and consumed and, eventually, becoming unnecessary waste. Society needs to develop sustainable changes that allow the health of the public and the planet to thrive. Individuals involved in the fashion industry, whether consumers, producers, or sellers, will be the ones responsible for this critical shift. Simple changes to the current consumer culture in many nations can have a tremendous impact, and healthy differences within the clothing industry can be fashioned to create environmental sustainability and to ensure healthy workers and consumers as well. The earth provides all the resources we need to live, and all the resources to produce clothing and the fashion that we may love so dearly. Choosing to support a healthy planet and society is a commitment to ourselves and our future.

The enduring phrase "reduce, reuse, recycle" is one of the best guides for achieving a healthy, sustainable life for the planet and societies alike. First, simply reducing the amount of clothing purchased is a step in the right direction. The demand to grow cotton, extract oils for polyester, raise and kill animals for leather, and further degrade the environment to produce other clothing materials will decrease if consumers purchase less—if no one is buying at rapid rates, then production will decrease. Consciously choosing sustainable fashion-buying habits may seem challenging, but it is necessary in order to change the current, unsustainable way some societies are living. Deciding between whether to save money or save the world is a personal choice that should come with the best intentions. Changing unsustainable purchasing habits to oppose unjust textile industry practices is not impossible, and it could result in a new paradigm wherein technology and innovations fall into the hands of caring, compassionate people.

A second step toward sustainability in fashion would be to find ways to reuse the clothing itself or its fabric. Repurposing and upcycling used clothing items keeps them out of the landfill while also reducing the demand for materials and causing a decrease in production. Ways to "repurpose" include making worn clothing into cloth materials used for cleaning; "upcycling" old clothing involves more innovative thinking, such as turning a sock with a hole in it into a hair accessory; both are sustainable ideas. Another way of reusing clothing is through donation—once clothes are outgrown or no longer liked, they can be donated to a charitable organization or directly to another person. Shopping at thrift stores or buying "previously-owned" clothing from other outlets also keeps perfectly usable clothing in circulation and another step away from becoming garbage.

Recycling is a modern technology that has become necessary in overly wasteful societies. Specifically, textile recycling—disassembling, sorting through, or recreating apparel—can reduce our use of resources and eliminate textiles in landfills. This is the third option for a textile's lifespan, but textile recycling does require energy, so reducing the production and consumption of apparel and increasing the reuse of clothing are the preferable ethical practices.

Today's shoppers need to choose whether they wish to be remembered as part of the era that left billions of tons of perfectly usable clothing as garbage while allowing the mistreatment of industry workers and the environment, or as part of the generation that took responsibility for making ethical choices and started a revolution with sustainable intentions in mind. "Reduce, reuse, recycle" can transform our fashion world into a fun, unique, and viable industry. Take a moment to consider the ethical, conscious changes that you can make in your daily life, and realize that even your small actions can result in huge victories toward a more livable and sustainable way of life..

Works Cited

International Labour Organization (ILO). *Final report of the discussion: Global Dialogue Forum on Wages and Working Hours in the Textiles, Clothing, Leather, and Footwear Industries.* Sectoral Policies Department, 2015.

Luebker, Malte. *Minimum wages in the global garment industry.* ILO Regional Office for Asia and the Pacific, 2014.

United States Environmental Protection Agency. *Reducing and Reusing Basics,* 2017

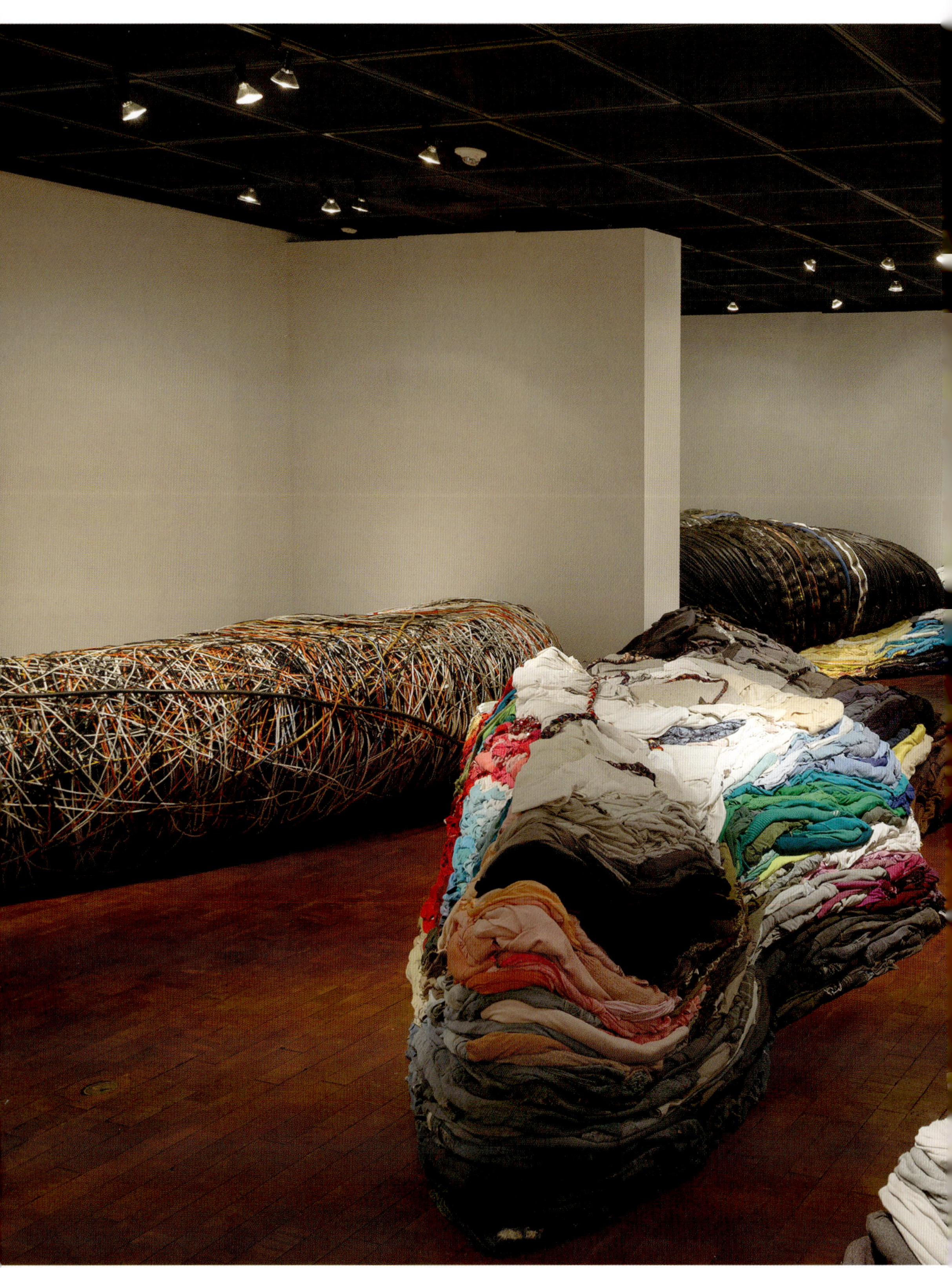

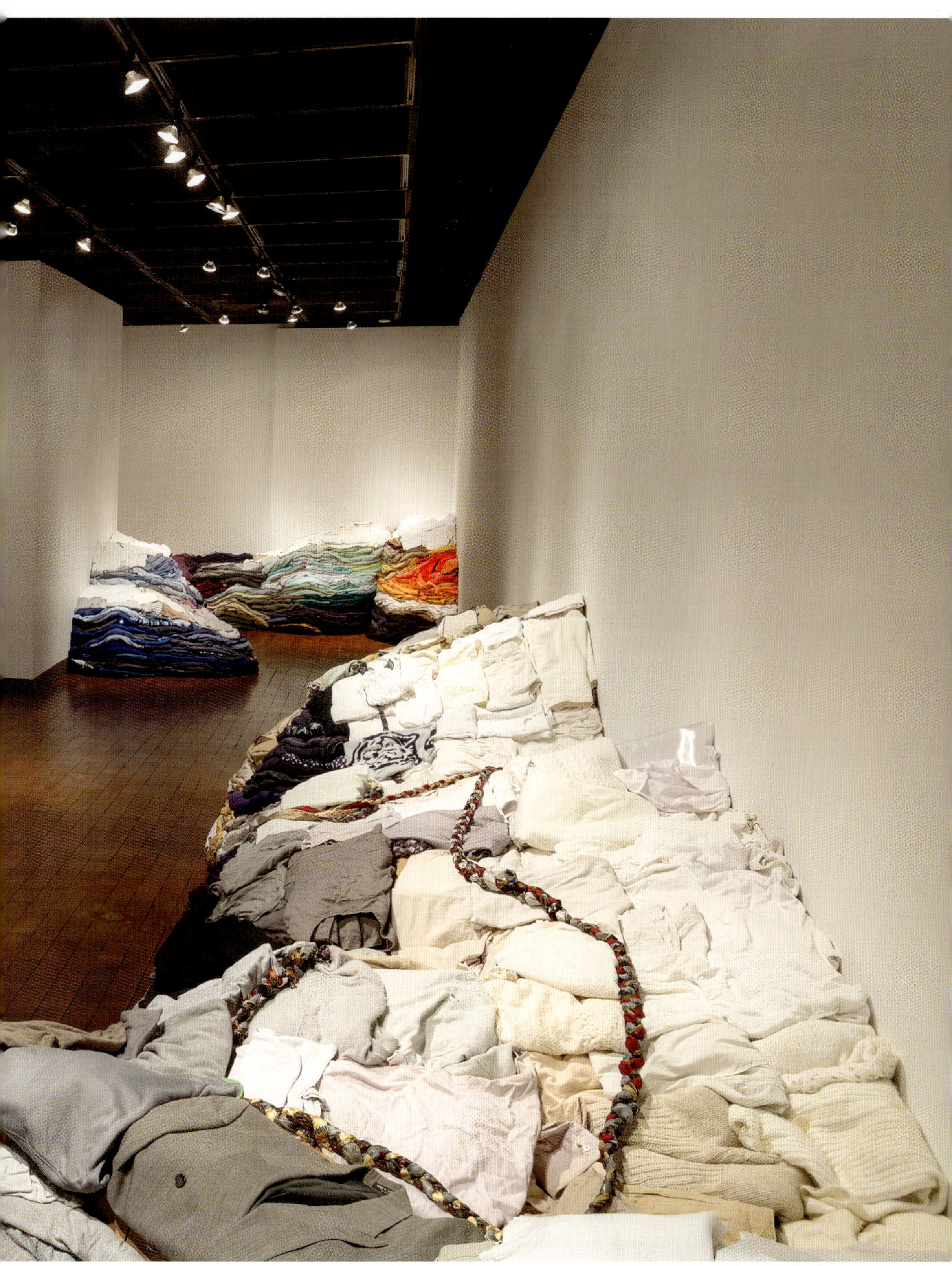

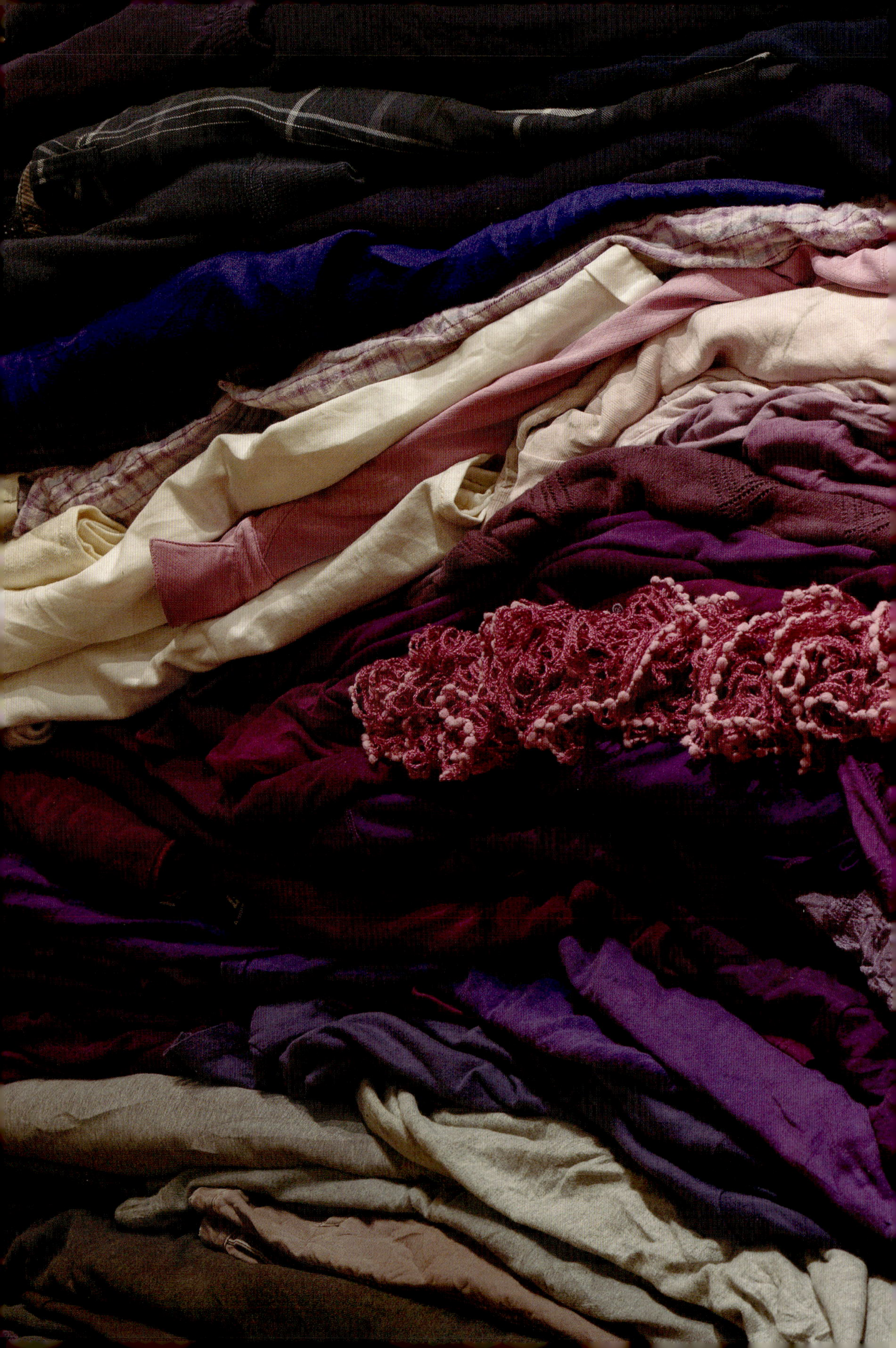

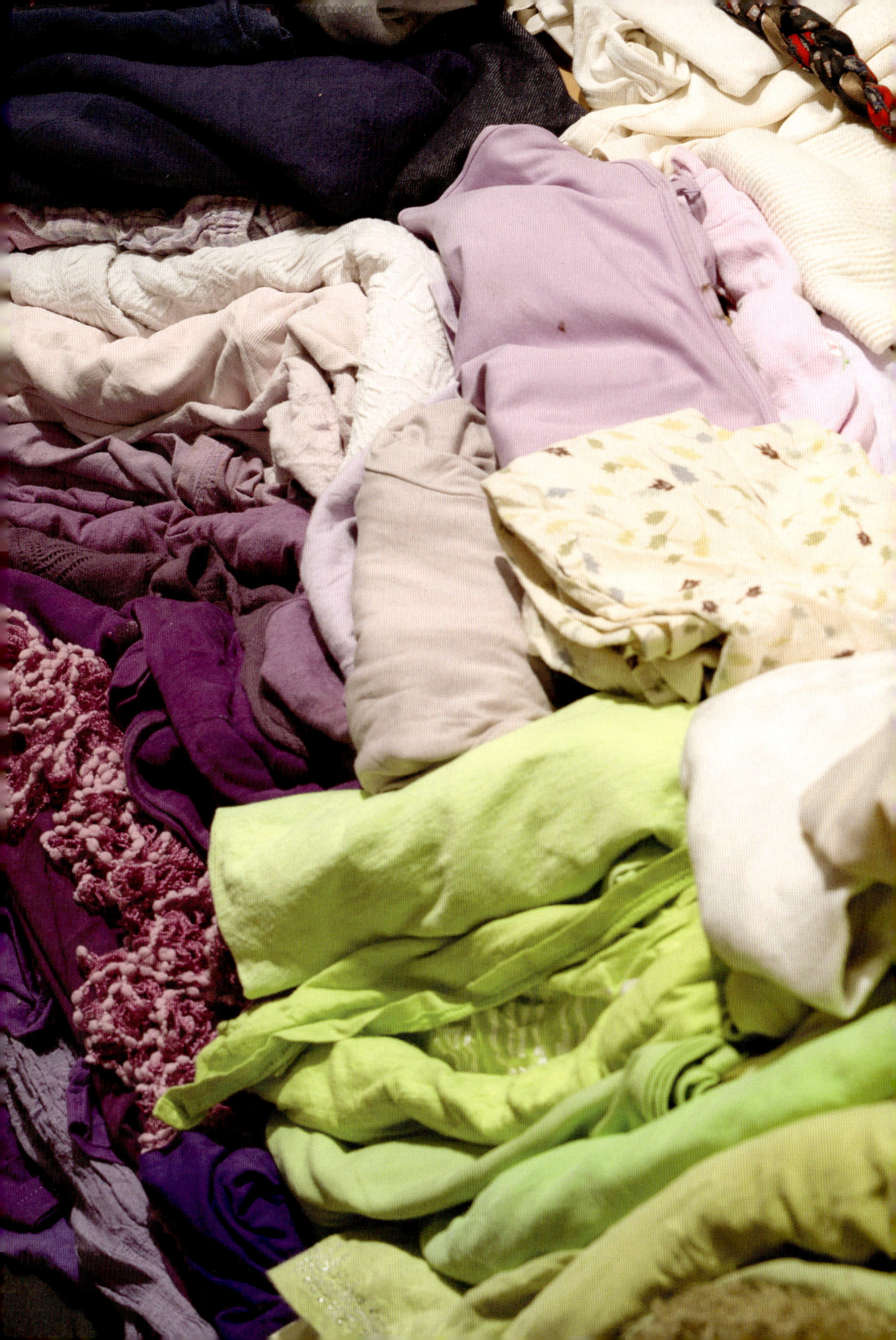

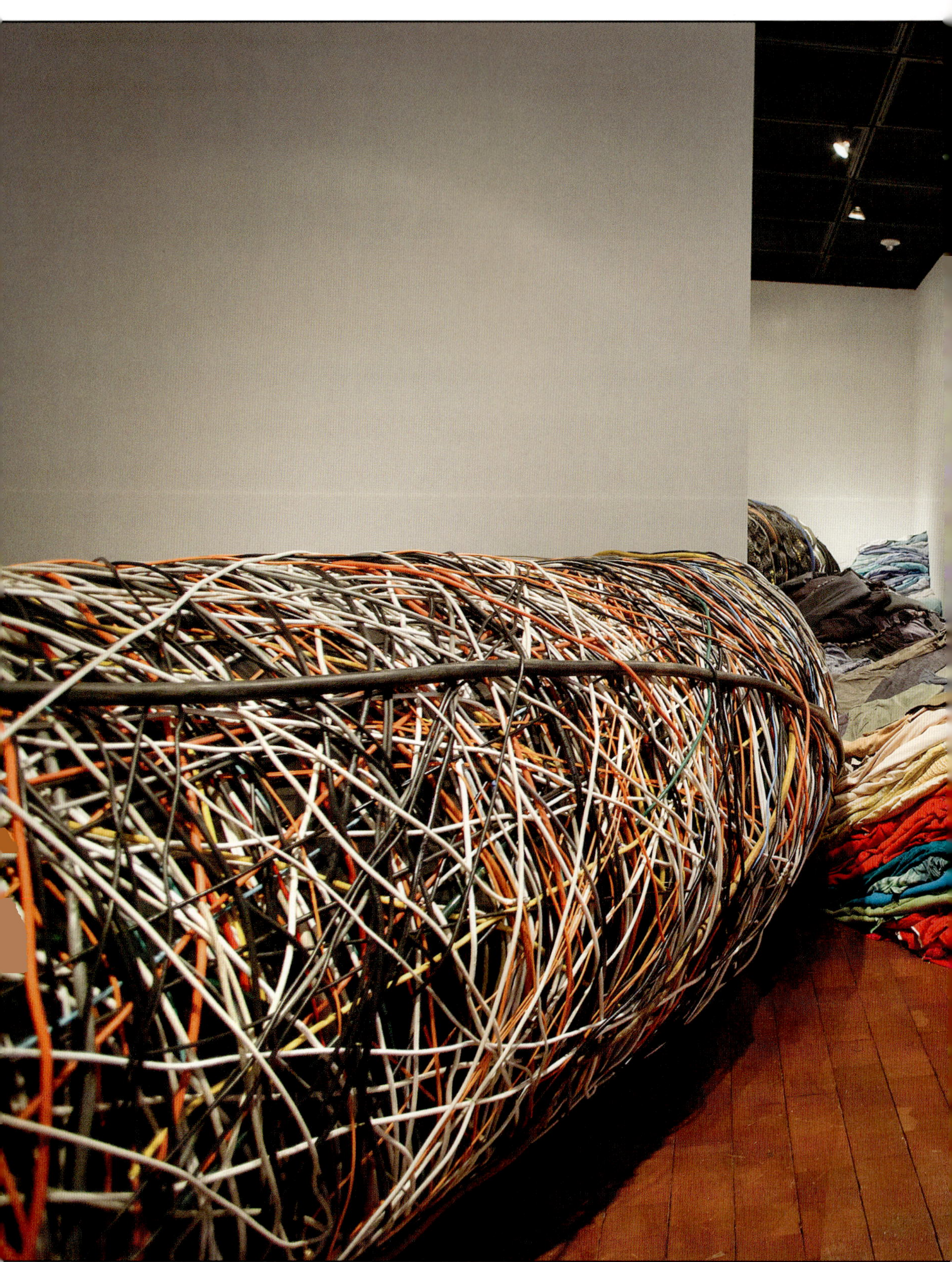

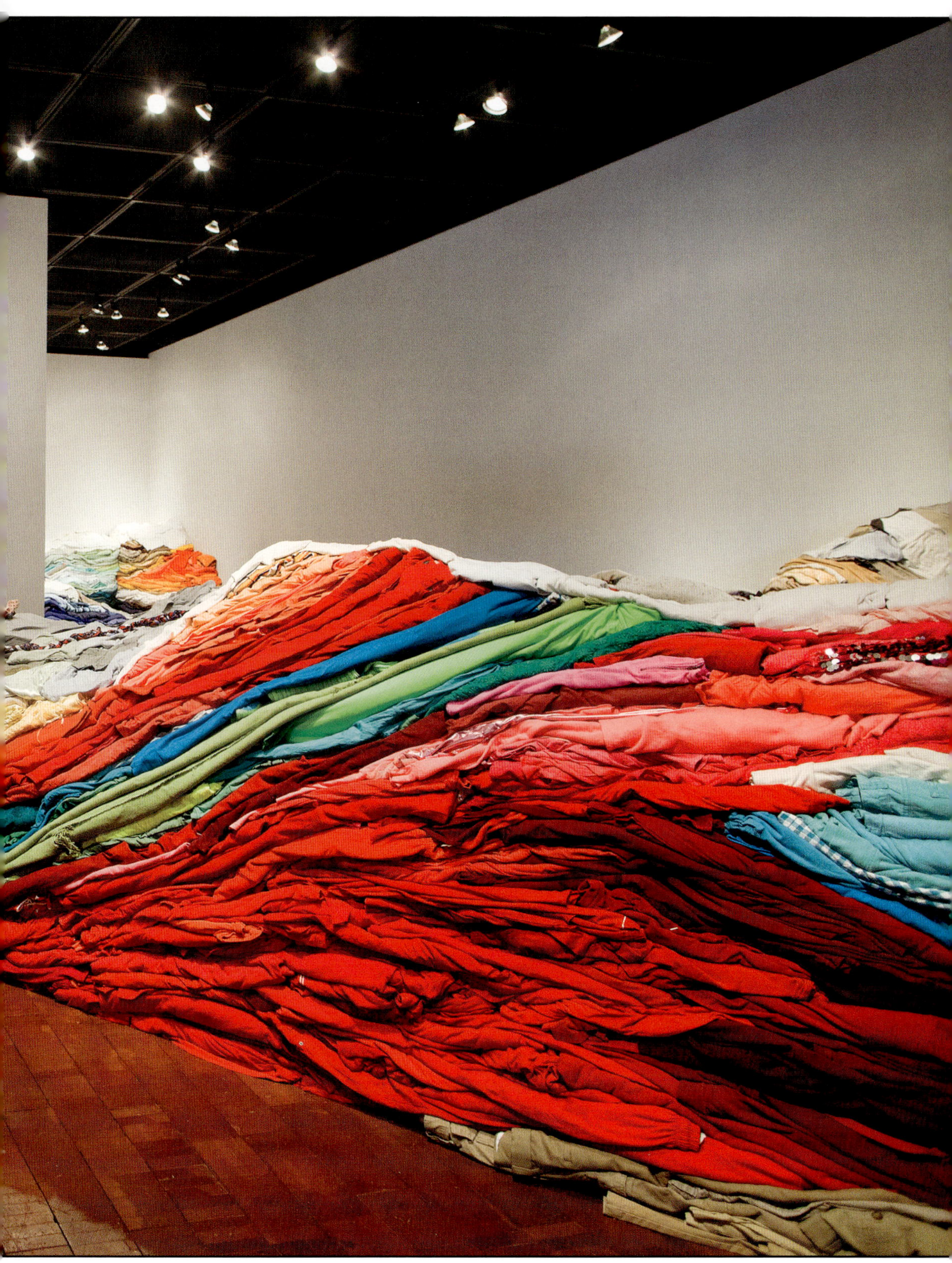

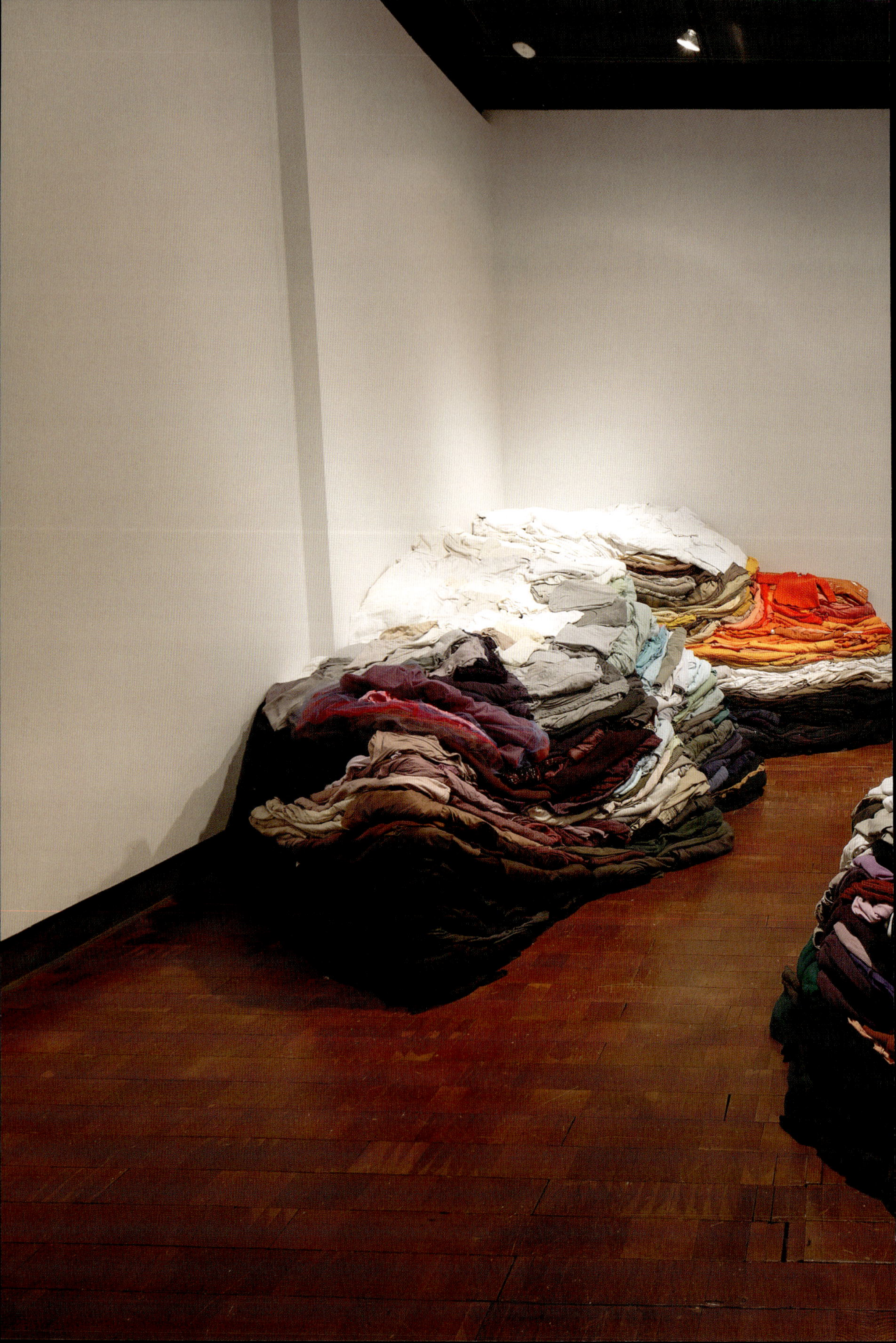

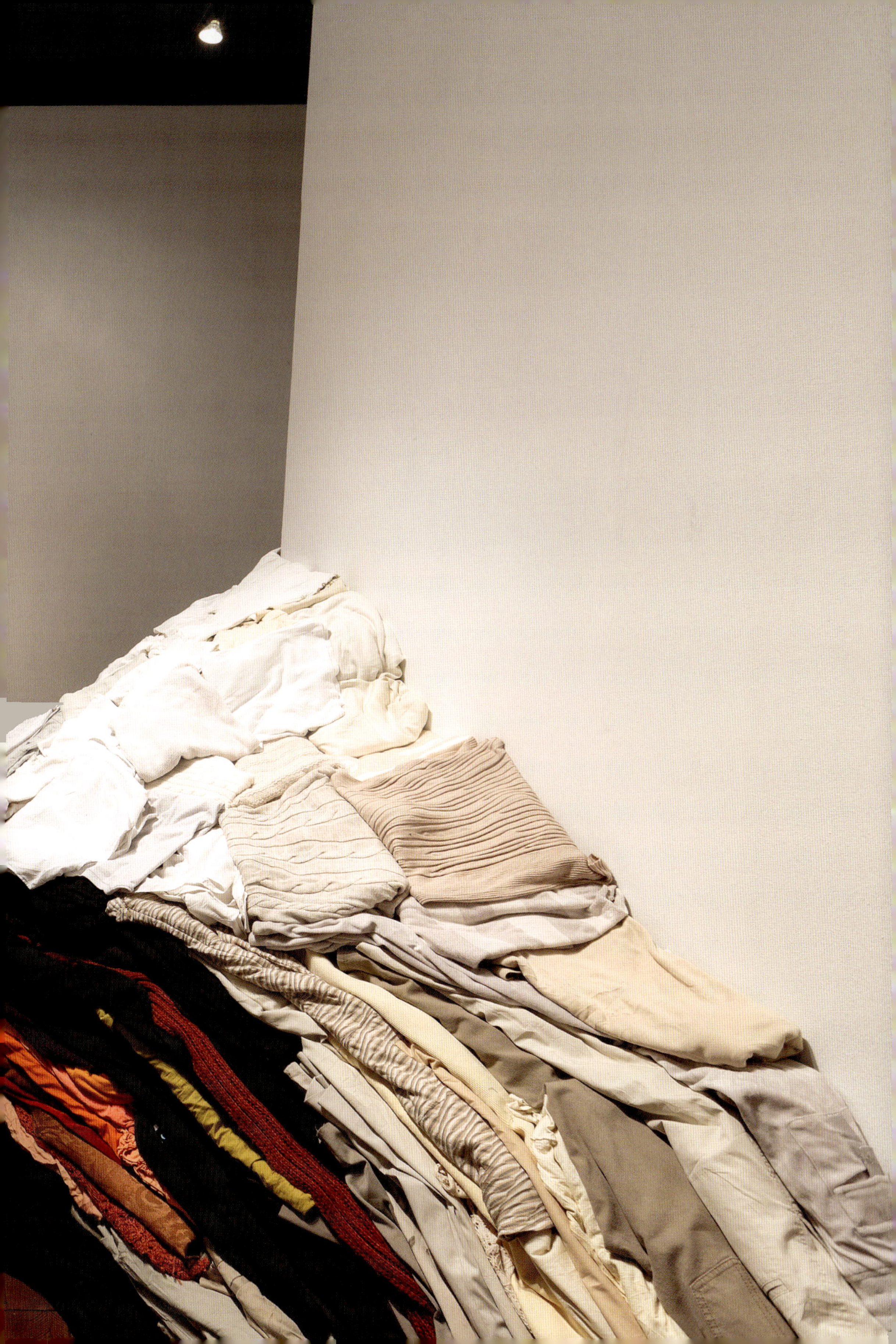

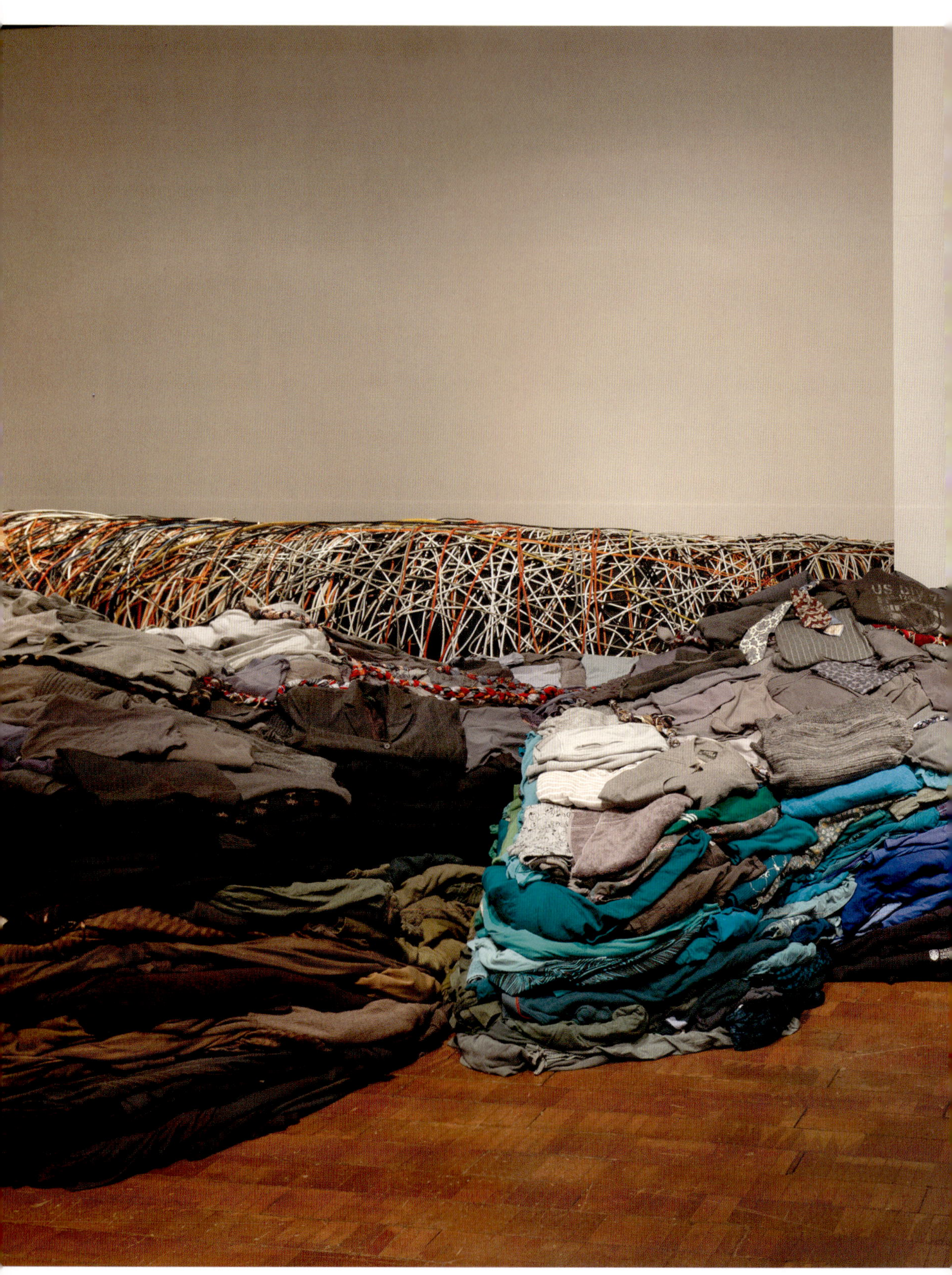

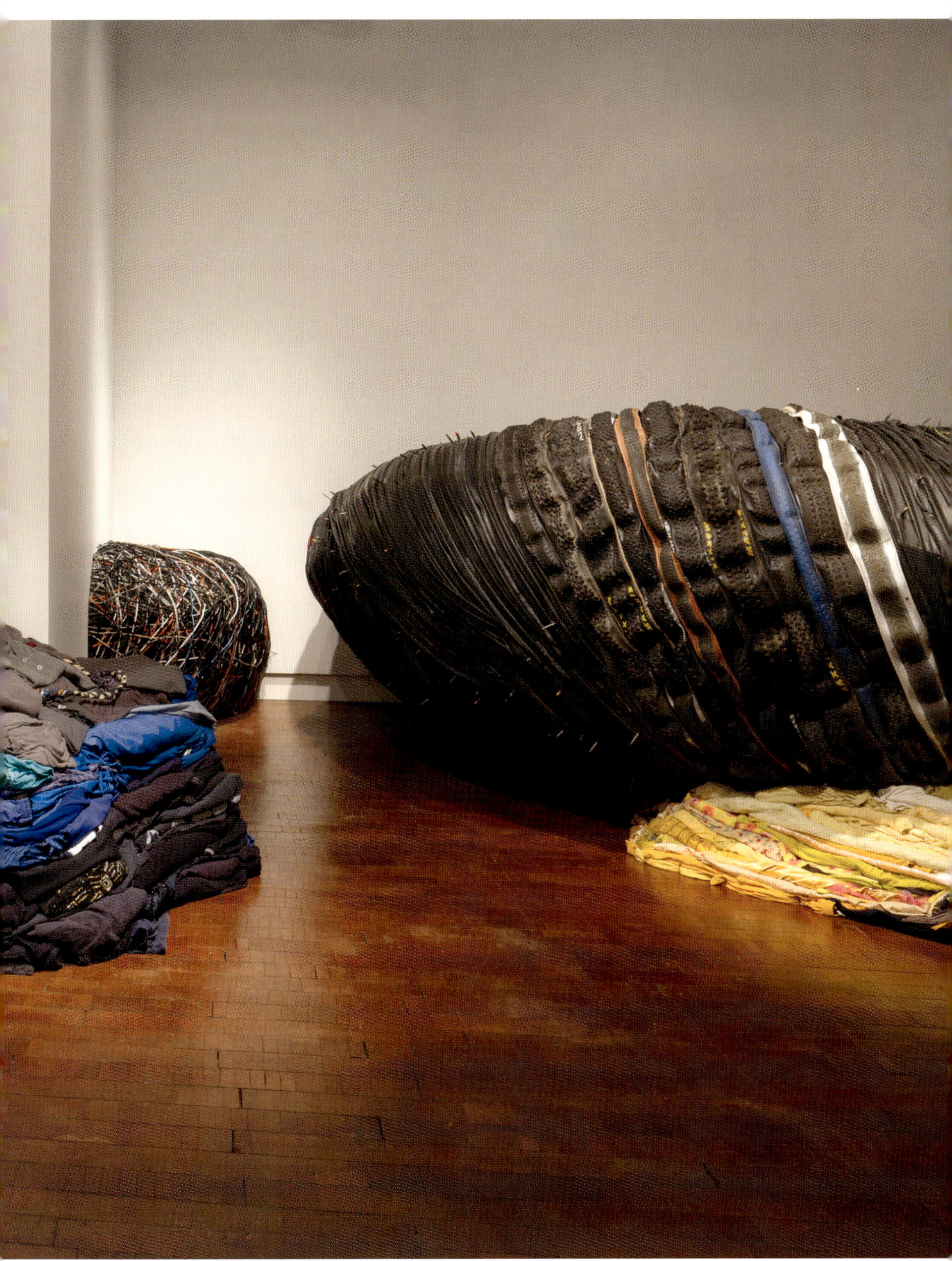

THE ECONOMICS OF FAST FASHION

Ganit Singh

"My grandmother has only one shirt in her wardrobe. My mother has three. My daughter's generation, 50. And 48 percent of them, she never wears."

— Jack Ma, Founder and Executive Chairman of Alibaba.[1]

Imagine if everything in your wardrobe grew by 50 percent. Do you think you would notice the sudden rise in tops, bottoms and accessories? Surely you would notice the increase in options to wear before a day of work or leisure. While you may believe this to be true however, statistics would prove you wrong.

Over the course of just seven short years, the apparel industry has entered into a boom that is accelerating astronomically. Valued at over 1.4 trillion dollars, and experiencing a market increase of over 50 percent, apparel is one of the hottest growing industries in the world, and economic indicators show no sign of the market slowing. Compounding yearly, the market has been increasing at a 4.6 percent rate since 2012.[2] *(See table.)*

Annual Clothing Consumption (In Billions)	2011	2012	2013	2014	2015
Menswear	329.1	340.1	355.1	373.0	663.8
Womenswear	558.7	578.0	603.7	634.3	663.8
Childrenswear	163.8	170.3	178.7	188.8	199.3

(Marketline Advantage)

To give you an enhanced perspective, growth of GDP for all global goods and service markets was just 2.6 percent at that time. Simply put, these statistics infer that each year we are buying more

[1] Stanford Graduate School of Business (30 Sep 2015). Jack Ma, Alibaba Group: Stanford GSB 2015 Entrepreneurial Company of the Year. Retrieved June 1, 2018, from https://www.youtube.com/watch?v=kh_wPWQrWZA

[2] Marketline Advantage. "Global—Apparel Retail." (13 Sep 2017). http:// advantage.marketline.com.login.ezproxy.library.ualberta.ca/Product?ptype= Industries&pid= MLIP2070–0018.

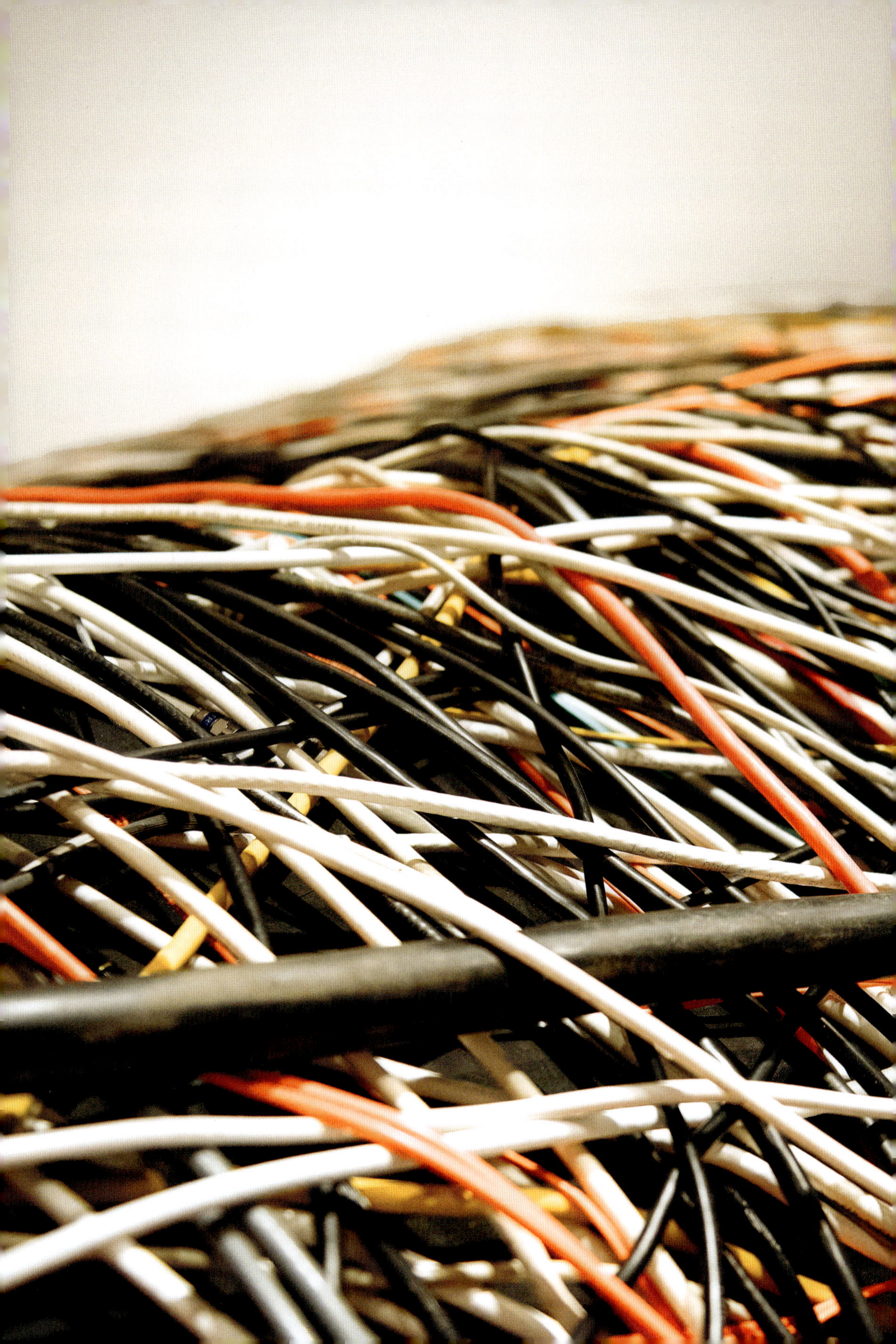

and more clothes to feed a growing addiction. Indeed, we have become a society that is obsessed with clothing, as global employment in the textile and sector was reported to grow to a staggering 57.8 million jobs by 2014.[3]

It's likely that these growing numbers would be praised by conservative economists, as an increase in expenditure is thought to bring forth a rise in standard of living. Beyond its reference in the UN's Millennial Development Goals, economic growth is a term that is conventionally associated with improving well-being.[4]

While a great deal of academic literature demonstrates the positive effects of economic growth, much is still to be learned about the adverse effects of income inequality. Although as a society our standard of living has increased dramatically over the past century, last year the world's top 1 percent of the population took home 50.1 percent of all household wealth.[5]

Apparel is a great market to study in this regard, as it presents goods that have a limited shelf life and a frequent need to be replenished. With an examination of the global apparel market, we can understand why there is a sudden boom and what implications it has on suppliers and purchasers involved. To better understand the boom, we must draw our attention to the world of fast fashion.

"Fashion constantly changes and so do our customers."

— Stefan Persson, son of H&M Founder Erling Persson[6]

Welcome to Fast Fashion

Fast fashion is a term used to depict apparel that is quickly and cheaply produced in hopes to recreate trendy designs from the high-fashion world. Known for creating goods with a limited shelf life and a minimal life cycle, H&M, Zara, and Forever 21 are among the top fast-fashion companies today. Backpacking off of the concept of "52 micro-seasons of fashion," each representing a given week in a year, these companies specialize in producing apparel at a lightning-fast speed to sustain extremely quick turnovers in inventory. Products sold at these stores typically reflect trends

Sourced from Forbes, 2018	High Fashion	High Fashion	Fast Fashion	Fast Fashion
The World's Most Valuable Brands	Louis Vuitton	Gucci	H&M	Zara
Rank	#20	#47	#36	#51
Brand Value	28.8 Billion	12.7 Billion	14.2 Billion	11.3 Billion
Brand Revenue	9.9 Billion	4.7 Billion	21.6 Billion	17.2 Billion
1 Year % Change	6%	5%	-11%	6%

(Forbes)[8]

---

[3] World Bank. "World Bank Open Data," 2017. data.worldbank.org

[4] United Nations Millennium Development Goals. (n.d.). Retrieved June 1, 2018, from http://www.un.org/millenniumgoals

[5] Credit Suisse Group. "Global Wealth Report 2017: Where Are We Ten Years after the Crisis?" Retrieved June 1, 2018, from https://www.credit-suisse.com/corporate/en/articles/news-and-expertise/global-wealth-report-2017-201711.html

[6] D'Souza, Nandini. "Will the See Now/Buy Now Fashion Model Really Work?" Harper's BAZAAR, Harper's BAZAAR, 28 Mar. 2018, www.harpersbazaar.com/fashion/fashion-week/a14343/fashion-industry-changes/.

seen in the music and film industry, as many global celebrities have partnerships or are in good standing with fast-fashion brands.[7]

Despite the notoriety, fast-fashion companies are extremely powerful. By selling designer clothing at pennies on the dollar, the industry's growth has led to several brands being placed on the coveted Forbes 500 list of most valuable brands.

Celebrity	Beyonce	Pharrell Williams	Nicki Minij	David Beckham	Iggy Azalia	The Weeknd
Endorsed By	H&M	Uniqlo	H&M	H&M	Forever 21	H&M
Twitter Followers	15.2 M	10.8 M	21.3 M	N/A	8.06 M	8.46 M
Instagram Followers	111.3 M	10.5 M	85.7 M	42.3 M	11.2 M	16.5 M

(Forbes)[8]

In 2016 alone, H&M opened 427 new stores; that's more than one store a day. Operating in more than 63 countries and employing more than 160,000 people worldwide, H&M is proving that fast fashion is more than just a trend.[9] Similarly, Zara houses more than 2,200 stores in 93 different countries.[10]   Zara founder Amancio Ortega boasts a net worth in excess of 70 billion dollars and, at the time of this writing, is the fourth richest man in the world.[11] In 2017 alone, he made over 1.5 billion dollars on dividends from Zara stock. Stefan Persson, son of H&M's founder Erling Persson, is no stranger to fast-fashion fortune, as he netted around $805 million in 2016. [12]

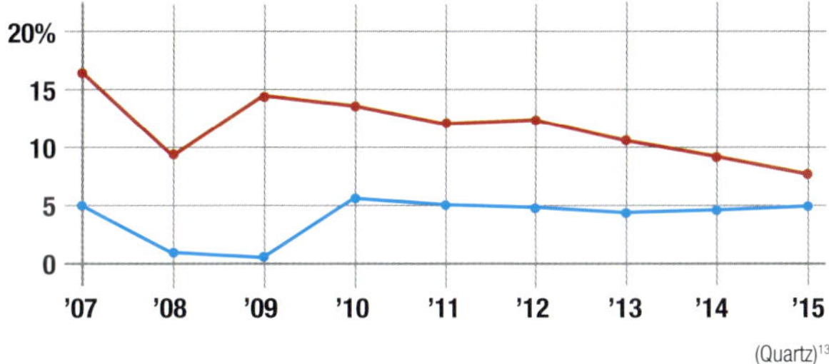

(Quartz)[13]

The Other Side

While there may be a lot of winners in the world of fast fashion, the industry is anything but glamorous. Beyond stealing the artistry of high-fashion designers, these companies are notorious for the poor working conditions experienced by their employees in developing countries. In 2010 H&M made headlines when a factory supplying their apparel in Bangladesh caught fire and took

---

[7] Answers Ltd. "The Celebrity Effect in Fast Fashion Industry." UKEssays, UK Essays, 22 Nov. 2018, www.ukessays.com/essays/marketing/the-celebrity-effect-in-fast-fashion-industry-marketing-essay.php.

[8] Forbes. "The World's Most Valuable Brands." *Forbes*, 2017. www.forbes.com/powerful-brands/list/.

[9] H&M. "Join the H&M Group." *H&M Career*, 2017, about.hm.com/en/career.html.

[10] Inditex. "Media." Inditex, 2017, www.inditex.com/about-us/our-brands/zara.

[11] Forbes. "Amancio Ortega." Forbes, Forbes Magazine, 2017, www.forbes.com/profile/amancio-ortega/.

[12] Catherine Clifford. "In 2017, There Was a New Billionaire Every 2 Days." *CNBC*, CNBC, 22 Jan. 2018, www.cnbc.com/2018/01/22/oxfam-report-in-2017-there-was-a-new-billionaire-every-2-days.html.

[13] Marc Bain. "One Chart Shows How Fast Fashion Is Reshaping the Global Apparel Industry." *Quartz*, 2 Nov. 2016, qz.com/825554/hm-zara-primark-and-forever-21-one-euromonitor-chart-shows-how-fast-fashion-is-reshaping-the-global-apparel-industry/.

the lives of 21 workers.[14] Despite being among the world's wealthiest companies, these factories are not audited vigorously for safety standards.

One might think a horrific tragedy would be enough to spur action from such a powerful entity, however despite signing the legally binding Bangladesh Accord on Fire and Building Safety in 2013 (alongside other fast-fashion companies), a second factory supplying H&M products caught fire in 2016.[15]

Fire safety is not the only concern for garment workers. A shocking 2016 report by The India Committee of the Netherlands compares the life of garment workers in Bangalore, India, to that of modern slavery. The report details the lives of young women who travel from different parts of India to join the garment industry. Producing clothing for brands such as H&M, Zara, Gap, and Tommy Hilfiger, the women are required to stay in hostels during their time of employment and are very limited in their personal freedom.[16]

Under constant surveillance by guards, the women are escorted to and from work and are allowed to leave the hostels for only two hours a week on Sunday. During this time they usually shop for groceries and personal items. Women who do not return during this two-hour window are subject to punishment, as they are not allowed to enter the hostel without the warden's permission. [17] Conditions of this sort are hard to imagine by workers living in a developed nation such as the United States, however these struggles are all but commonplace for textile workers all across the world.

While wages at these facilities are slightly above the minimum, these are hardly livable wages. Migrant women are often required to pay well above the free-market price for rent. Furthermore, these massively successful garment-manufacturing companies have put few safeguards in place to protect their female workers against abuse by the escorting guards hired to watch over them. The report goes into chilling detail about women fearing to speak about the abuse out of a fear of being fired by their employers. [18]

The Quality Trade-Off

By selling products at the lowest possible price, fast-fashion companies are constantly engaged in a race to the bottom. The success of this industry is founded in product design, which allows

---

[14] M. Hickman. (2011, October 22). "21 workers die in fire at H&M factory." Retrieved June 1, 2018, from https://www.independent.co.uk/life-style/fashion/news/21-workers-die-in-fire-at-hm-factory-1914292.html

[15] H. Timmons. (2016, February 02). "Another major factory fire in Bangladesh shows 'industry safeguards' are failing." *Quartz.* Retrieved June/July, 2018, from https://qz.com/608698/another-major-factory-fire-in-bangladesh-shows-industry-safeguards-are-failing/

[16] India Committee of the Netherlands. "Unfree and Unfair: Poor Living Conditions and Restricted Freedom of Movement of Young Migrant Workers in Bangalore." ICN – January 2016. (2016, January). Retrieved June/July, 2018, from http://www.indianet.nl/

[17] See India Committee of the Netherlands, "Unfree and Unfair."

[18] M. Bain. (2016, January 29). "'We cannot talk about it': Factory workers for major fashion labels live confined by guards." Retrieved June 1, 2018, from https://qz.com/605914/we-cannot-talk-about-it-factory-workers-for-hm-and-others-live-confined-by-guards/

for quality to lag behind in importance. Fast-fashion companies have no reservations in making cheap, low-quality clothing because they understand that the consumer is not looking for a long-term or sustainable product. Consumers are typically looking for a low-price trendy outfit and are not thinking about environmental sustainability or fair practices involved in production.

Styles are constantly changing, and with the price points of apparel so low, consumers are unafraid to routinely change their wardrobe. Ultimately it is the garment and textile workers who suffer the most in this race to the bottom. Workers in the garment industry are estimated to work anywhere from 10 to 18 hours per day, depending on the number of orders waiting to be filled. [19]

This quality trade-off has put the world of fashion is in a state of flux. Fast-fashion companies have used pull marketing strategies (e.g., search engine optimization, product placement in media), economies of scale (output beyond demand, to keep prices low), and sheer brute force (push marketing) to grab the attention of the onlooking customer. The end result is a price war, as retailers look to lower their prices and cut corners on quality as well as sustainability, safety, and fair compensation in order to become the low-cost leader.

The Tough Questions

Ultimately it is our responsibility as consumers to be answerable to the moral and financial dilemmas presented. What obligation should fashion brands have to take care of their garment workers? Is there something inherently wrong with making disposable clothing?

The silver lining of capitalist economies is that they allow us to vote with our income. Our faith in the fast-fashion industry can be quantified by our individual investments. Personally, I think lines should be drawn when it comes to the exploitation of a designer's artistry and of an individual's labor. Fast-fashion companies allow us to buy clothing at an extremely low price, but it's important to ask at what other costs. Do the few dollars you save on clothing justify the poor working wages and long hours for workers in a factory? Would you be willing to pay more for clothing if you knew it was created in a safe and fair environment?

As of now it seems that consumers are willing to support fast-fashion companies contingent on the prices being low. It is important to remember that consumers have power to change this industry in the form of their disposable income. If you don't want companies like H&M and Zara and others to persist in their malicious practices, one of the first things you can do is stop buying from their stores. Financial and verbal protest may help push fashion retailers to be more accountable for the workers they indirectly employ.

---

[19] See India Committee of the Netherlands, "Unfree and Unfair."

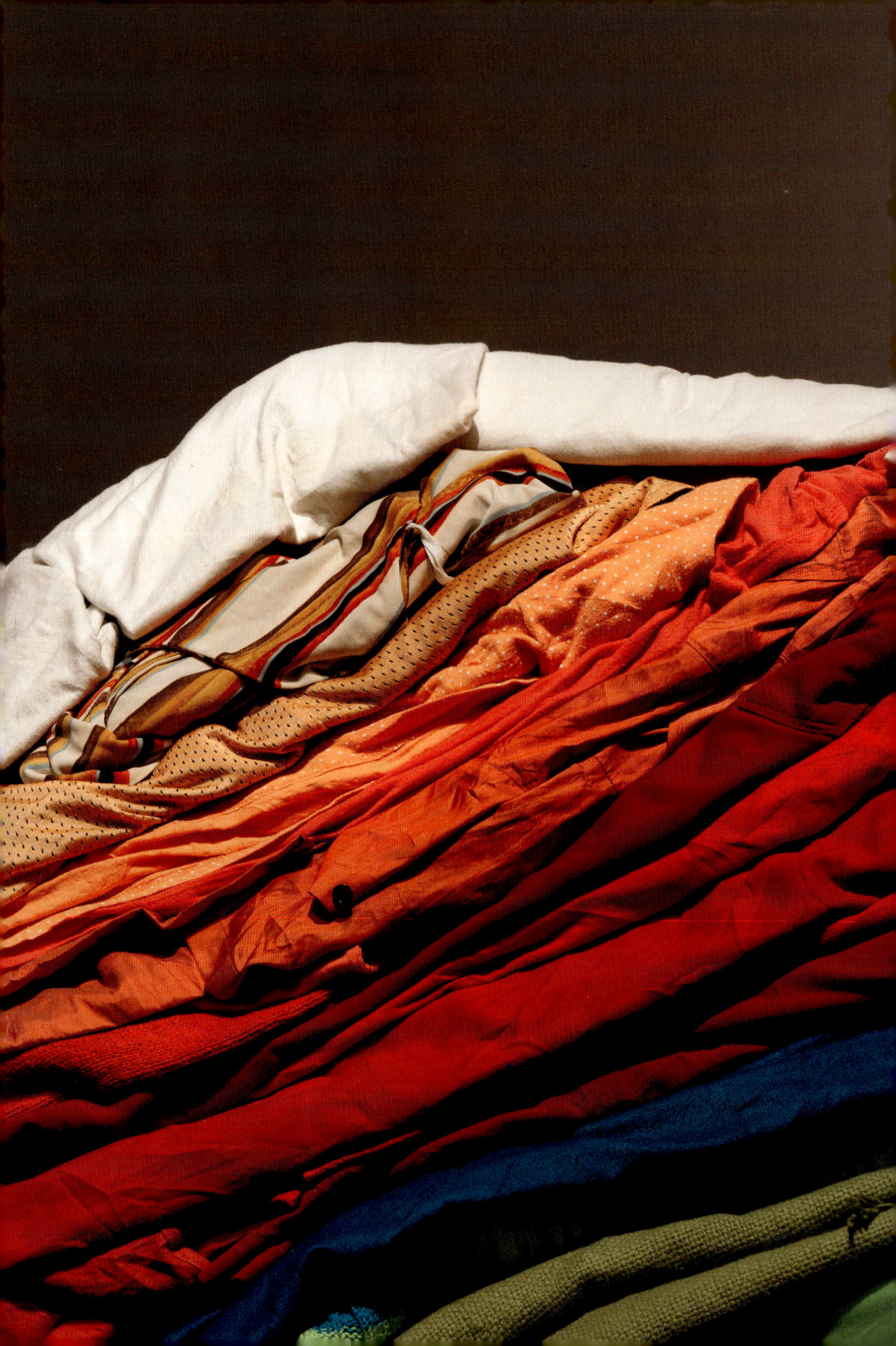

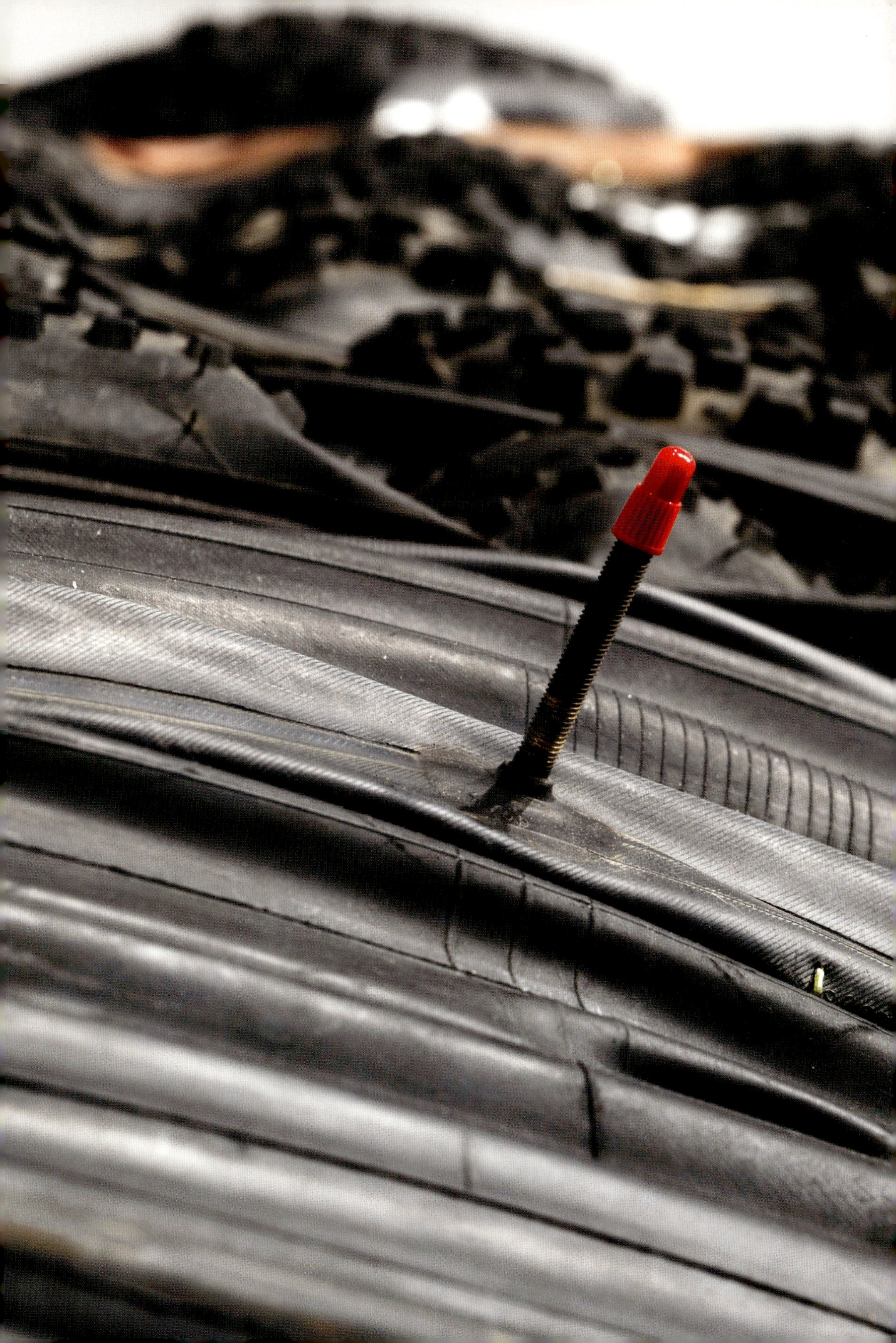

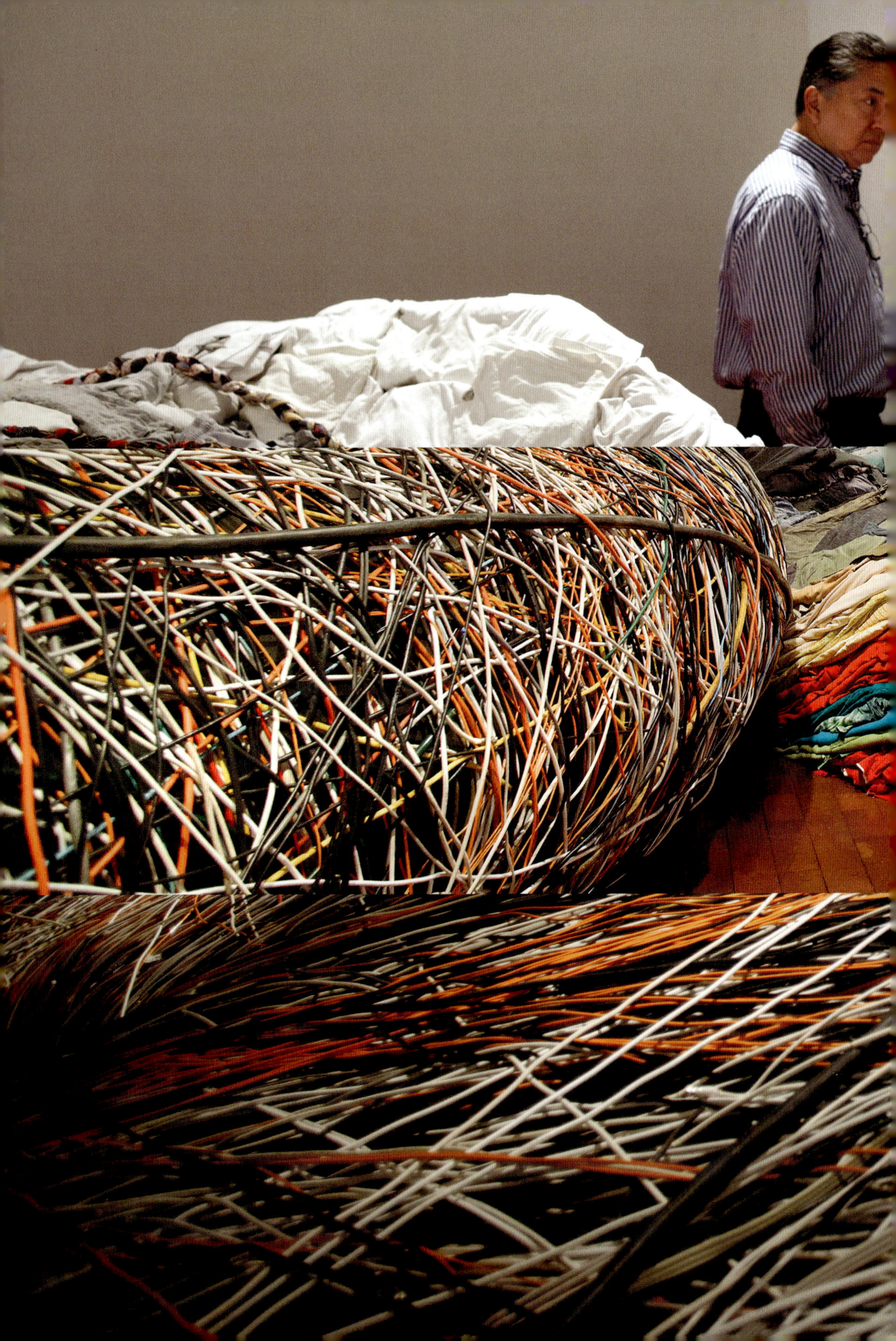

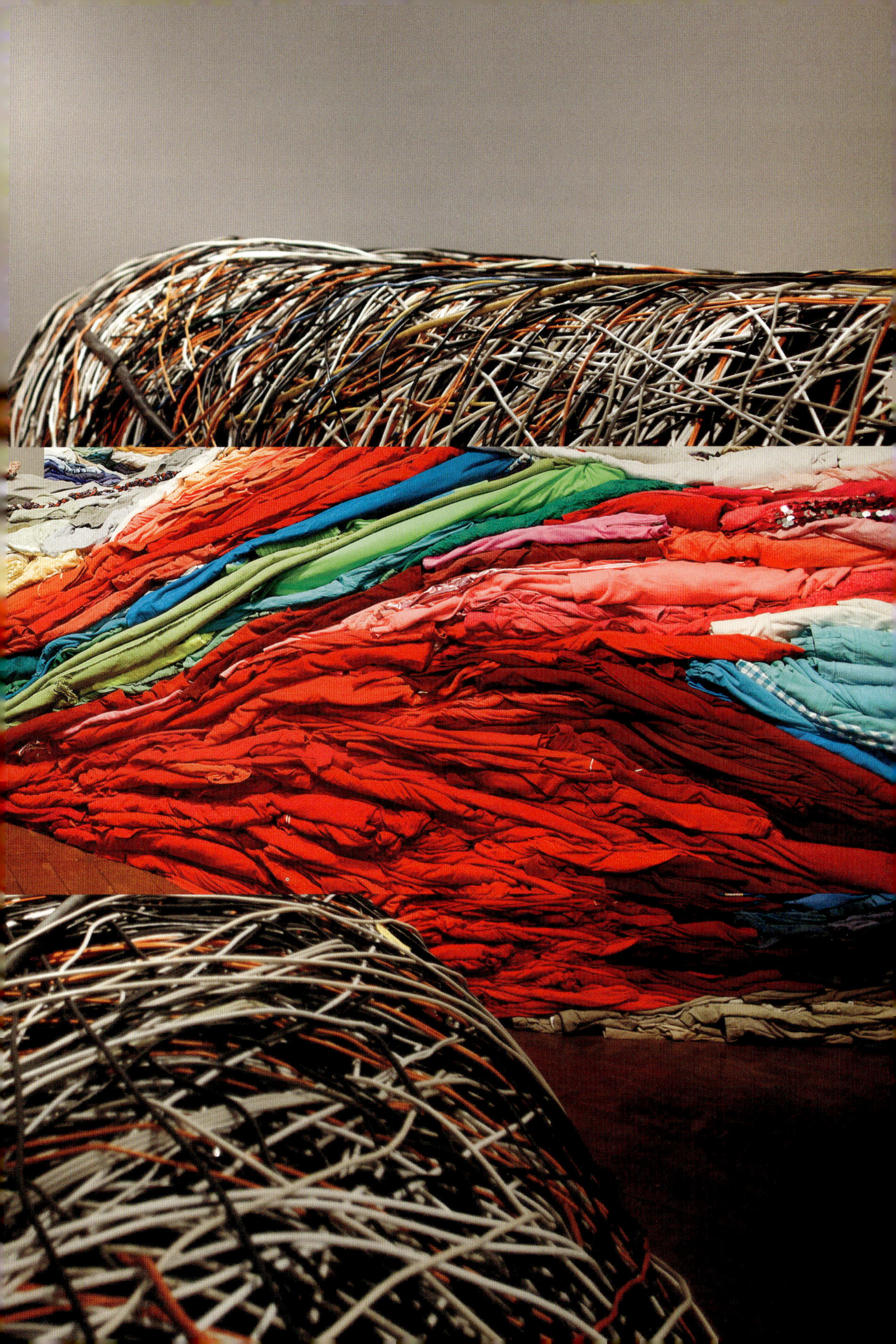

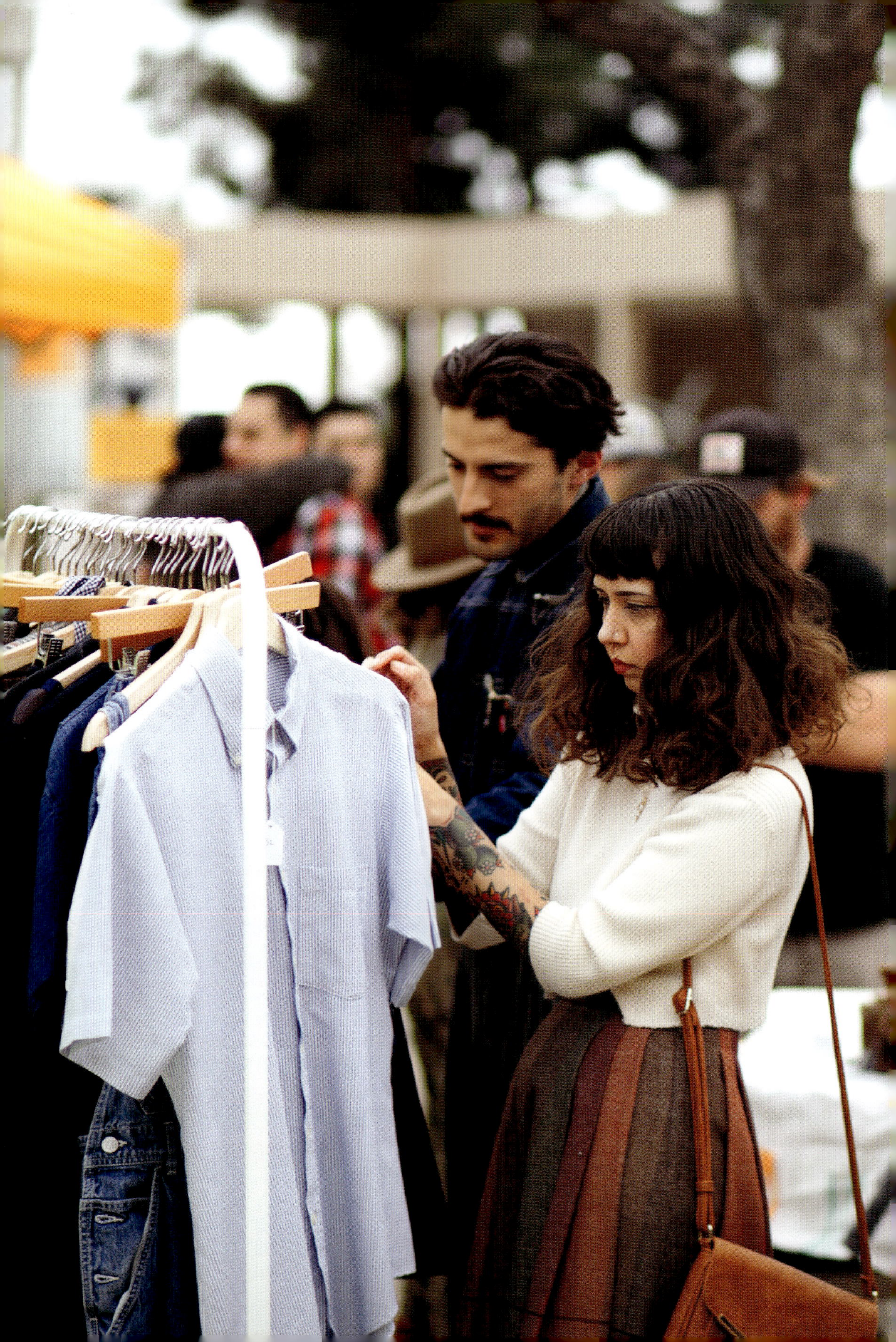

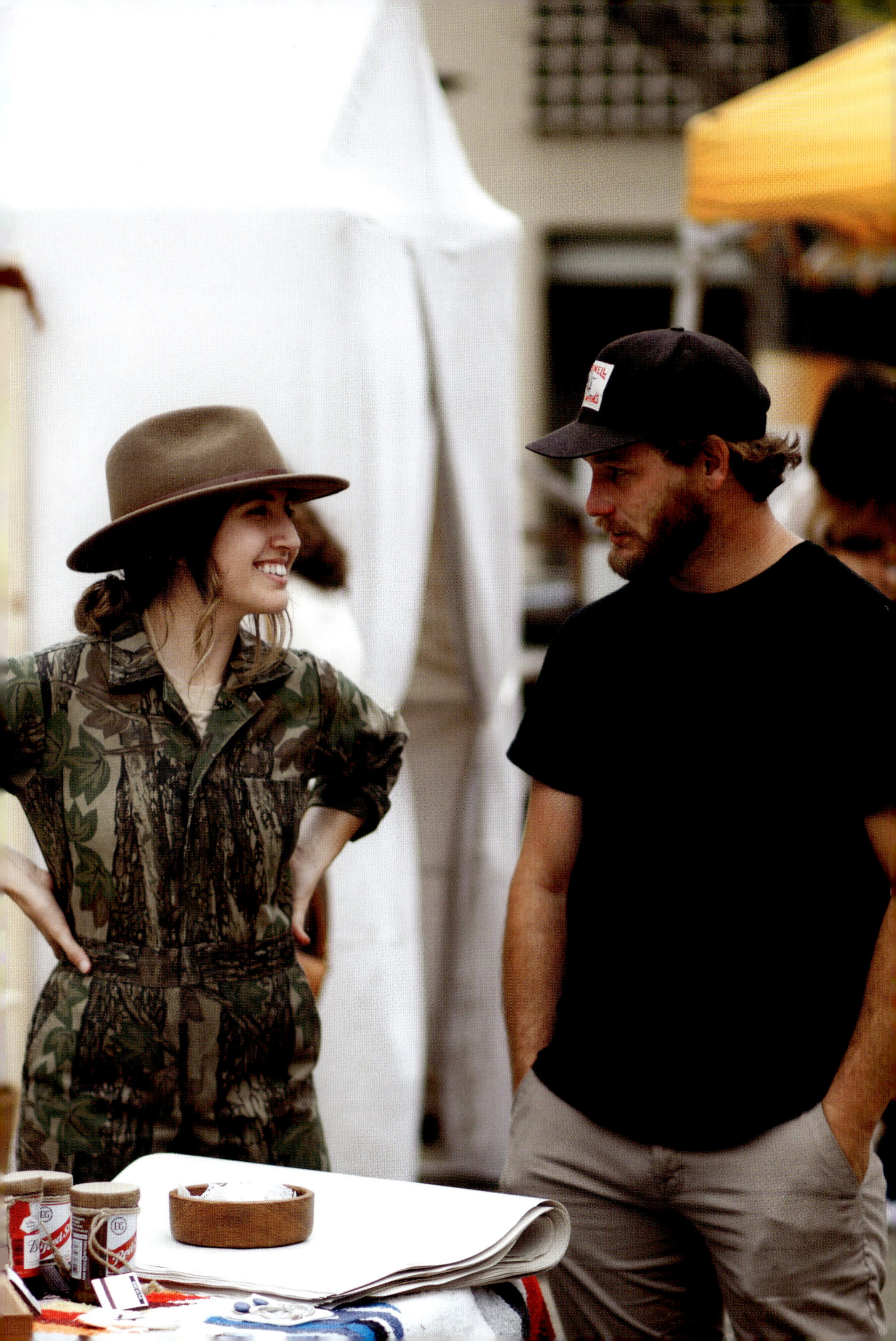

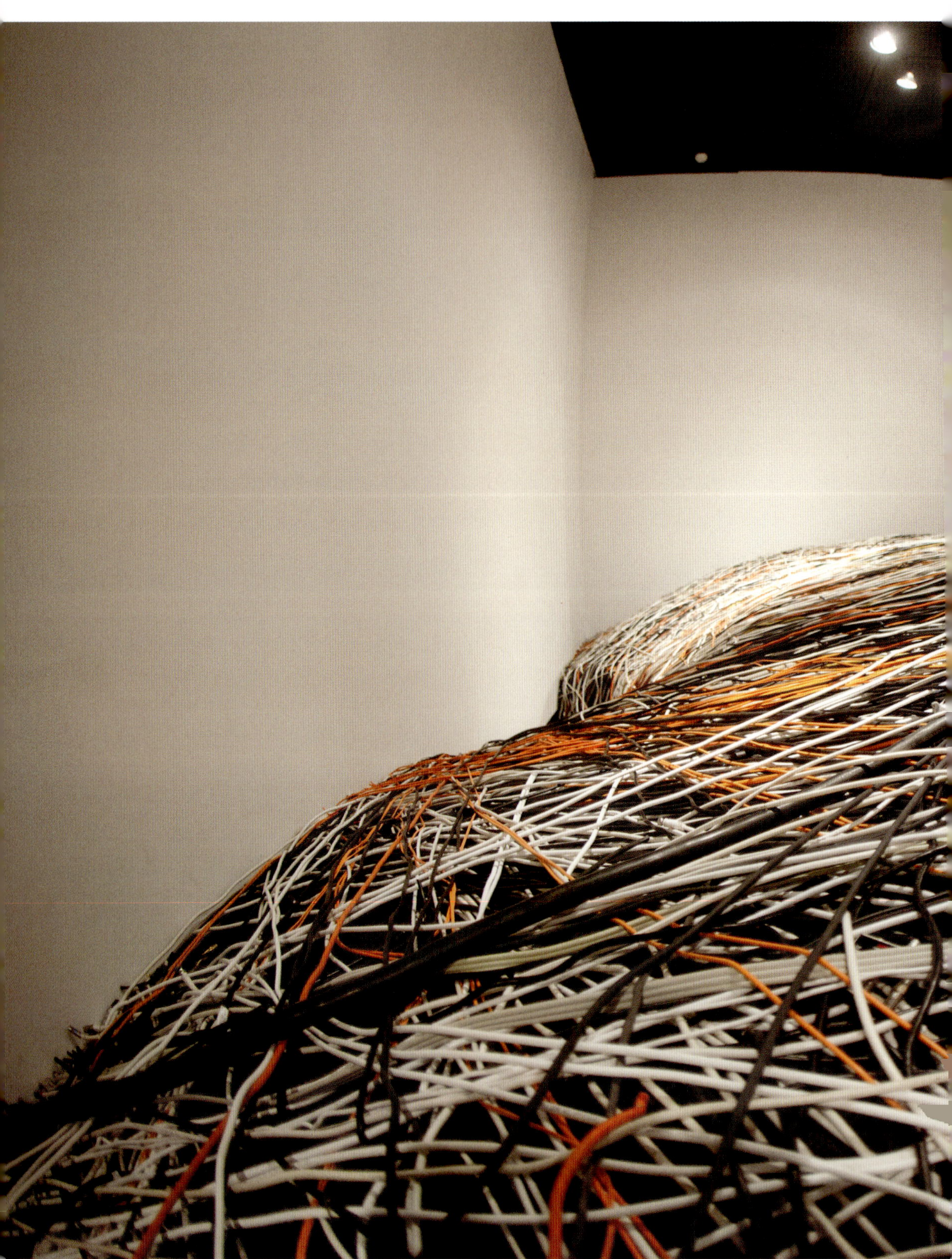

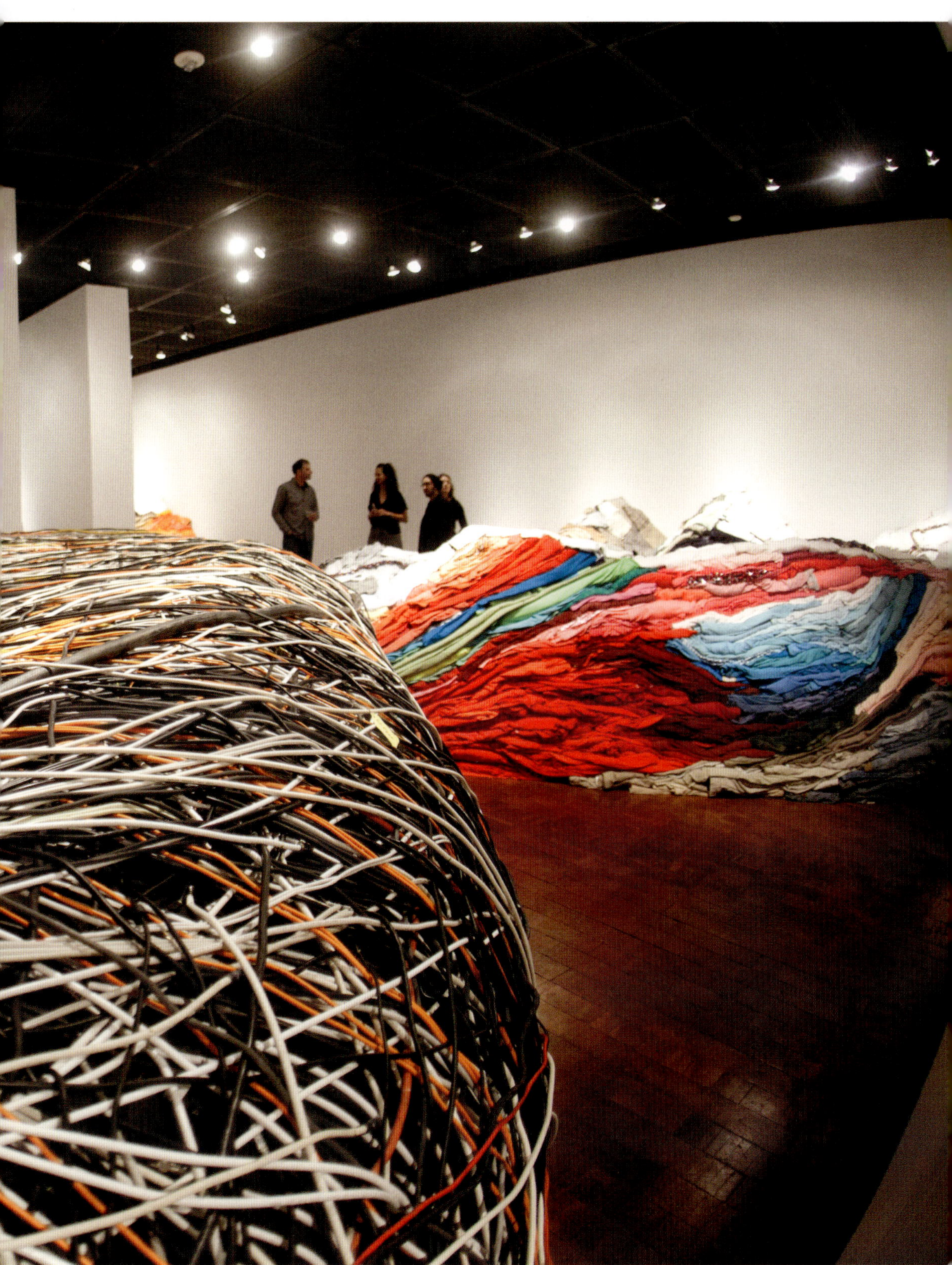

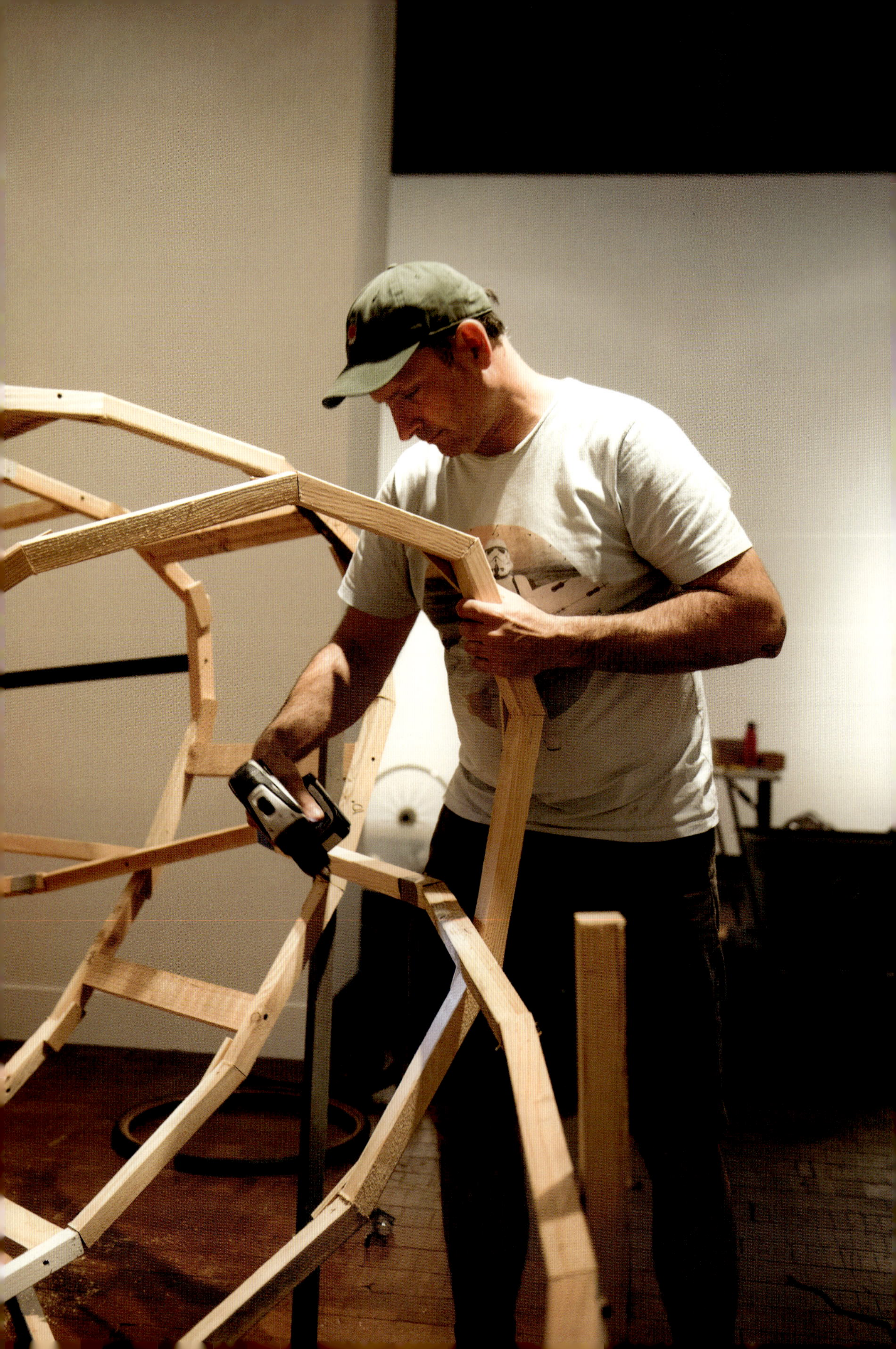

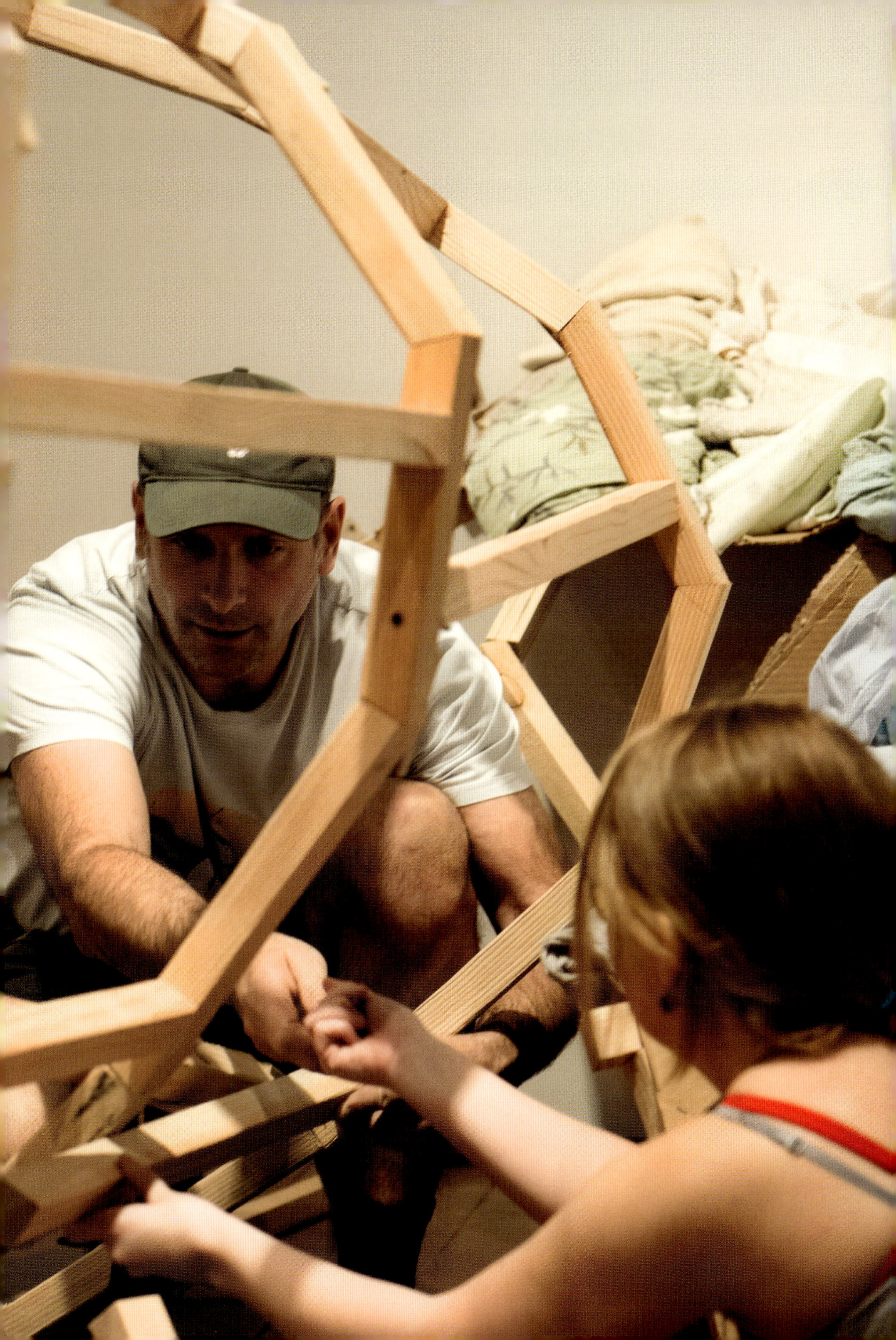

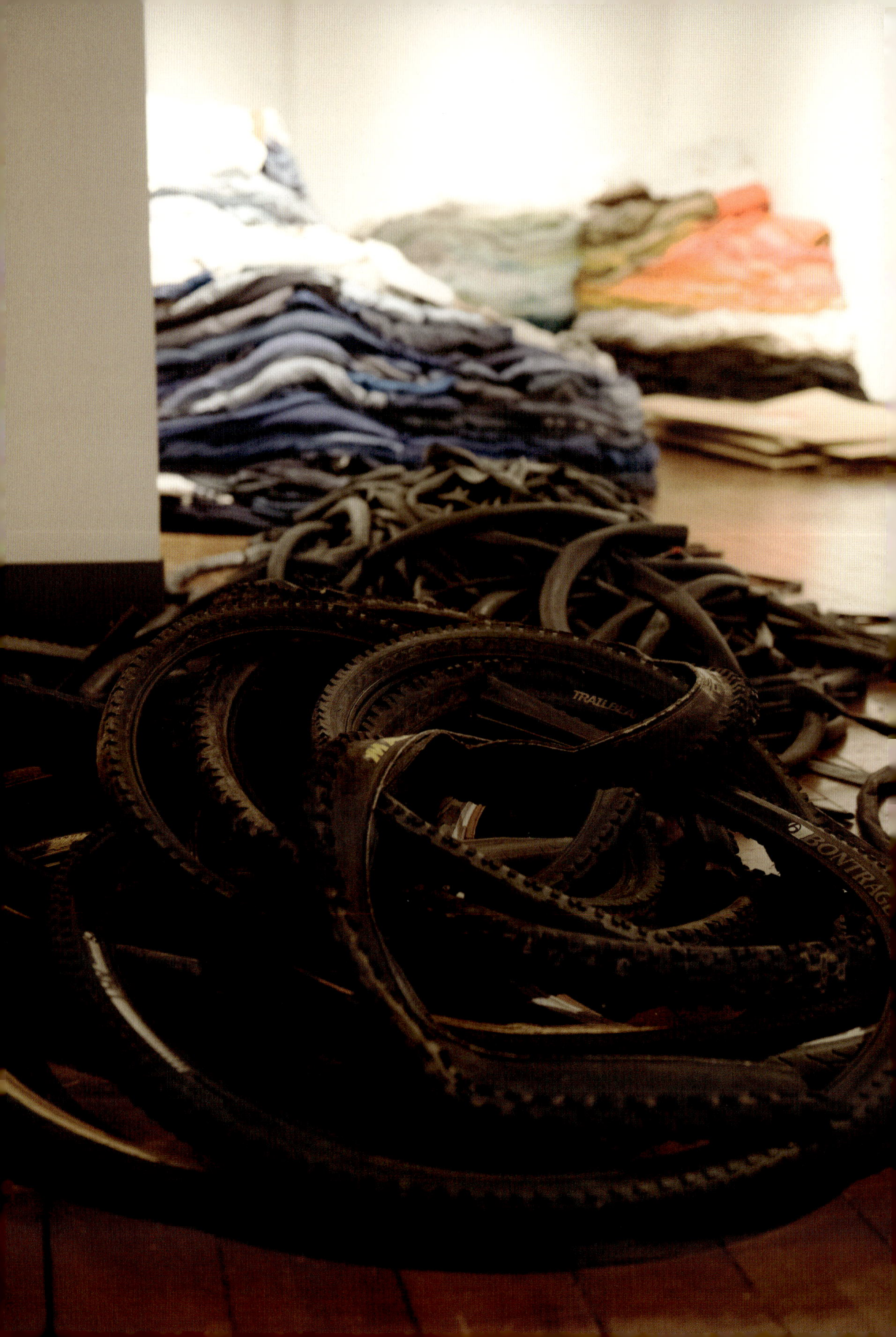

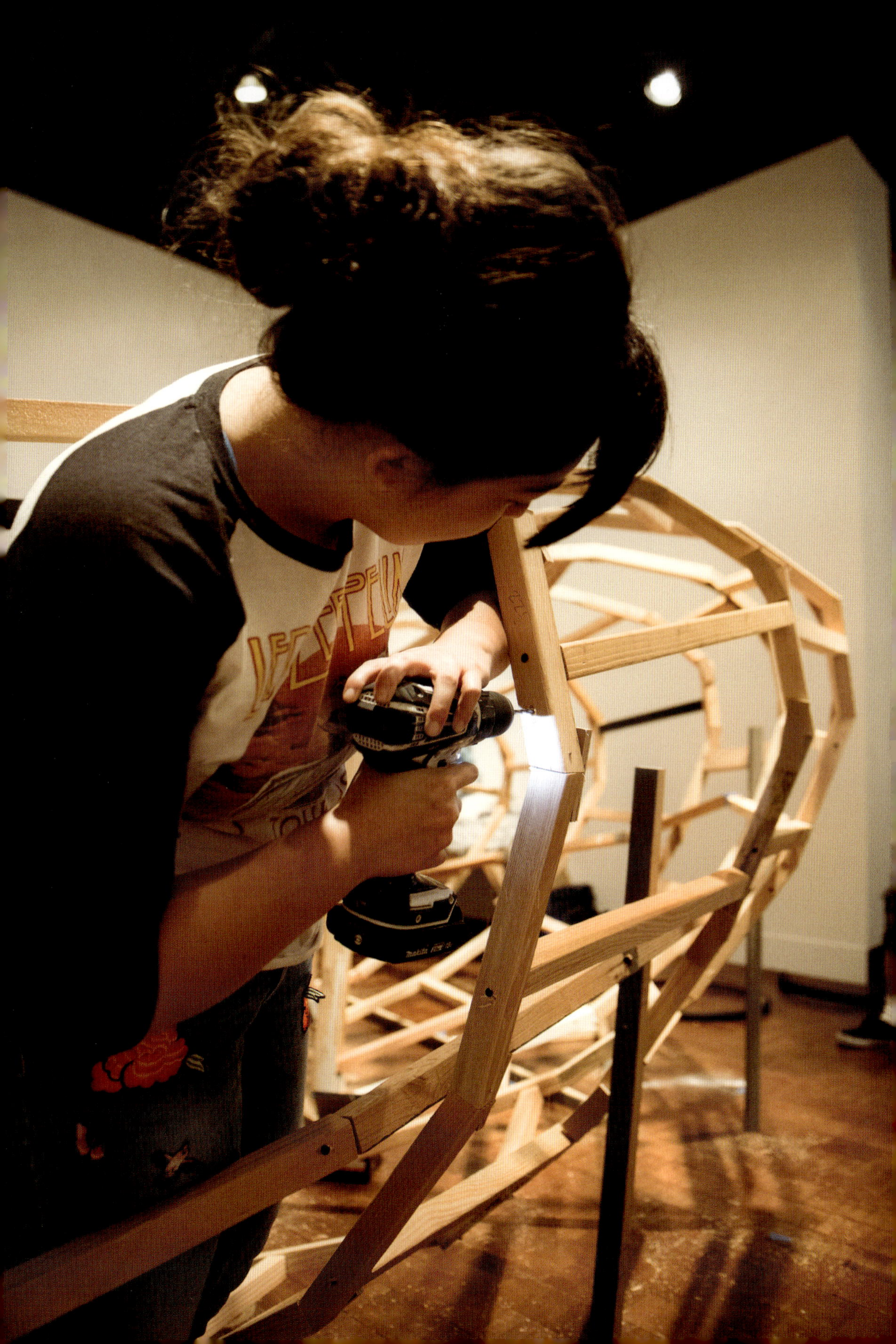

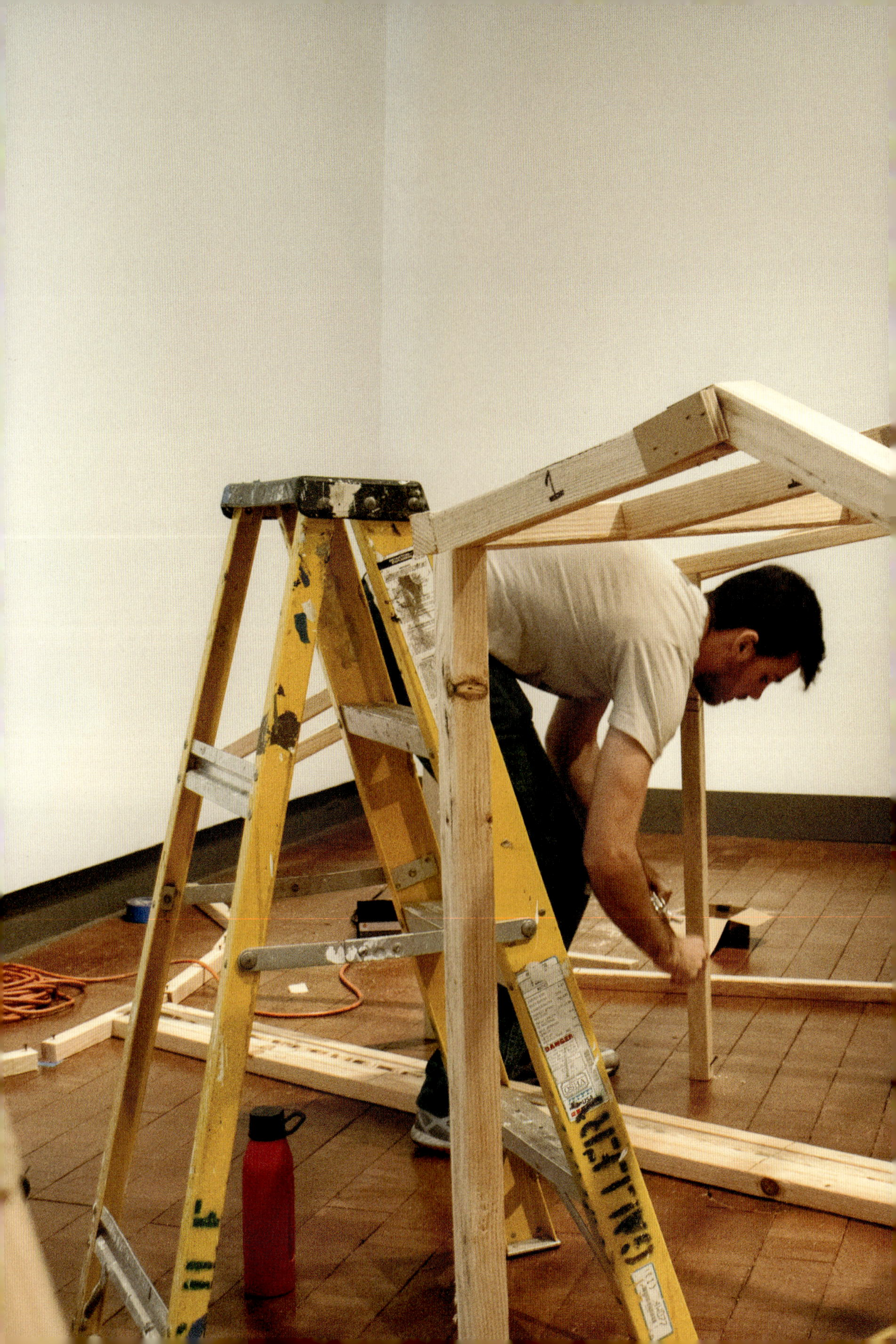

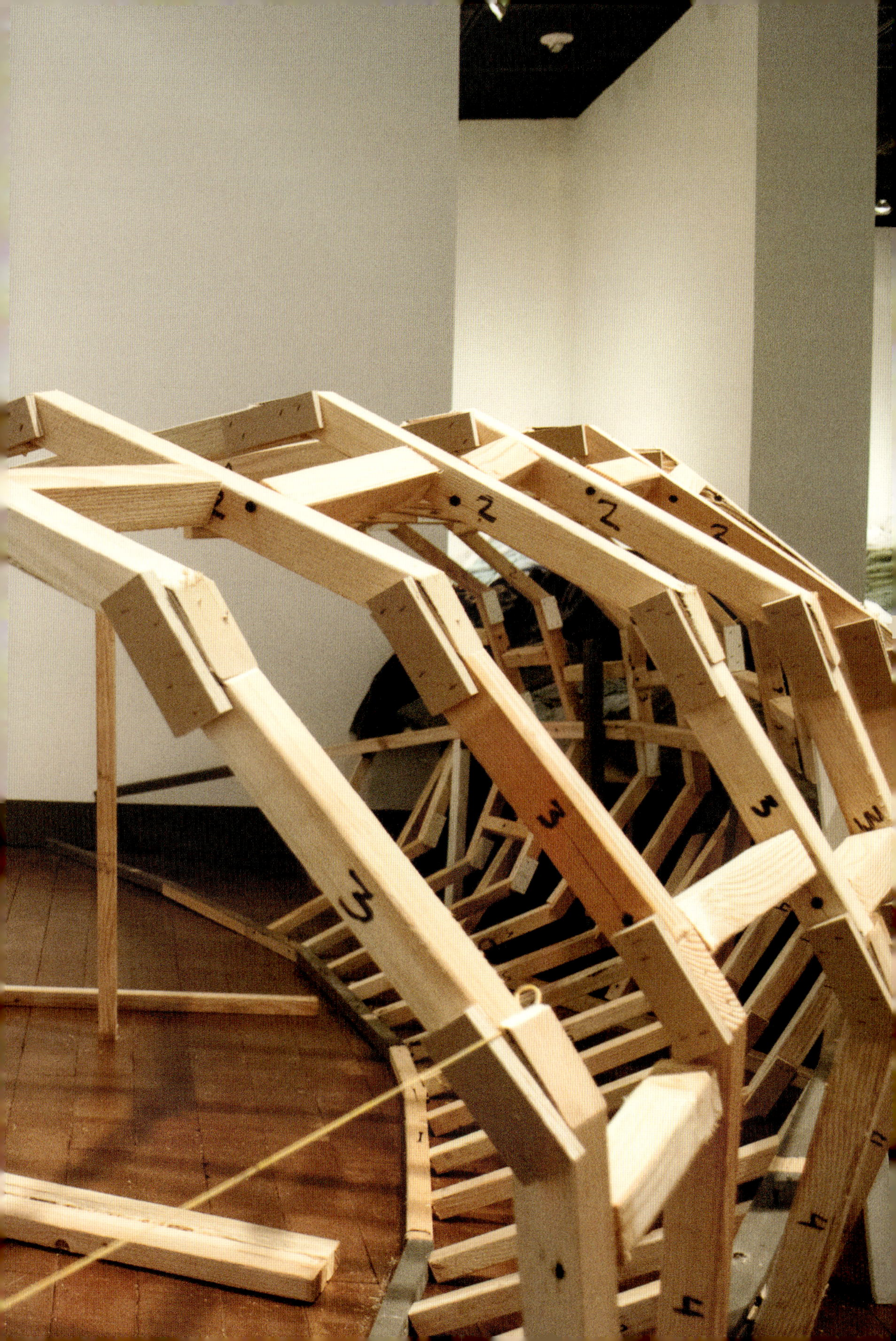

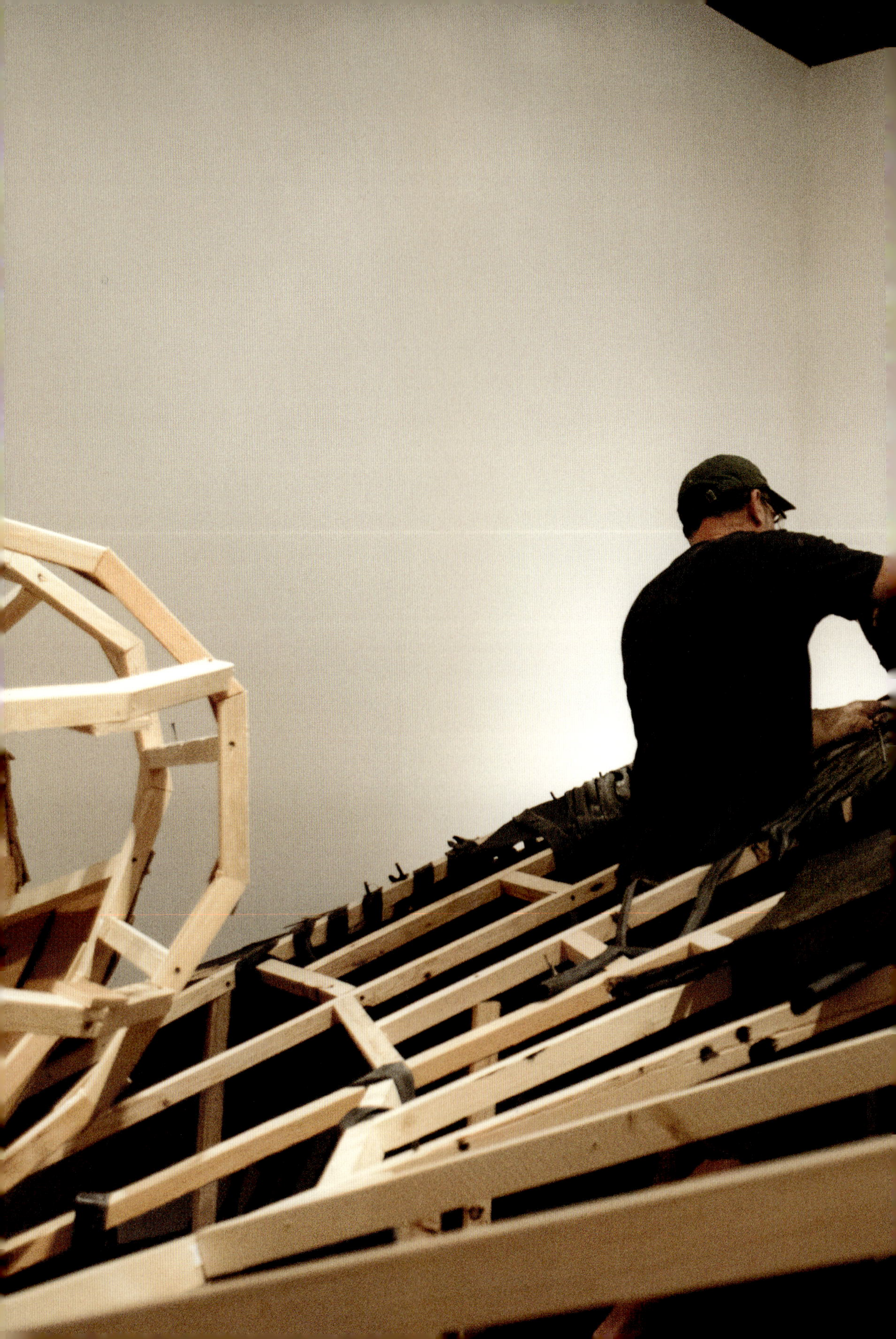

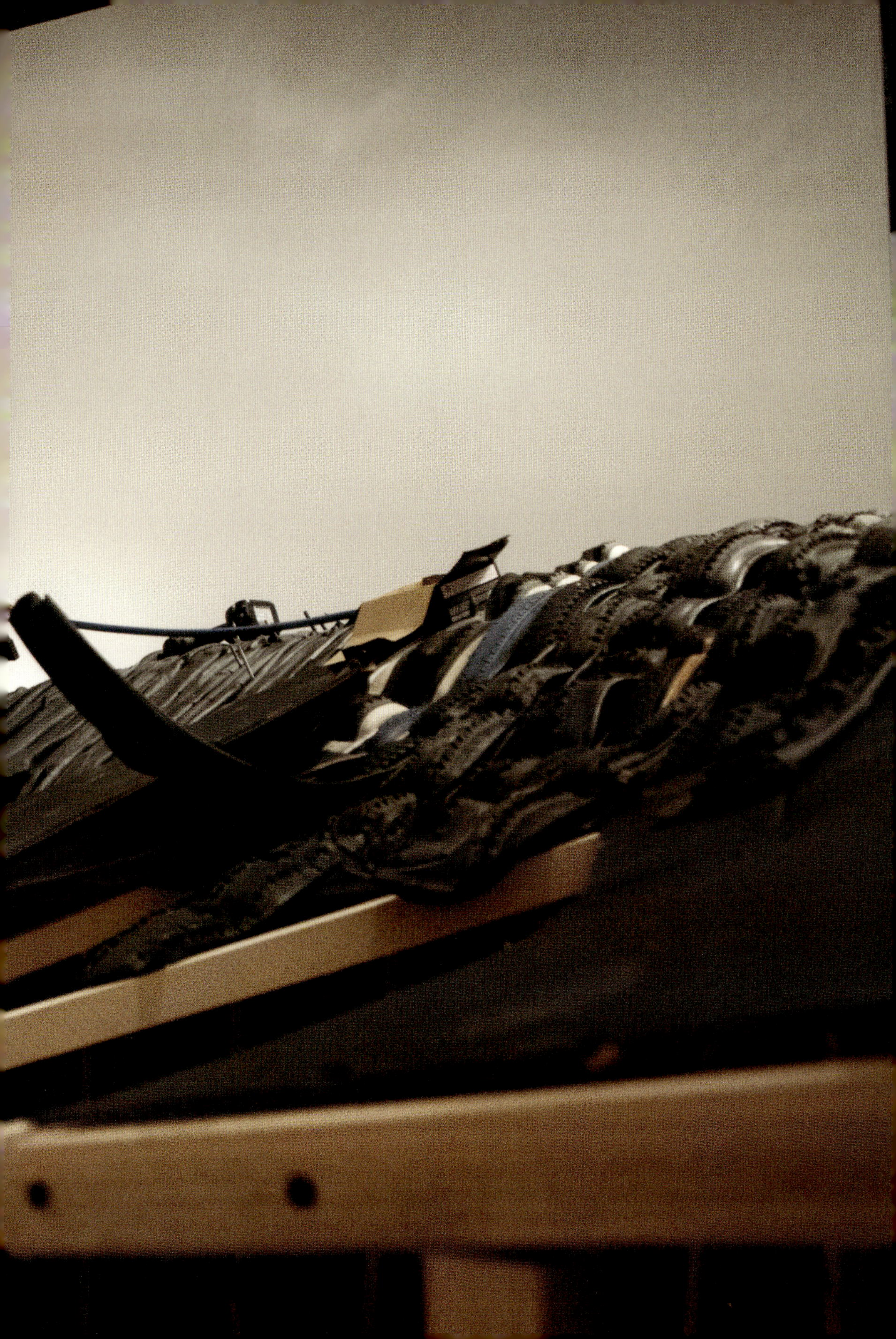

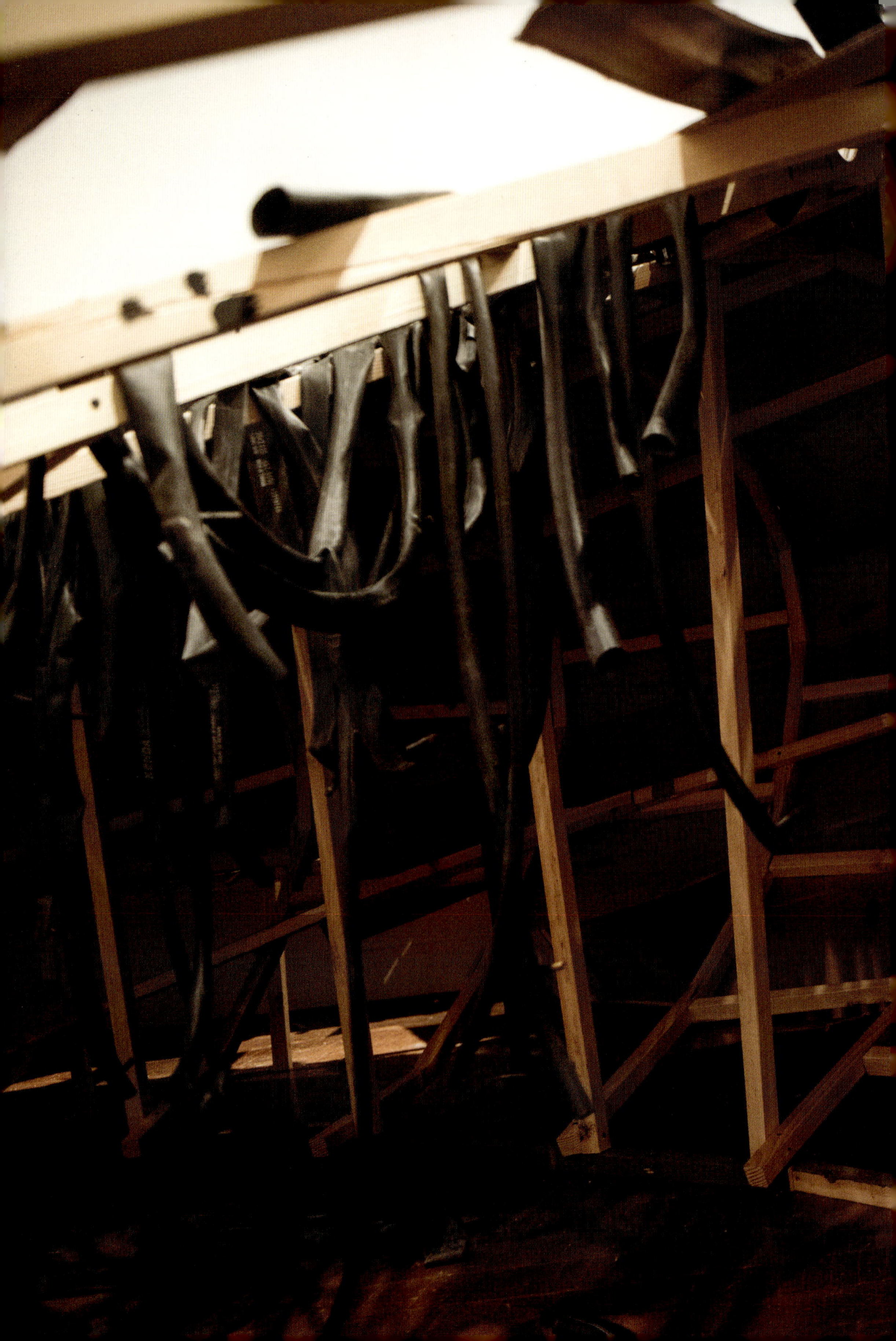

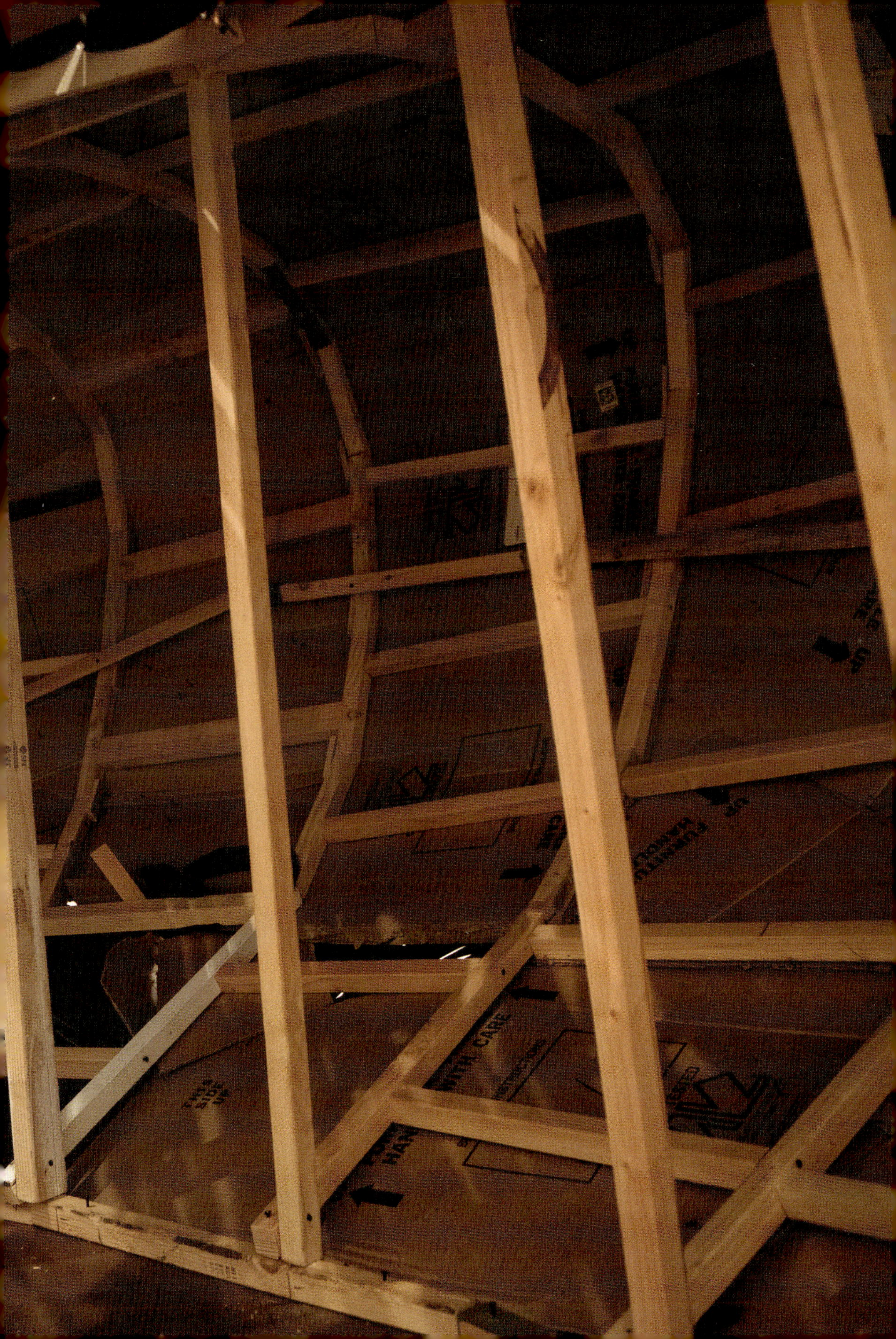

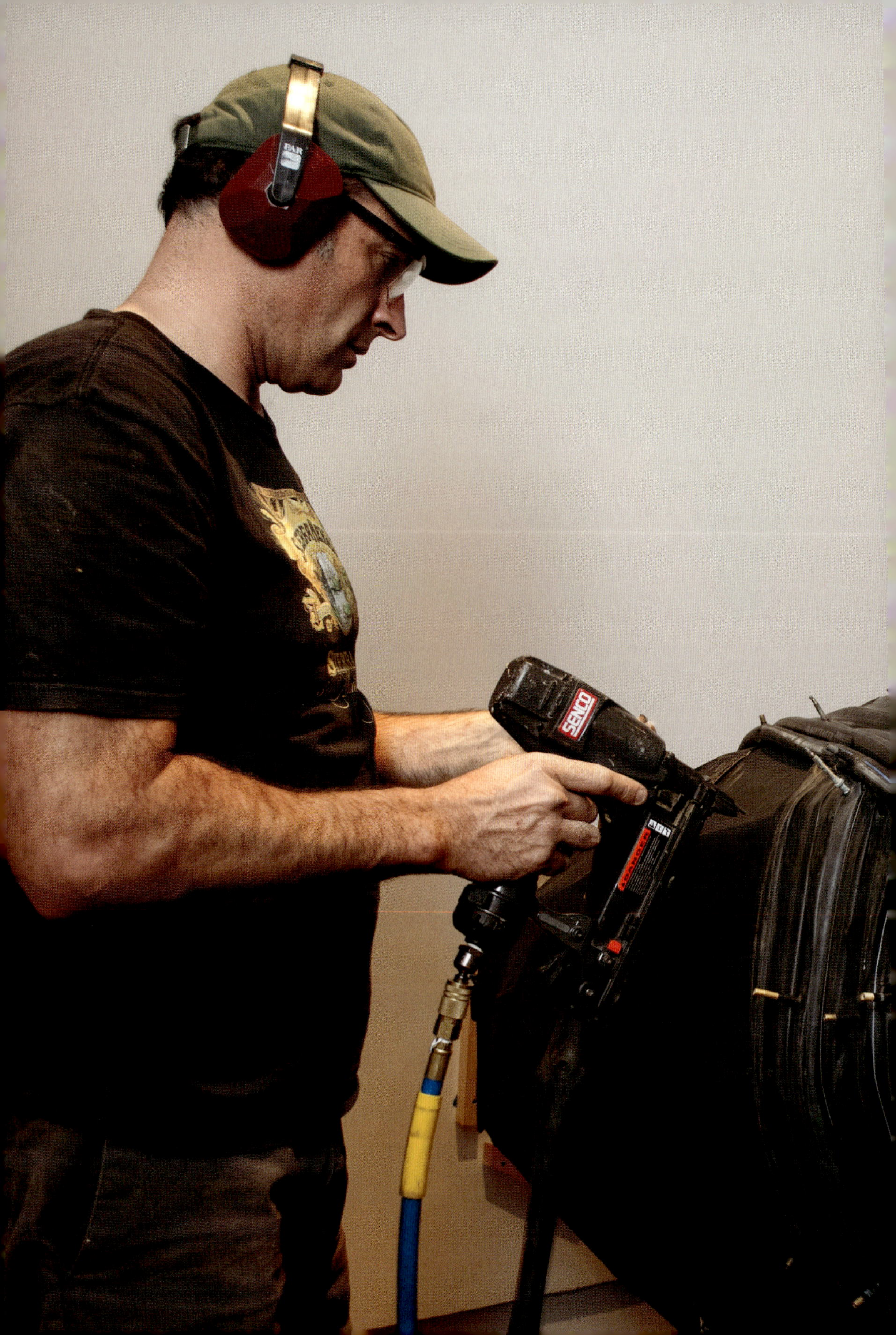

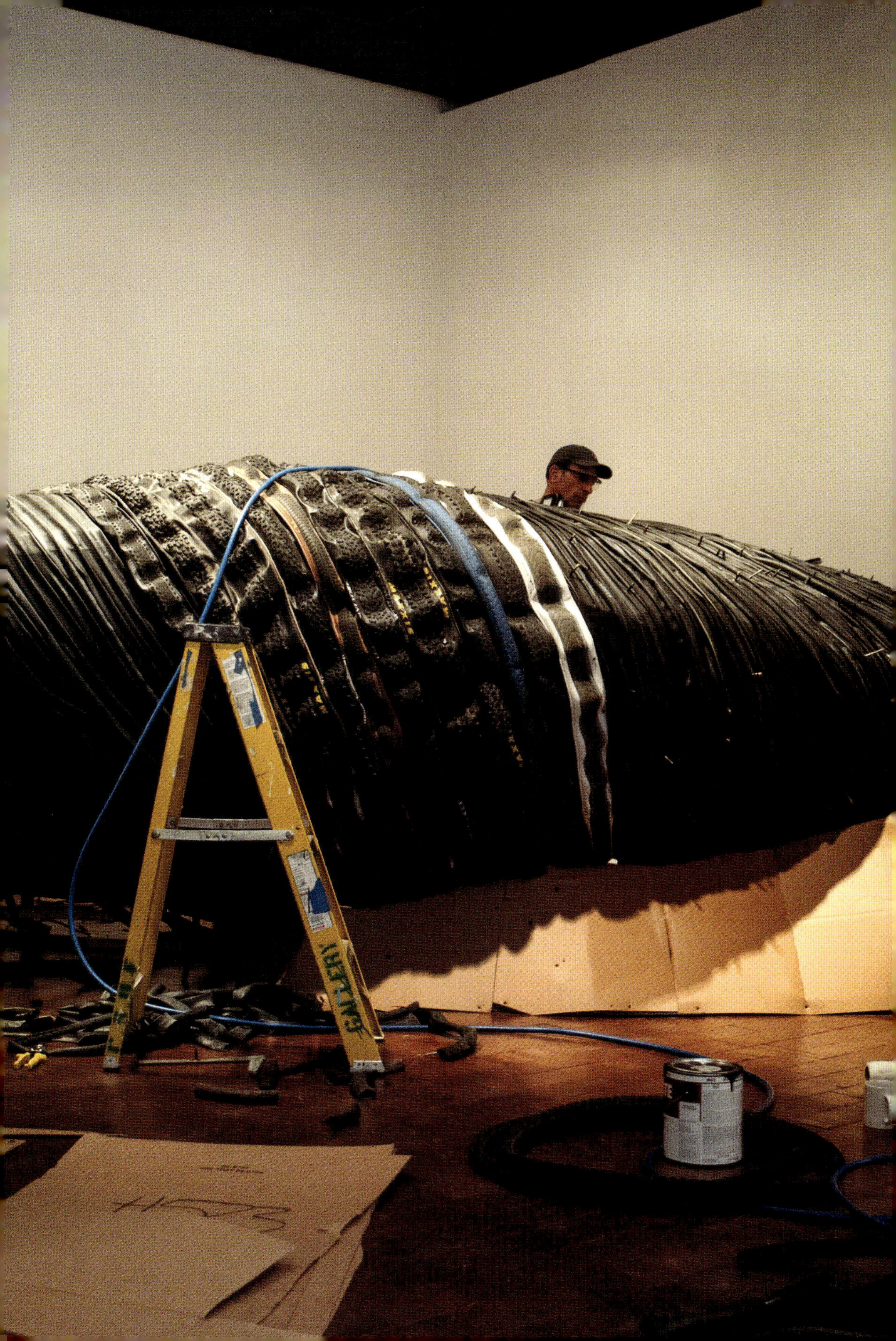

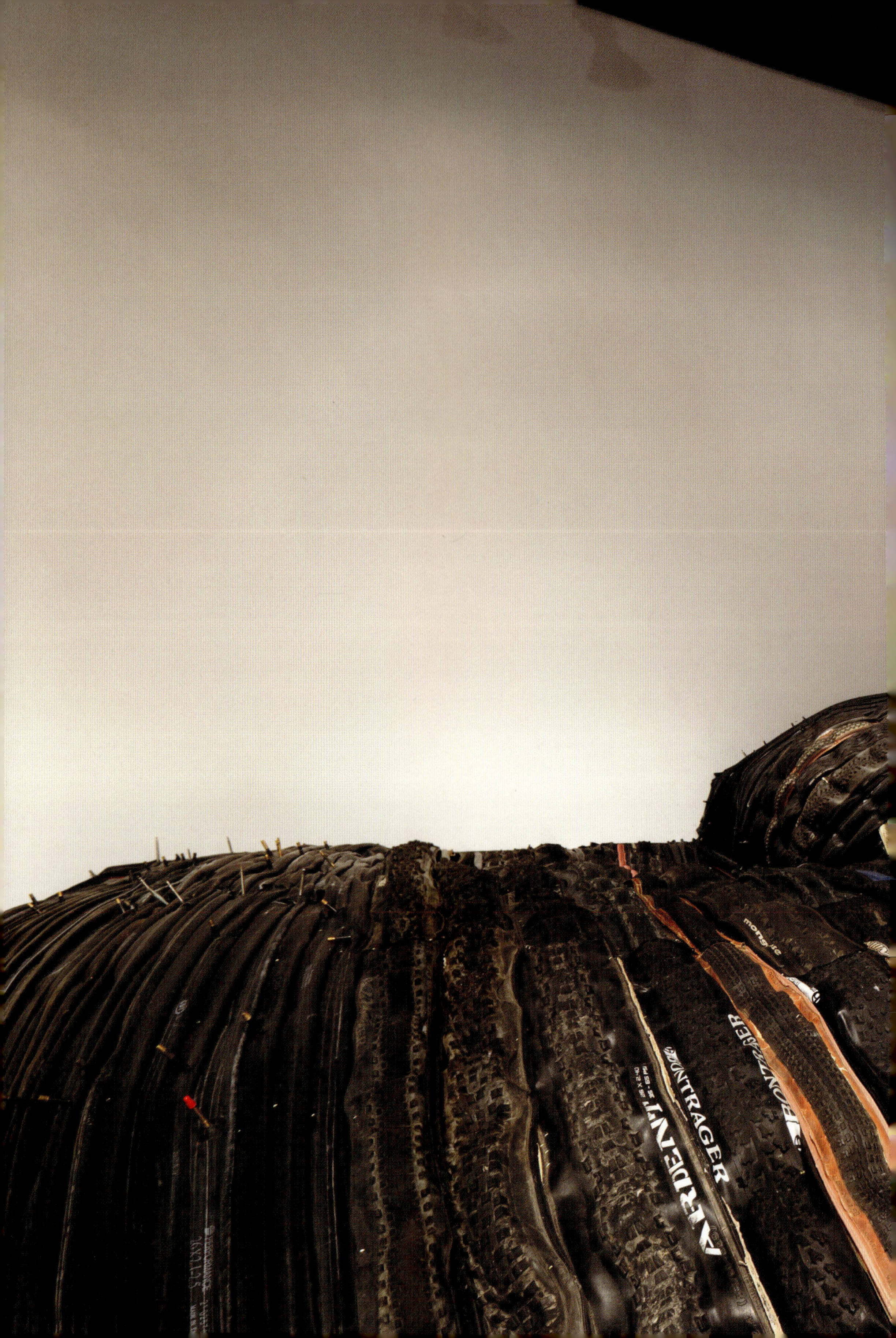

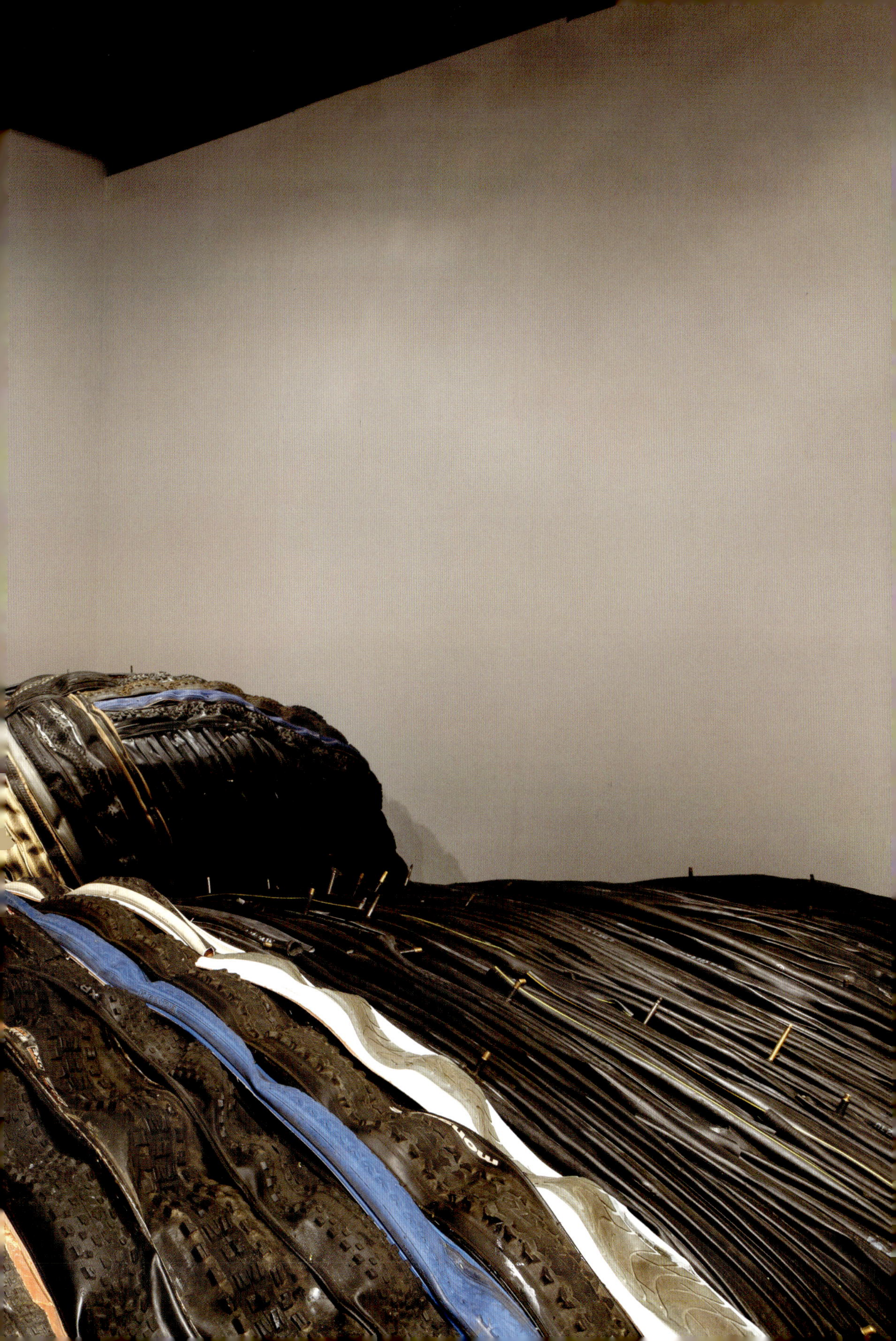

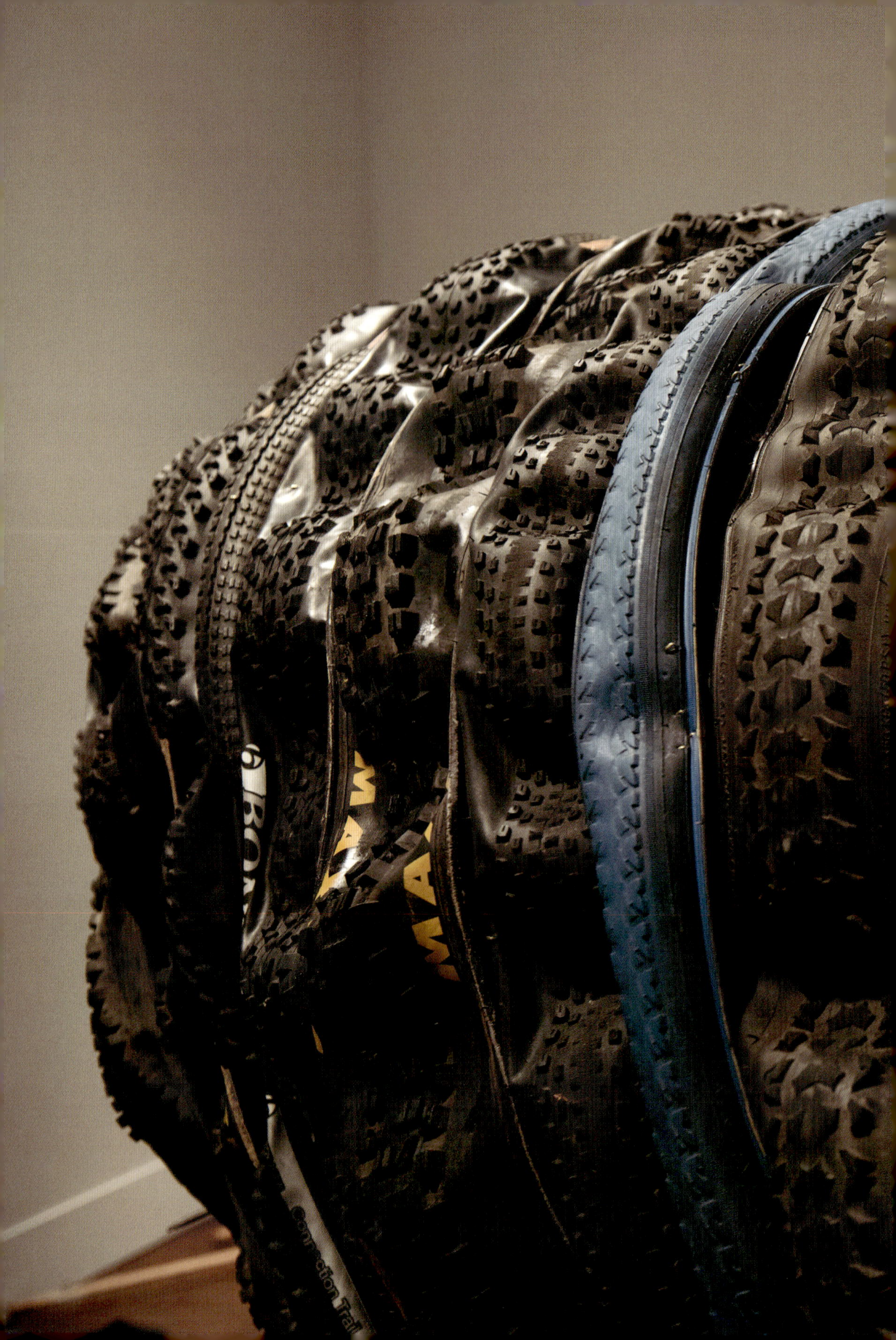

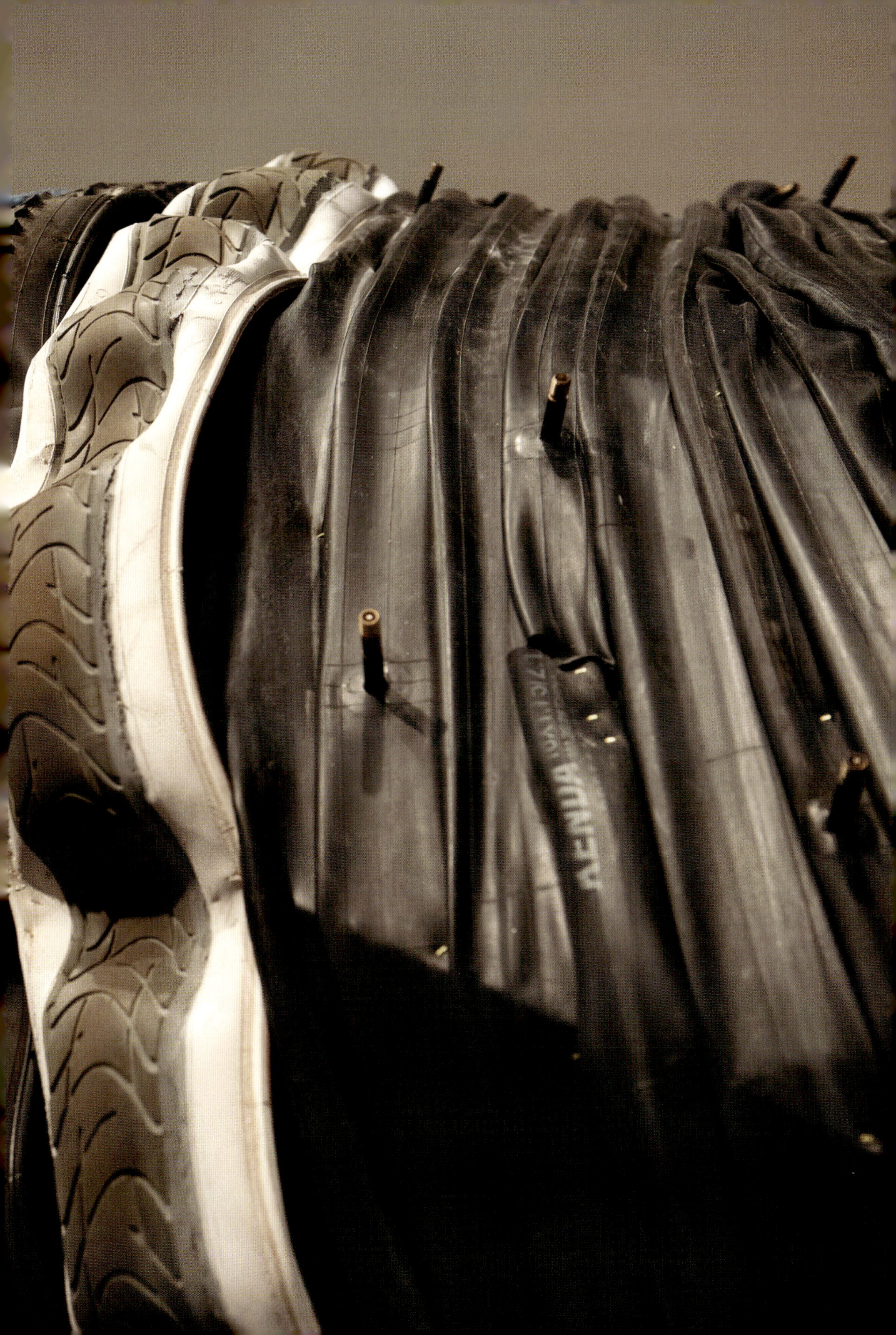

AUTHOR BIOS

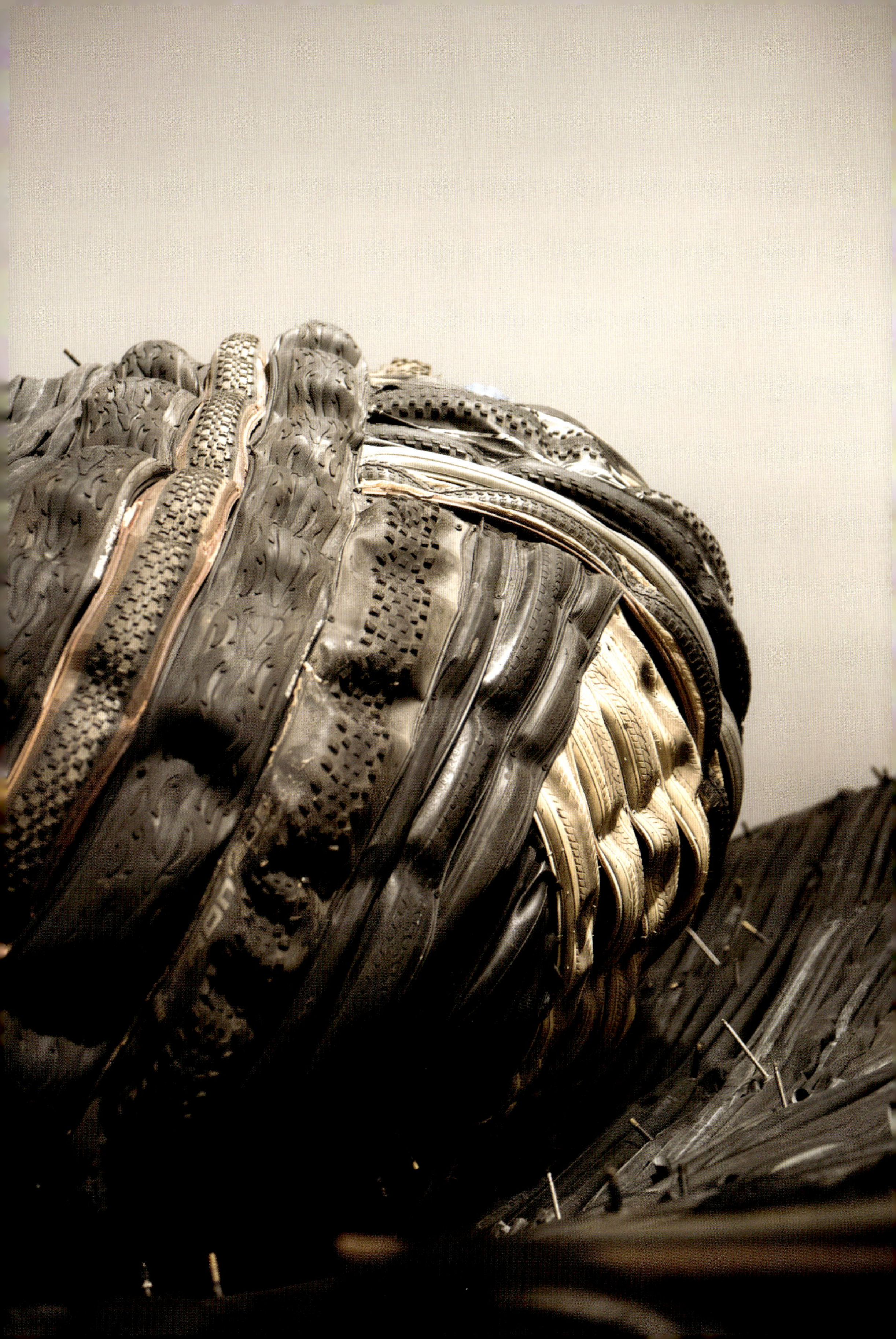

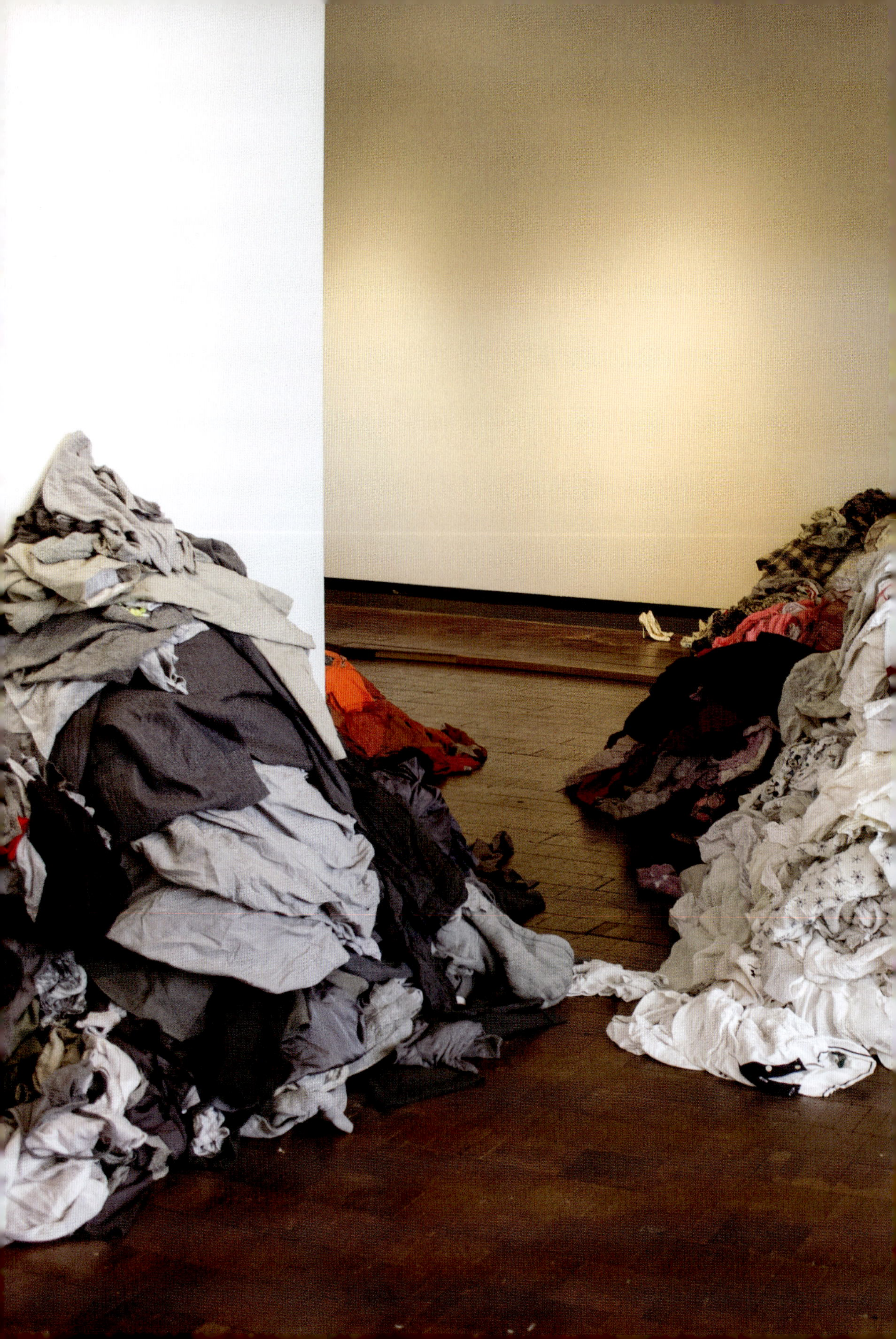

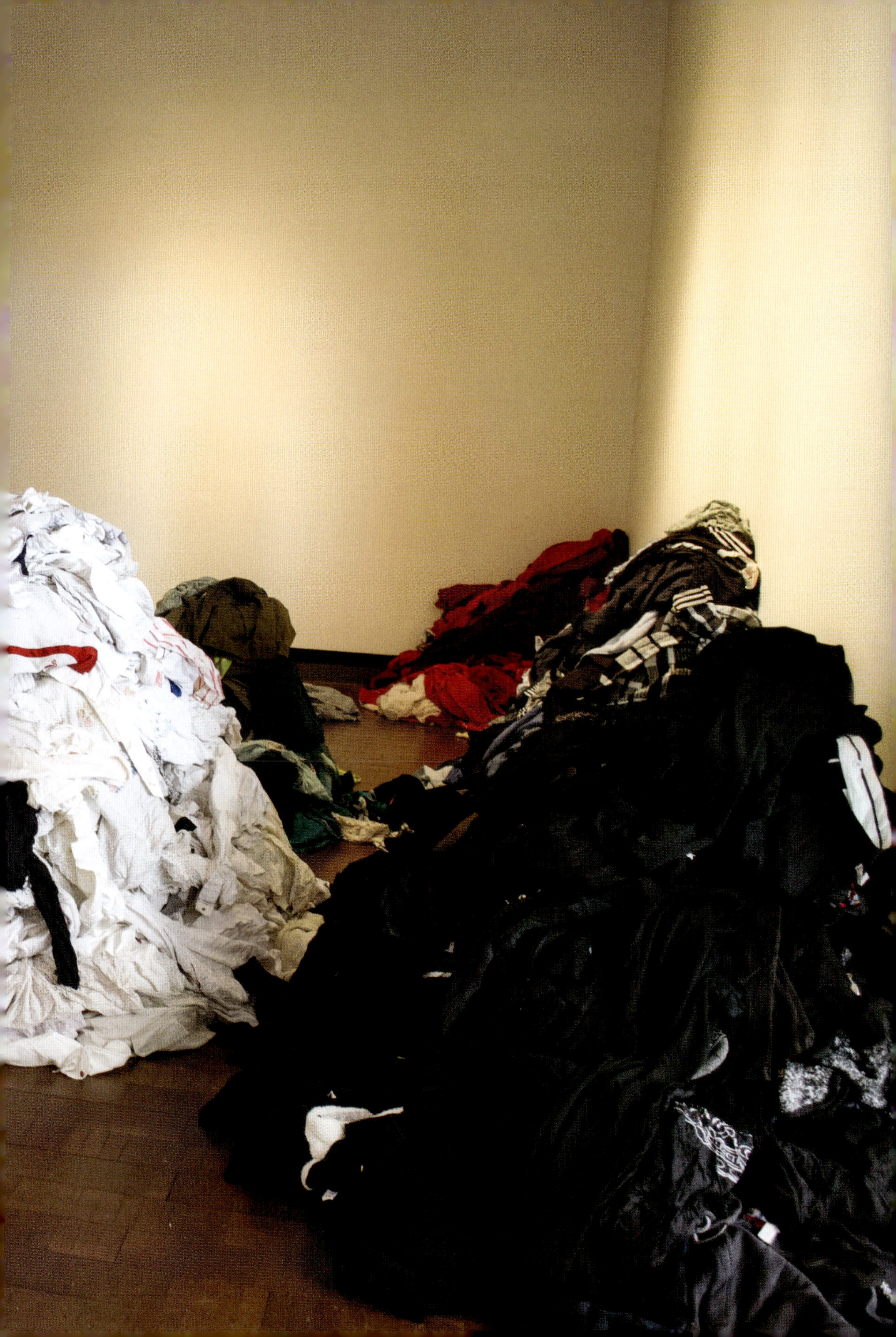

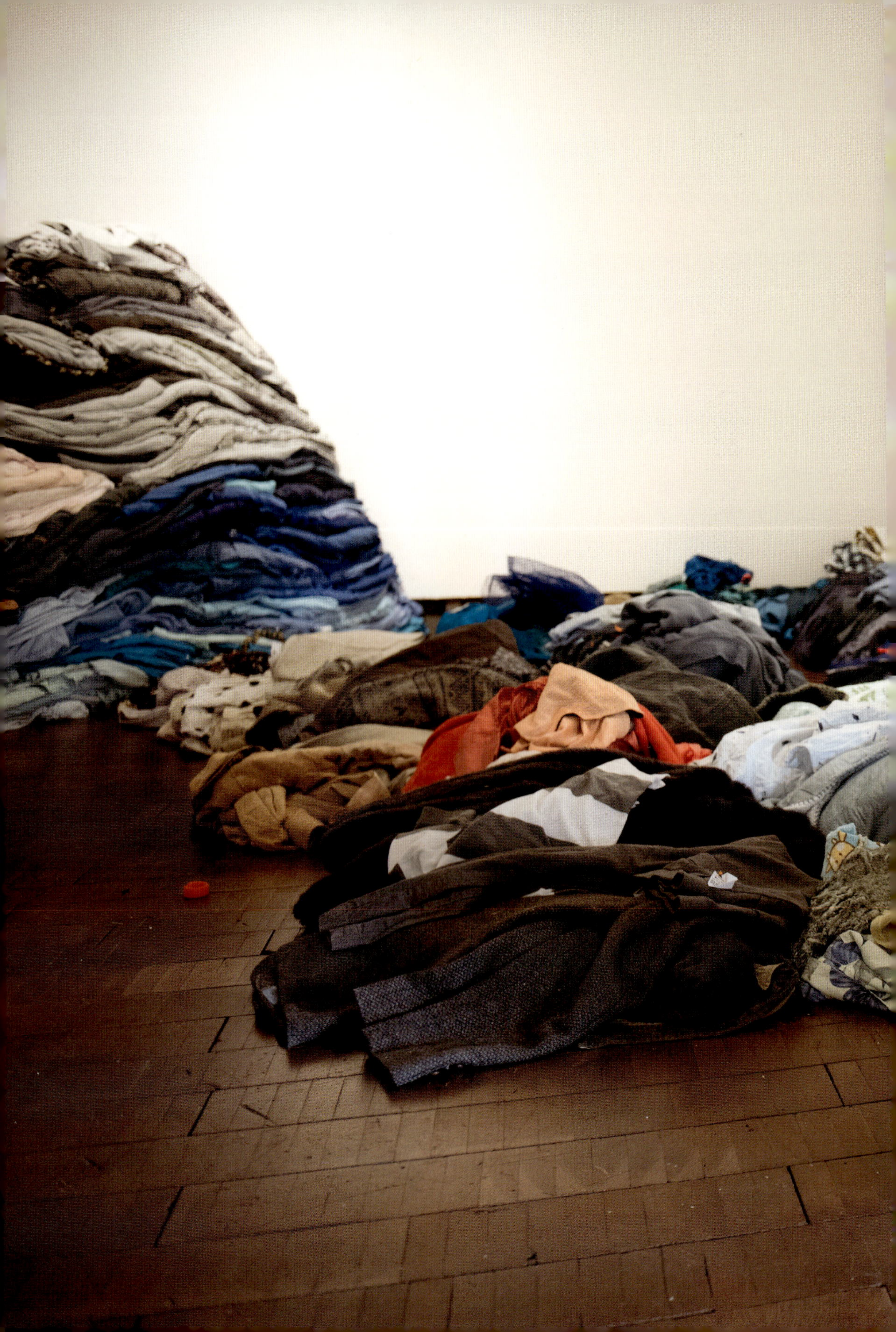

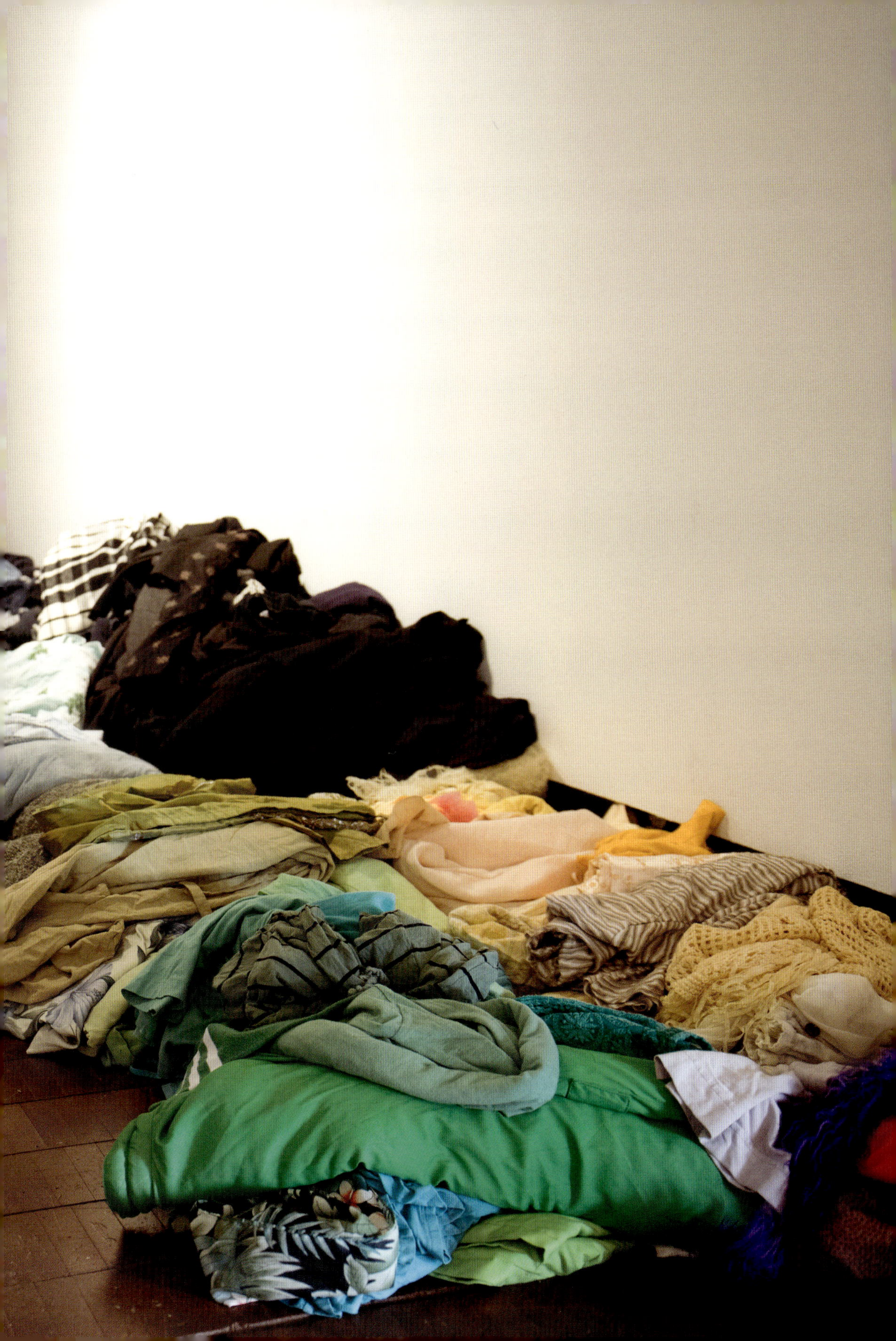

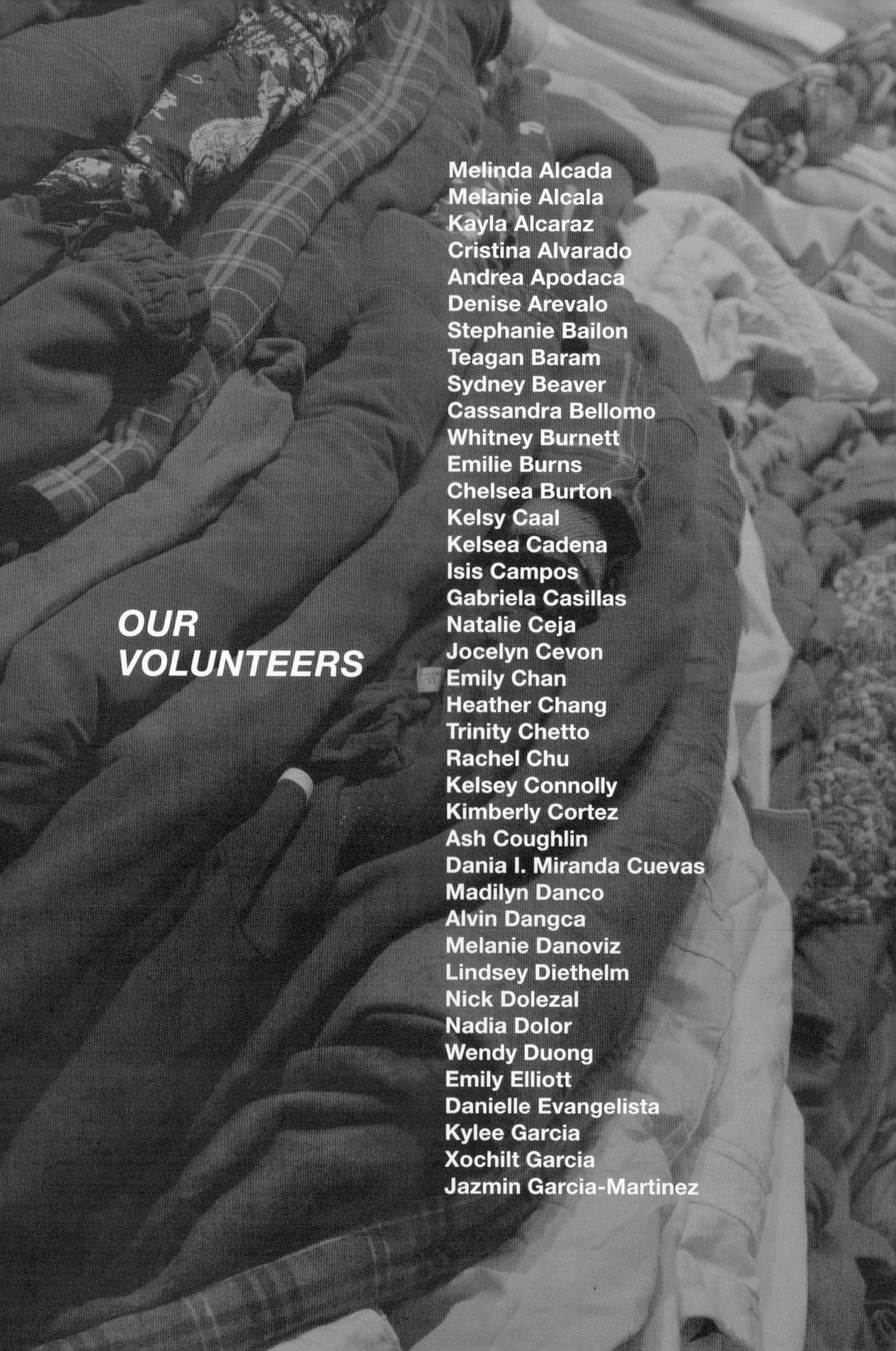

OUR
VOLUNTEERS

Melinda Alcada
Melanie Alcala
Kayla Alcaraz
Cristina Alvarado
Andrea Apodaca
Denise Arevalo
Stephanie Bailon
Teagan Baram
Sydney Beaver
Cassandra Bellomo
Whitney Burnett
Emilie Burns
Chelsea Burton
Kelsy Caal
Kelsea Cadena
Isis Campos
Gabriela Casillas
Natalie Ceja
Jocelyn Cevon
Emily Chan
Heather Chang
Trinity Chetto
Rachel Chu
Kelsey Connolly
Kimberly Cortez
Ash Coughlin
Dania I. Miranda Cuevas
Madilyn Danco
Alvin Dangca
Melanie Danoviz
Lindsey Diethelm
Nick Dolezal
Nadia Dolor
Wendy Duong
Emily Elliott
Danielle Evangelista
Kylee Garcia
Xochilt Garcia
Jazmin Garcia-Martinez

Janine Gess
Teresa Giltner
Laura Gonzales
Daniel Gonzalez
Paola Gutierrez
Dylan Hensley
Jessenia Hernandez
Valeria Herrera
Vivian Hill
Nhu Ho
Huong Hoang
Baoxin (Carrie) Jiang
Alyssa Jimenez
Cheyenne Johnson
Mason Jones
Christianne Kimberlin
Samantha Kimura
Maya Kuwahara
Stavros Kyriakopoulous
Riah Landin
Victoria Layman
Sandra Leo
Cassie Levin
Lily Lin
Daphne Love
Breanna Lovell
Allison Kent-Gunn
Matt Key
Breanna Martinez
Connie Martinez
Victor Martinez-Cortes
Demaris Martz
Ashley McGraw
Rebecca Mena
Victoria Mendoza
Sara Mirbaha
Emily Montgomery
Omar Montoya
Cindy Moreno

Rachel Murphey
Nasrean Nael
Jose Flores Nava
Ildiko O'Brien
Val Okamoto
Olivia Ordonez
David Padron
Gisela Paolinelli
Aubrey Patterson
Jerry Zenoh Ramirez
Alan Richards
Chris Rioux
Isaura Ruiz
Sarah Salcido
Lilian San
Noah Scaringi
Ashley Serrano
Cooper Stieglitz
Noah B. Swiatele (Rascon)
Nour Tarzi
Aileen Teruya
Tiffany Thompson
Lauren Tju
Valeria Tomaylla
Margaret Tran
Kenneth Truong
Jessica Vaage
Kara Veldheer
Marisa Velez
Chanelle Veltre
Nathan Vu
Erin Warren
Megan Watts
Olivia Wilcox
Brittney Wilson
Jeffrey Wong
Carly Yamashiro
Ryan Young
Lingzhi Zeng

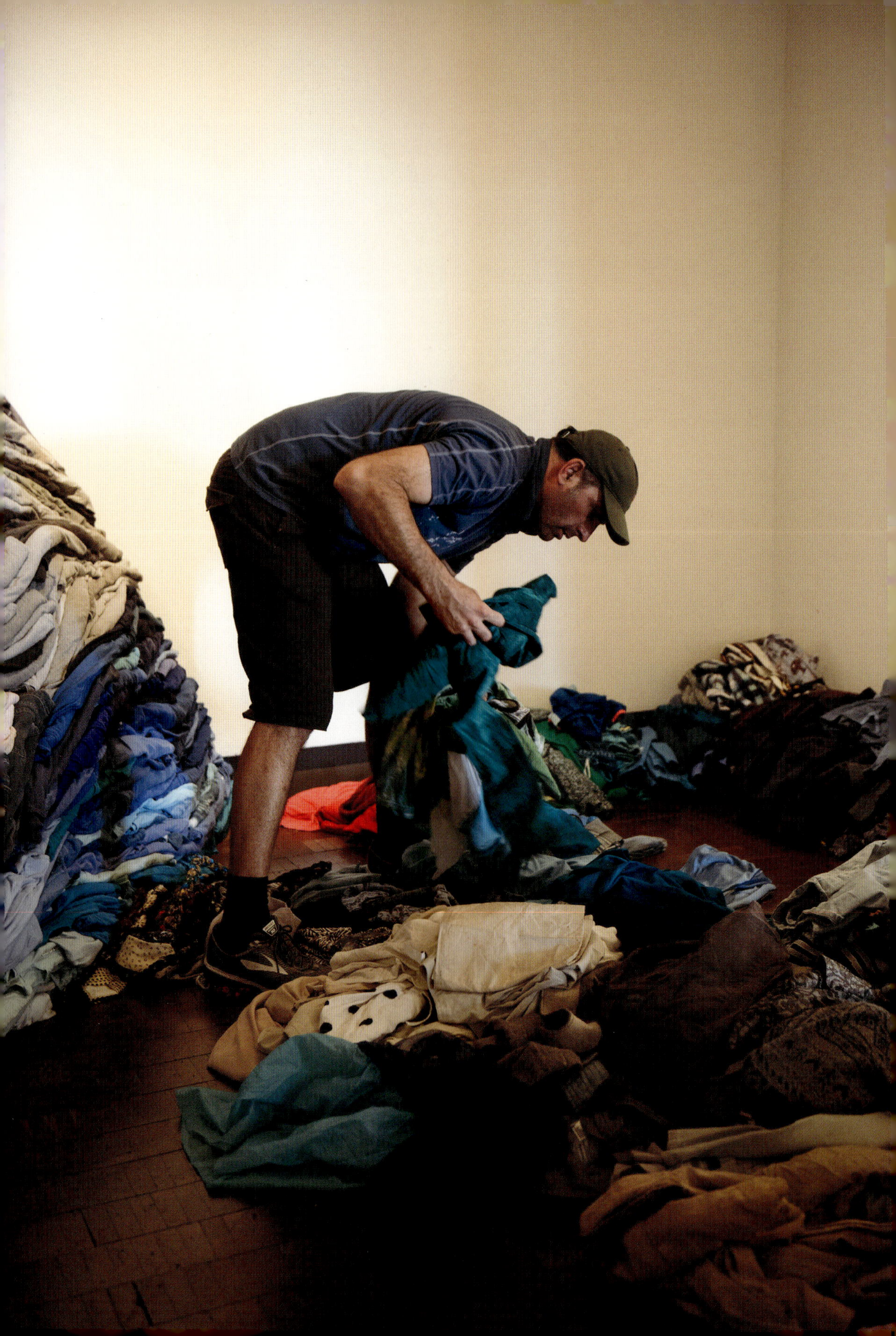

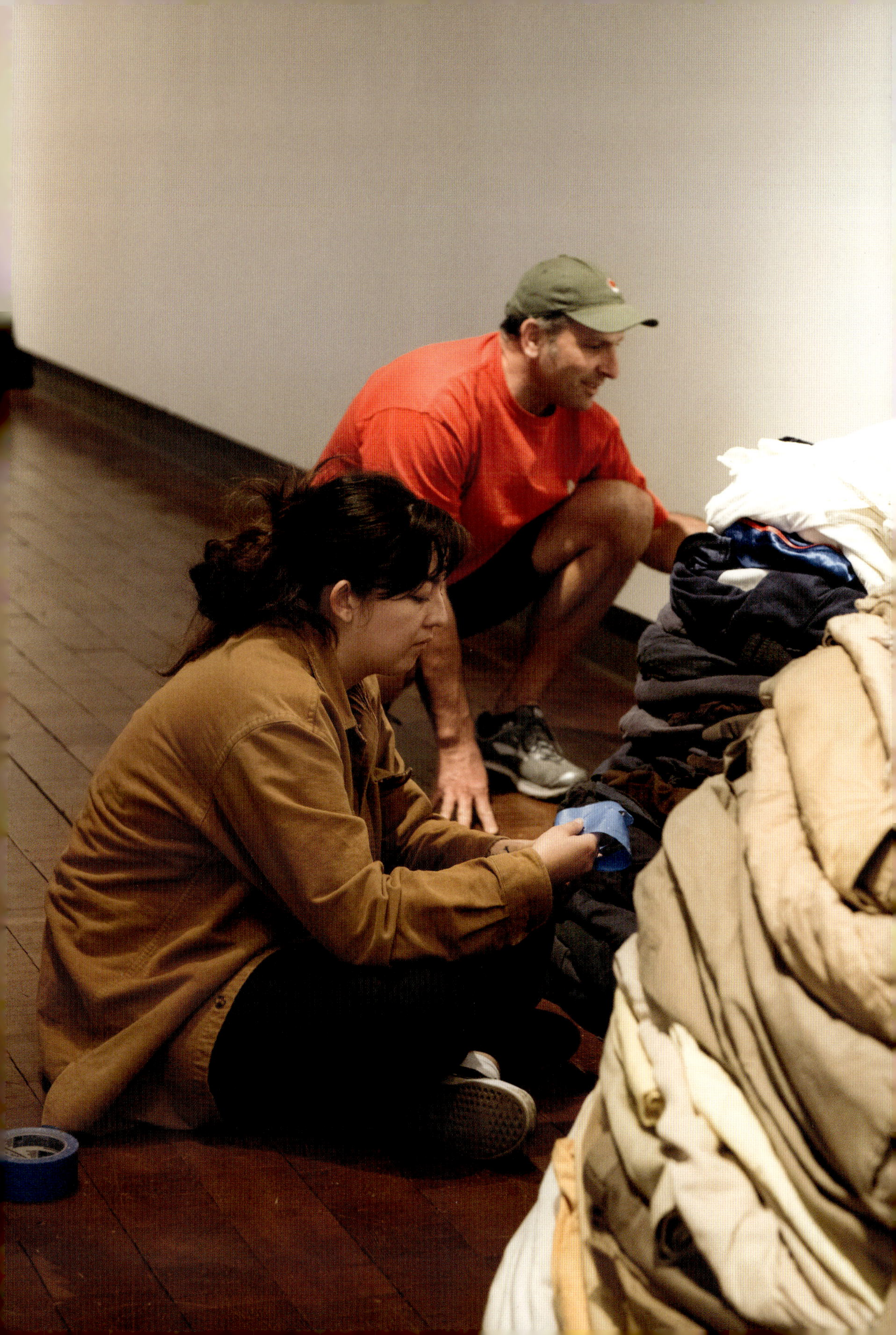

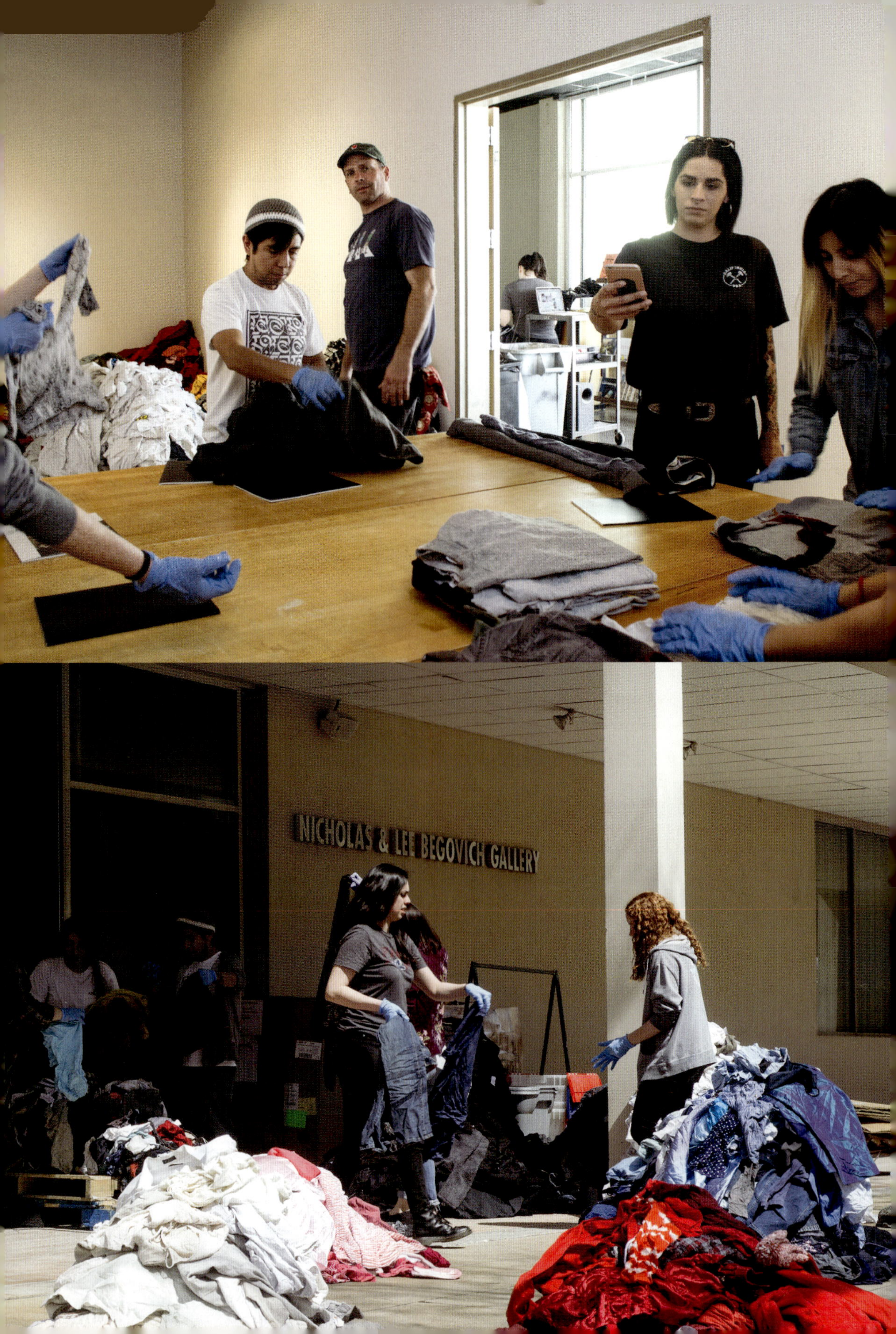

NICHOLAS & LEE BEGOVICH GALLERY

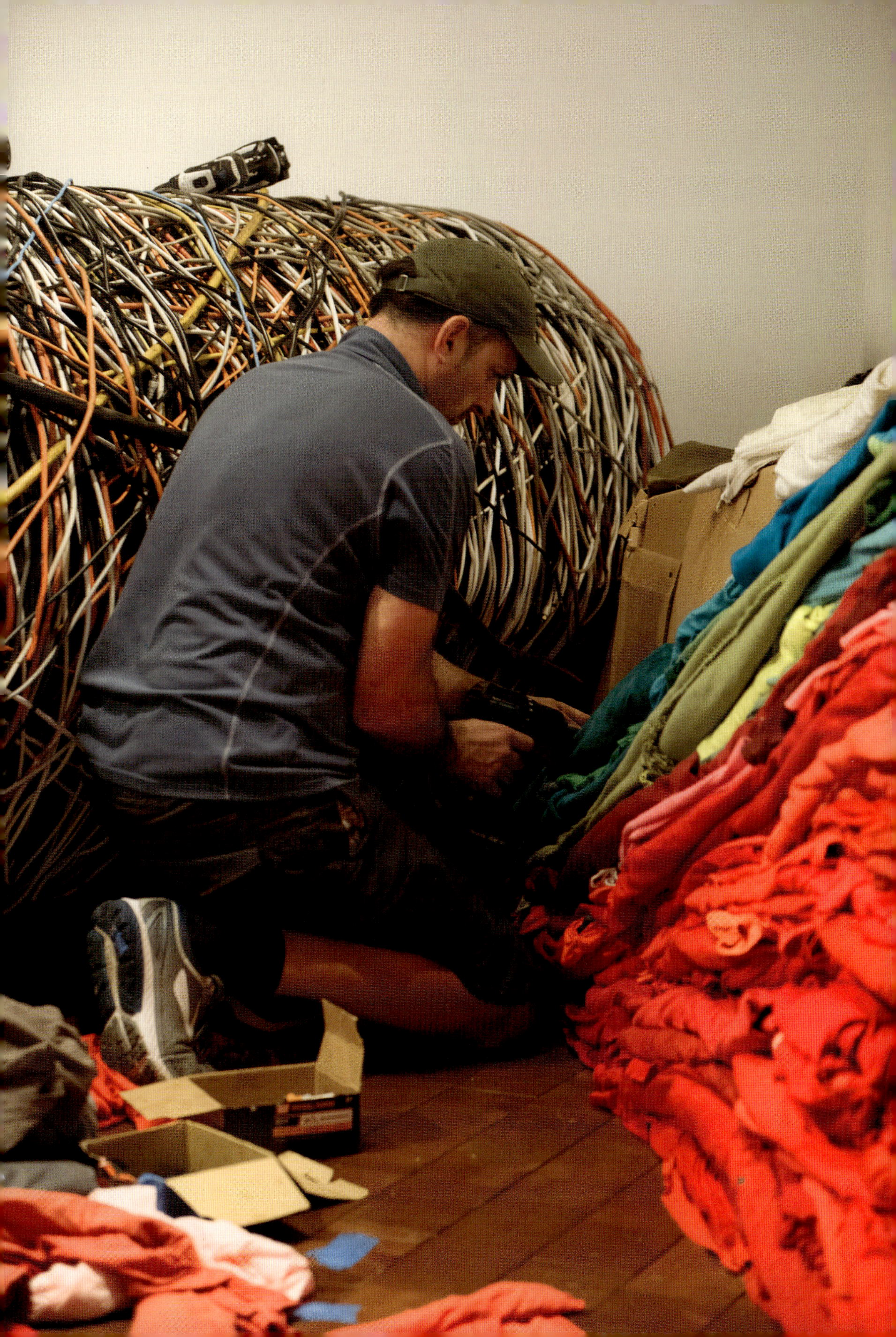

PHOTOGRAPHER CREDITS

© *D. Hill* -

Page: 4 *inset*, 16, 18, 20, 21 *bottom*, 46, 51, 61, 68, 103, 112, 118, 119, 120, 121, 123, 124, 126, 127, 128, 131, 133, 135, 138, 139, 140, 141, 144, 145, 148, 149, 150, 151

© *Eric Stoner* -

Page: 2, 10, 17, 21 *top*, 23, 27, 28, 29, 32, 36, 37, 38, 48, 49, 64, 84, 86, 96, 110, 114, 115, 117, 143, 152, 153

© *Michael Quinn* -

Page: 1, 4 *background*, 6, 8, 15, 19, 41, 44, 47, 54, 56, 59, 62, 66, 71, 74, 78, 80, 82, 89, 92, 94, 98, 100, 108, 109, 136, 146, 154, 155, 157, 158

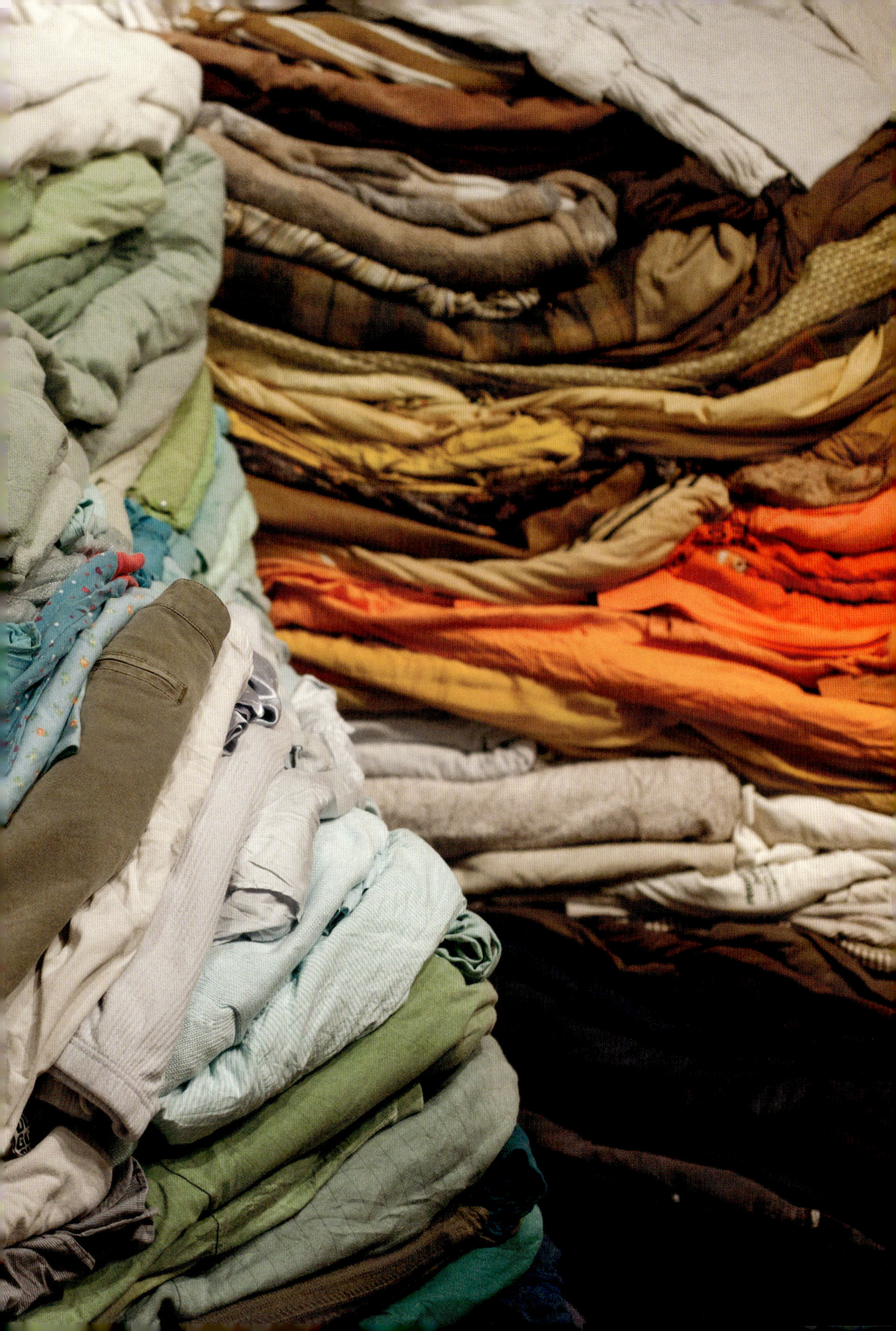

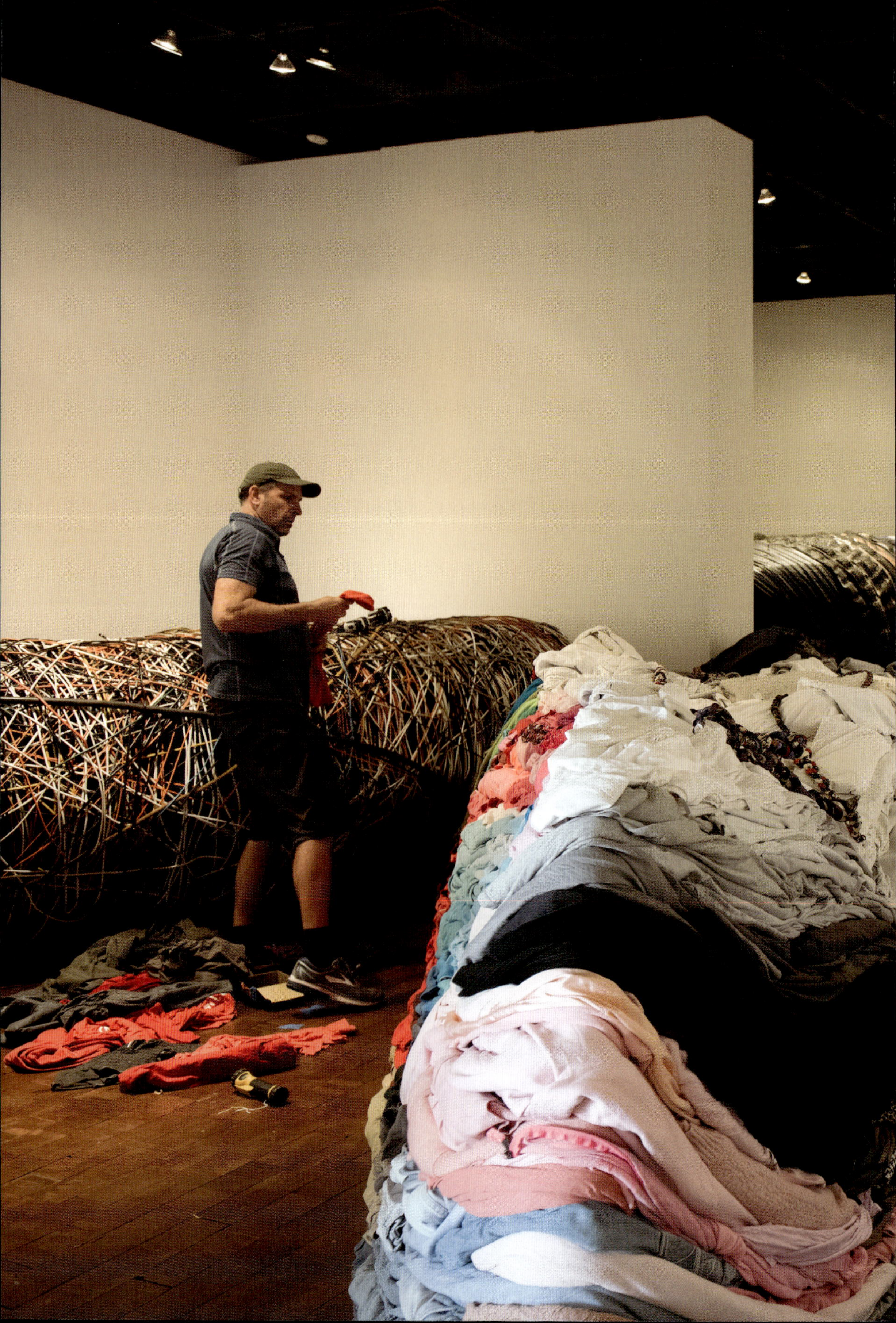

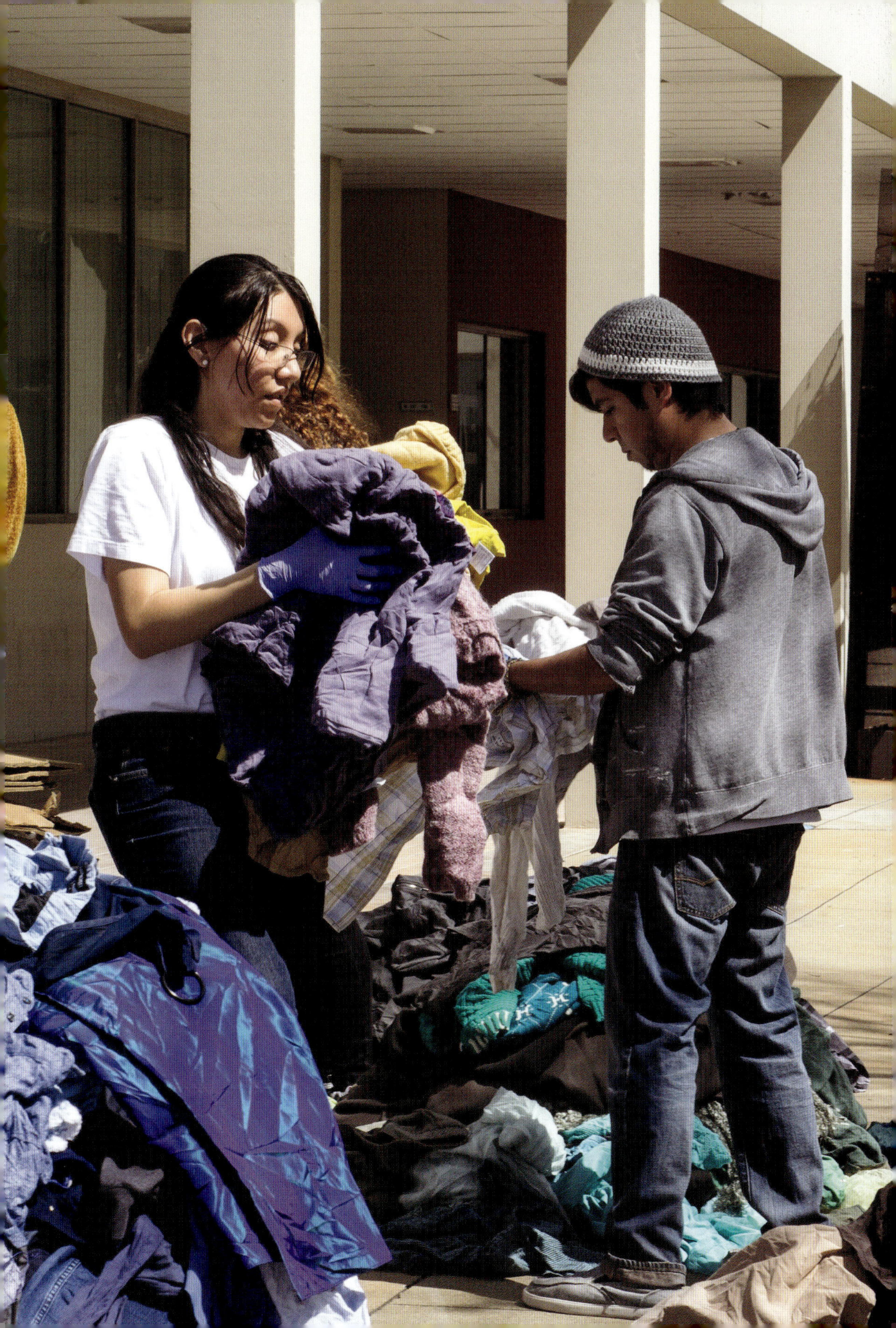

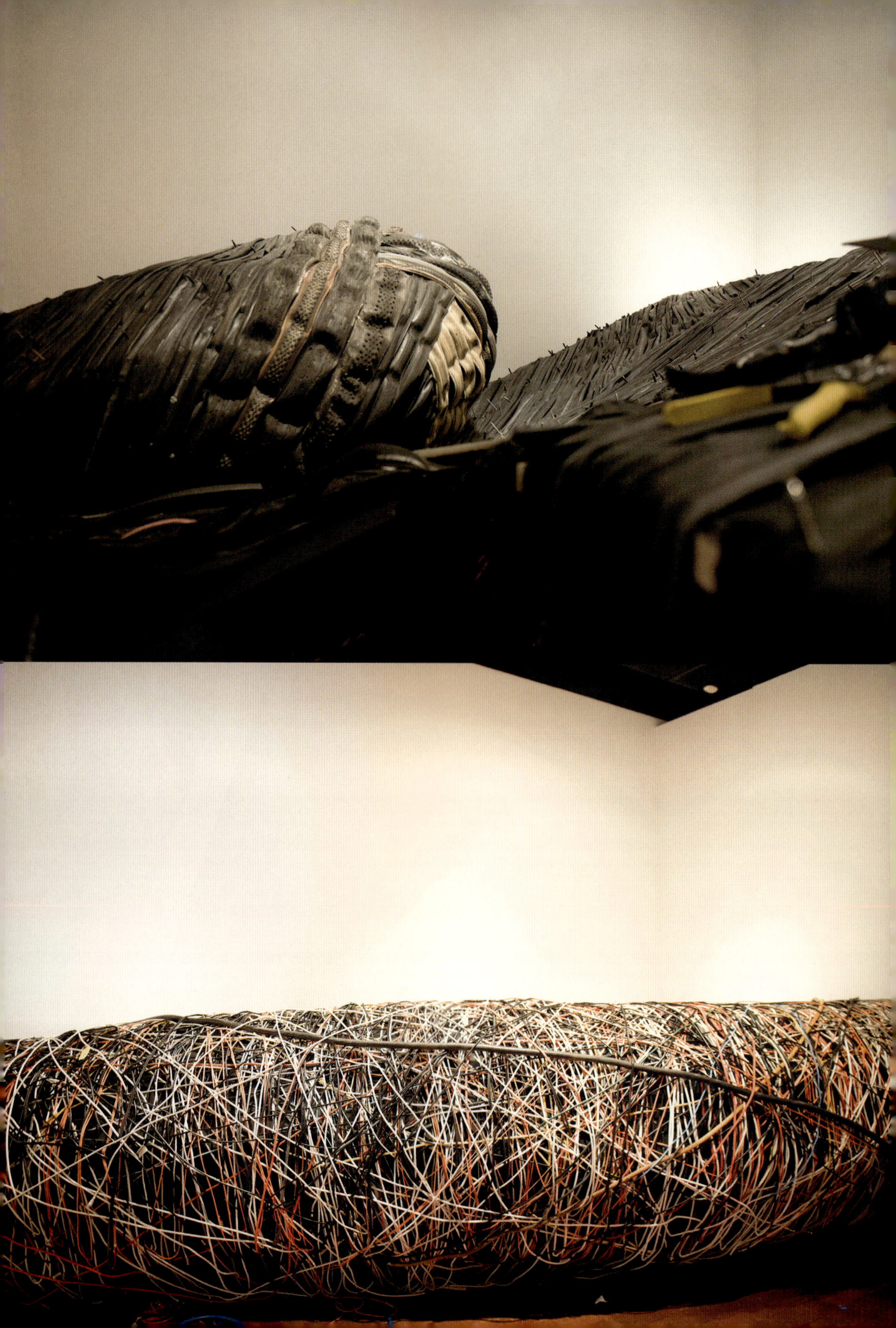

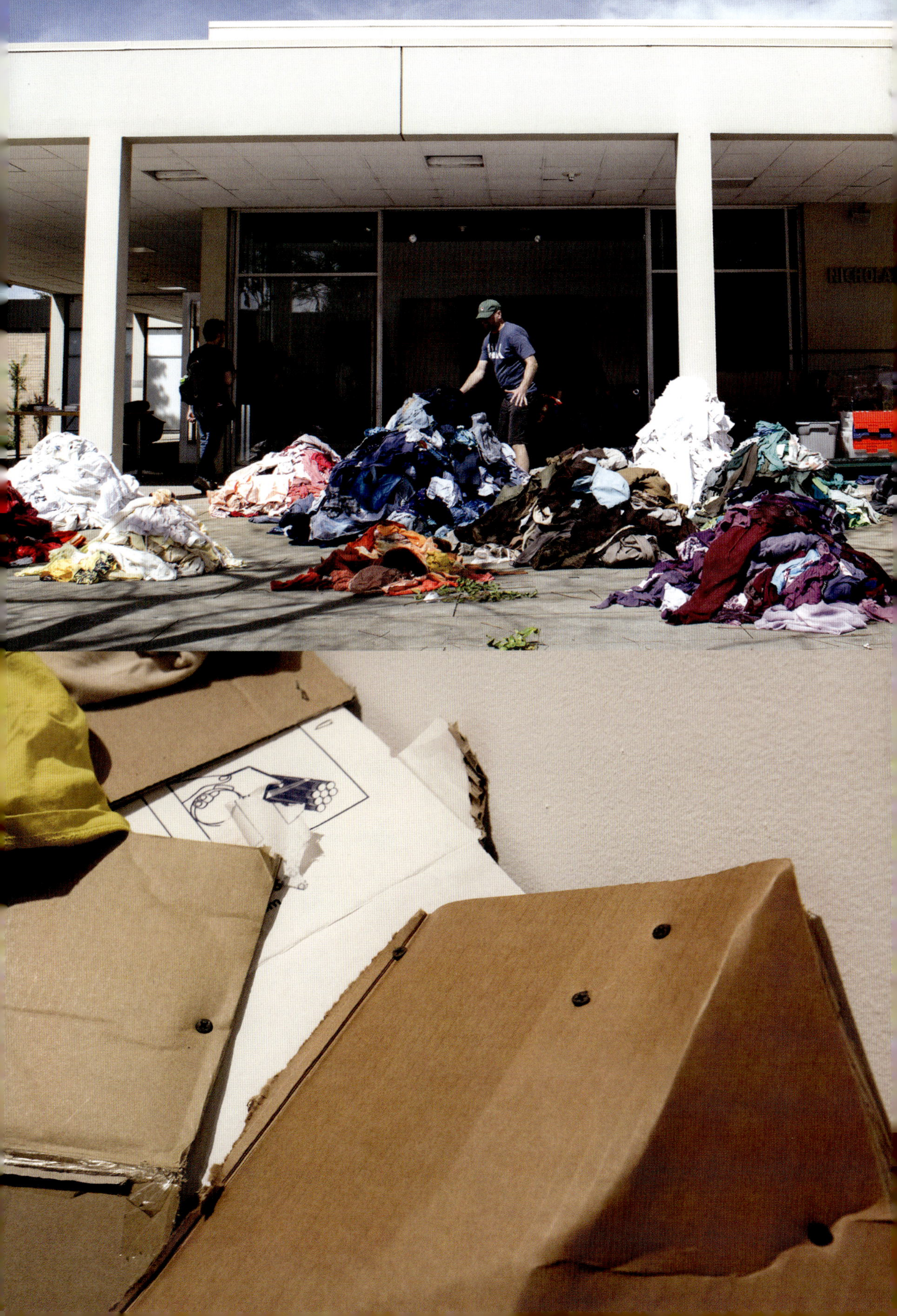

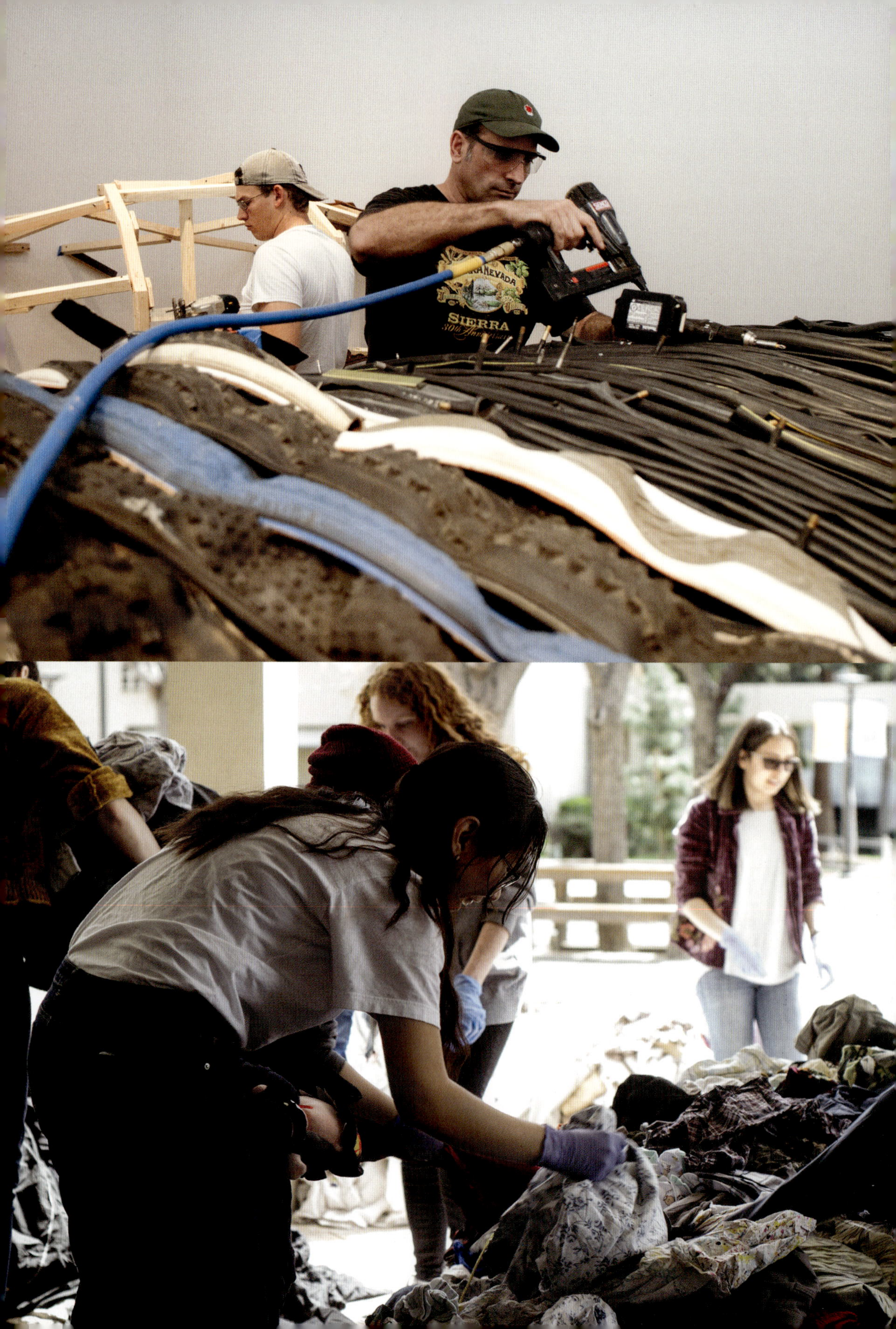

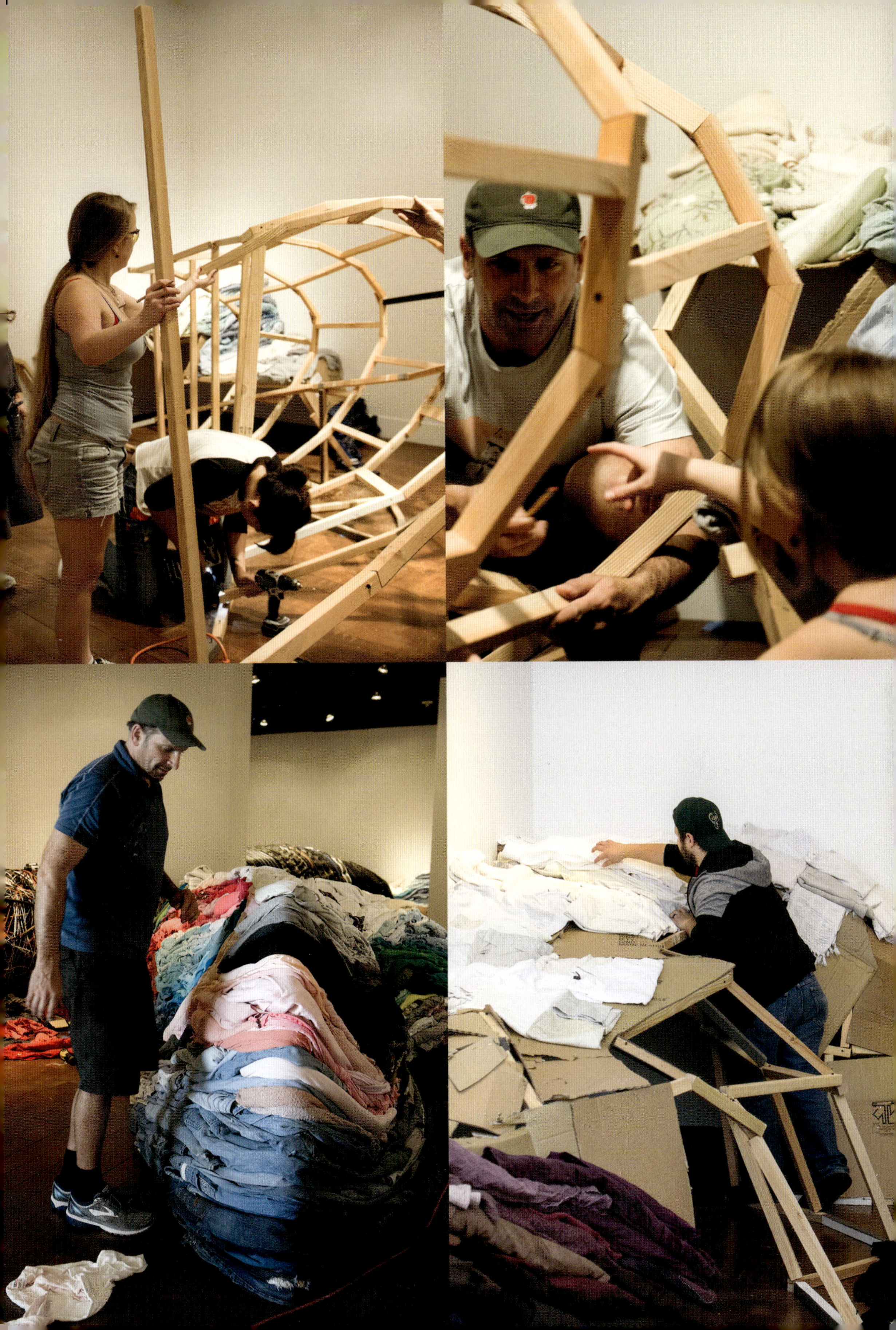

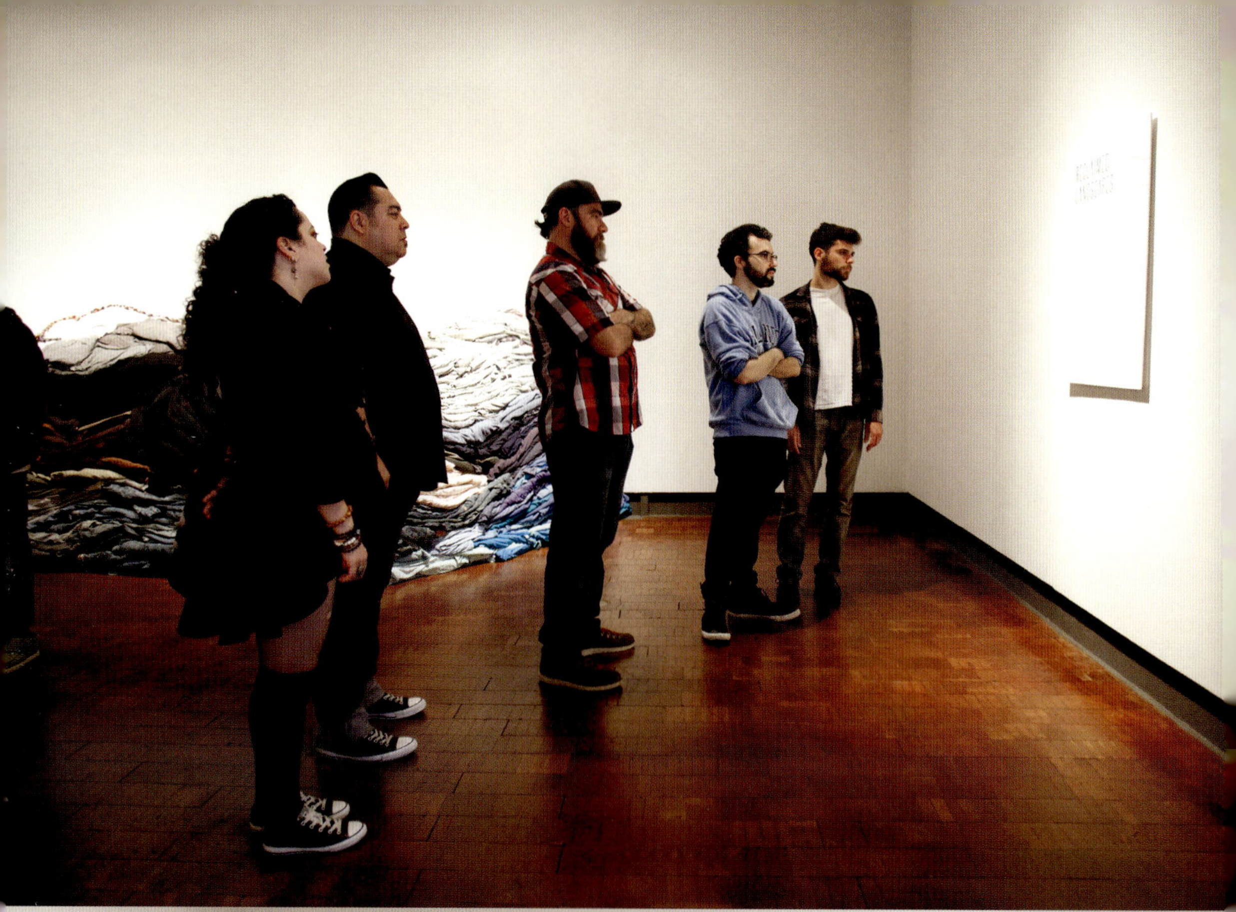

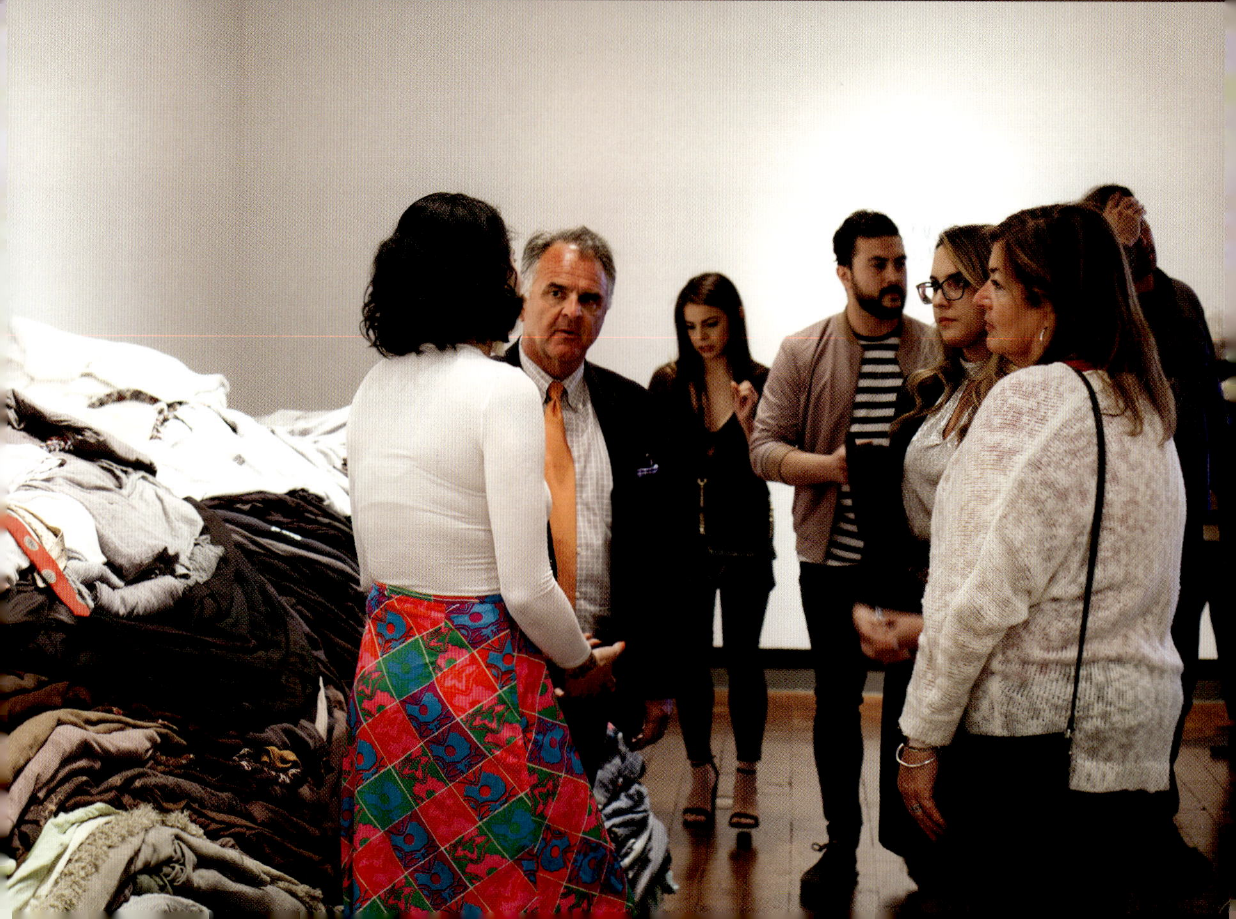

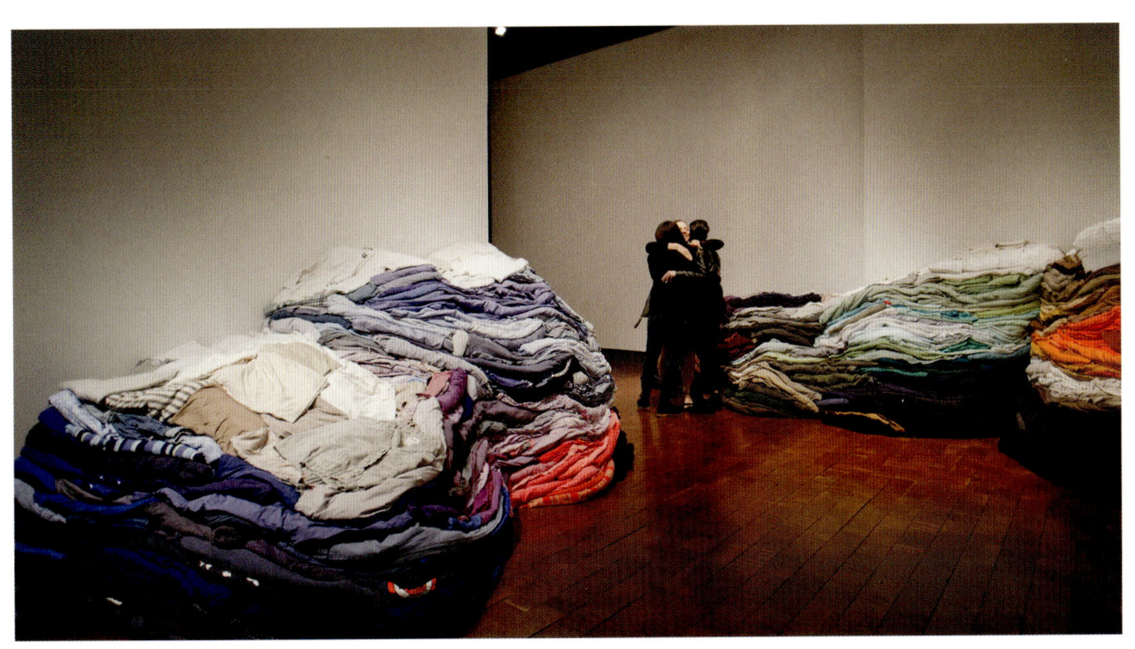

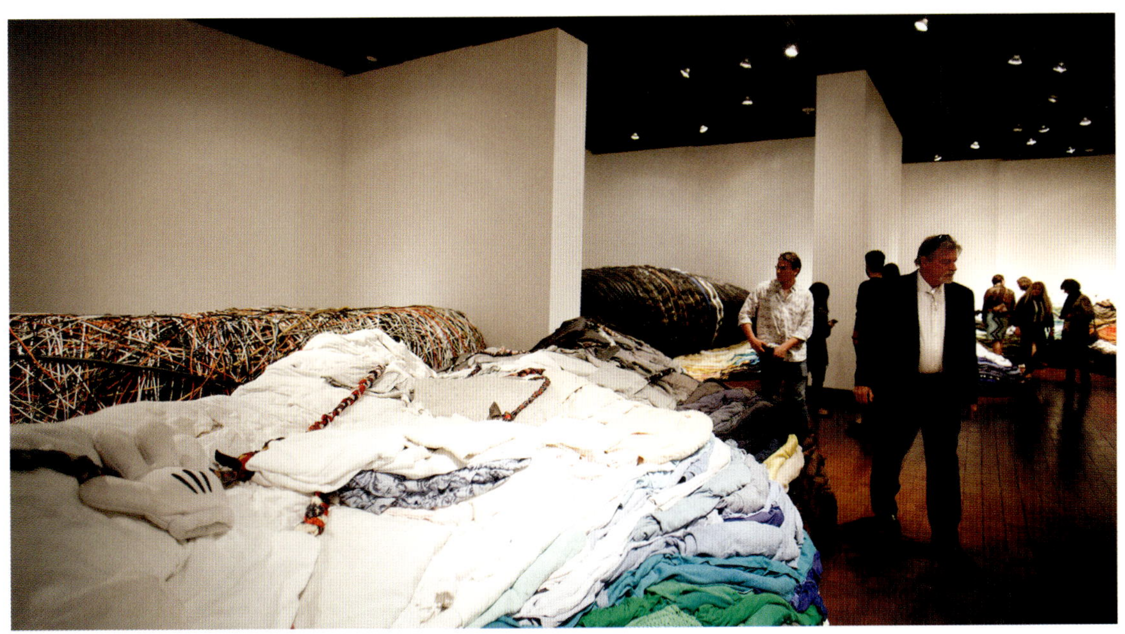

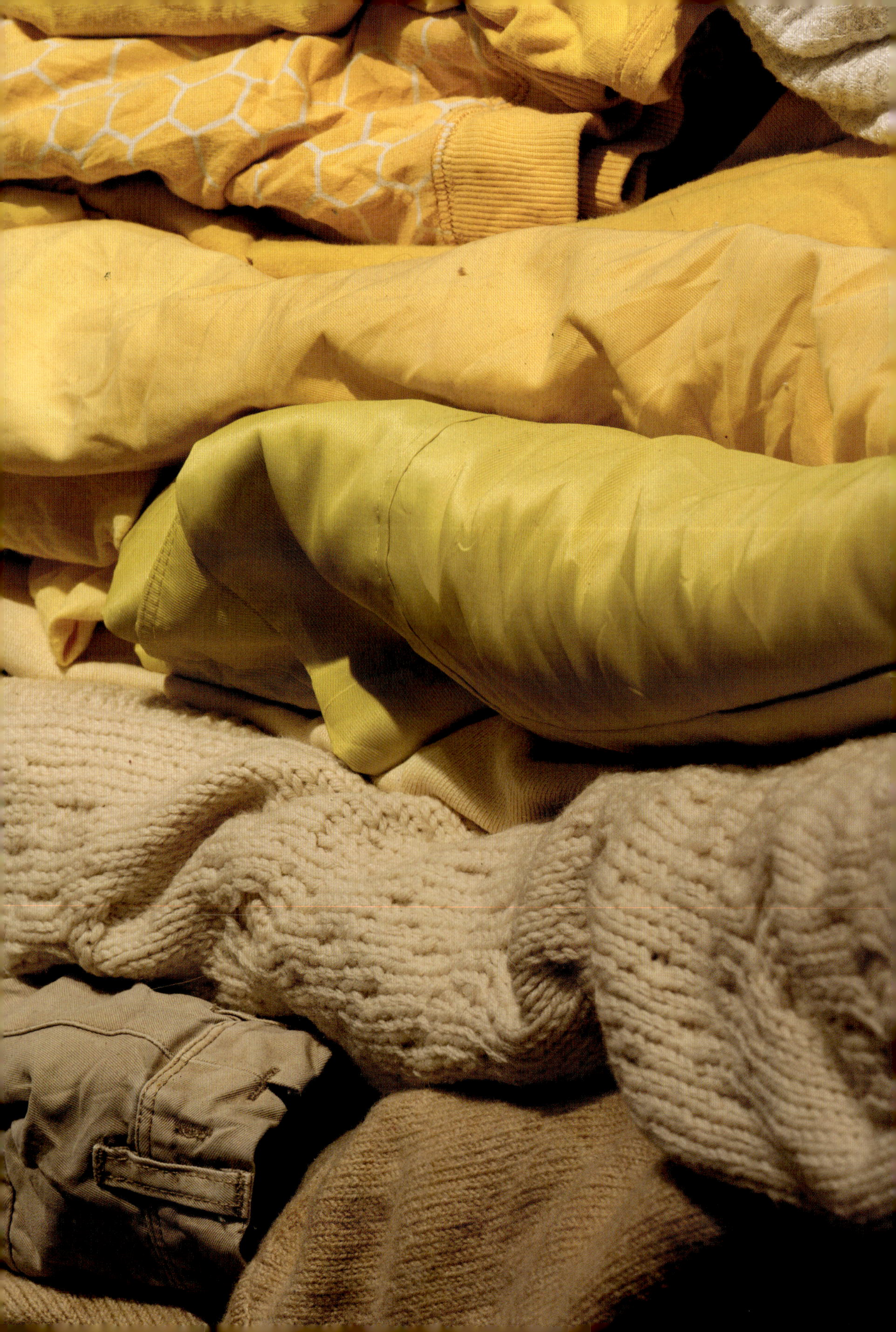

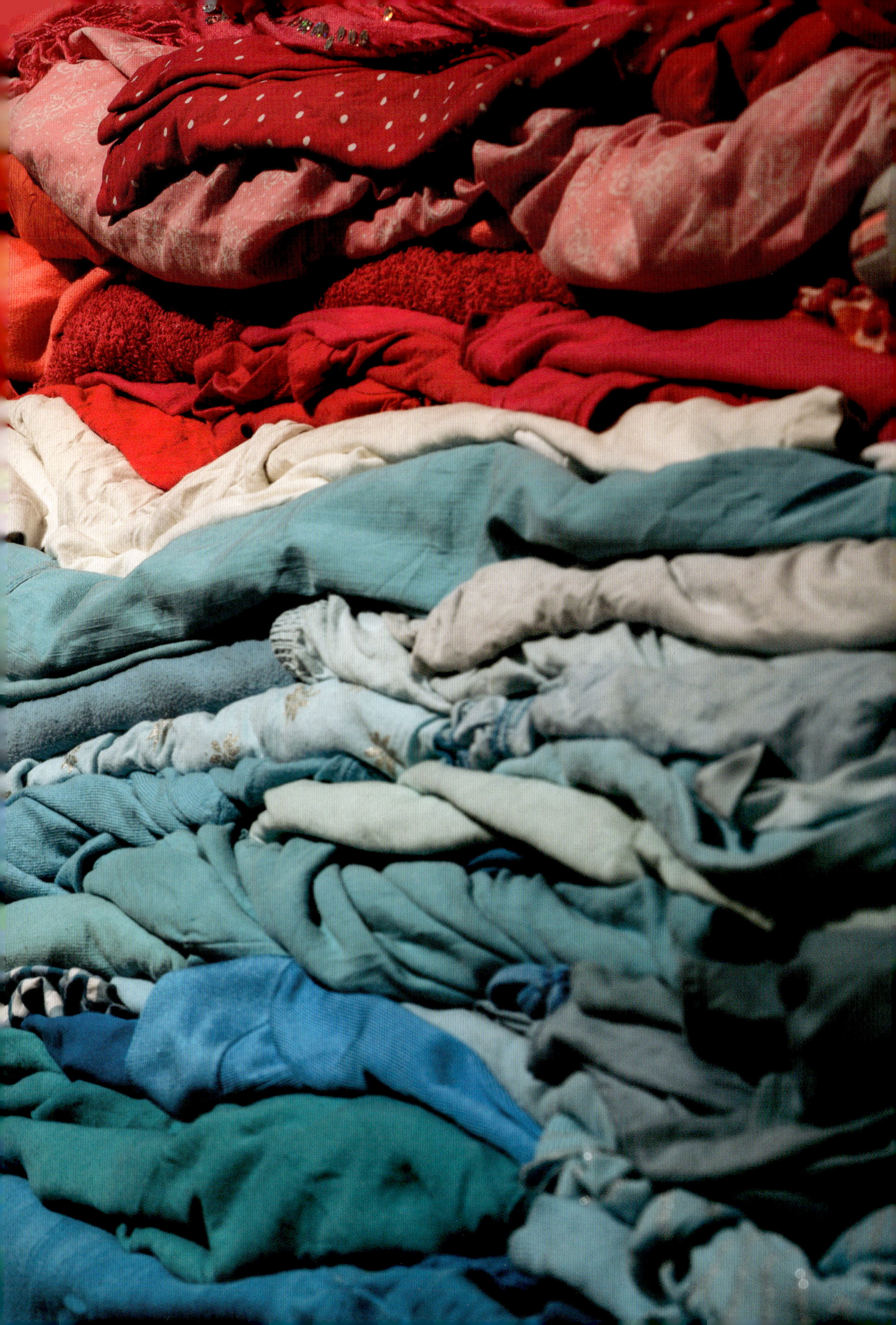

Published on the occasion of the exhibition
Reclaimed Landscapes: The Art of Jarod Charzewski
April 7 – May 17, 2018 at the Nicholas & Lee Begovich Gallery

Publisher: **CALIFORNIA STATE UNIVERSITY, FULLERTON**
College of the Arts, Nicholas & Lee Begovich Gallery
800 North State College Blvd.
Fullerton, California 92831

FIRST U.S. EDITION © 2020

ISBN
978-0-9997066-2-6

Title: *Reclaimed Landscape: The Art of Jarod Charzewski*
Authors: Jarod Charzewski, Jennifer Minasian and Danielle Clark

With Contributors:
Karen Crews Hendon
Dr. Nicole Seymour
Dr. John Bock
Joseph DeMarco
Tory Romero
Ganit Singh

Book Design: James Scott
Proofreader: Sue Henger
Distributed by SCB Distributors
Printed by Permanent Printing Limited, China

www.fullerton.edu/arts/begovichgallery

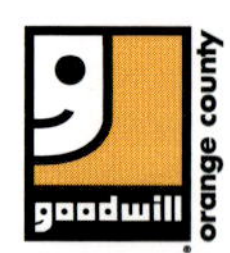
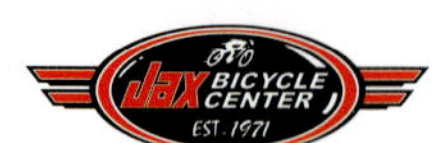
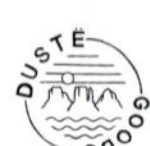

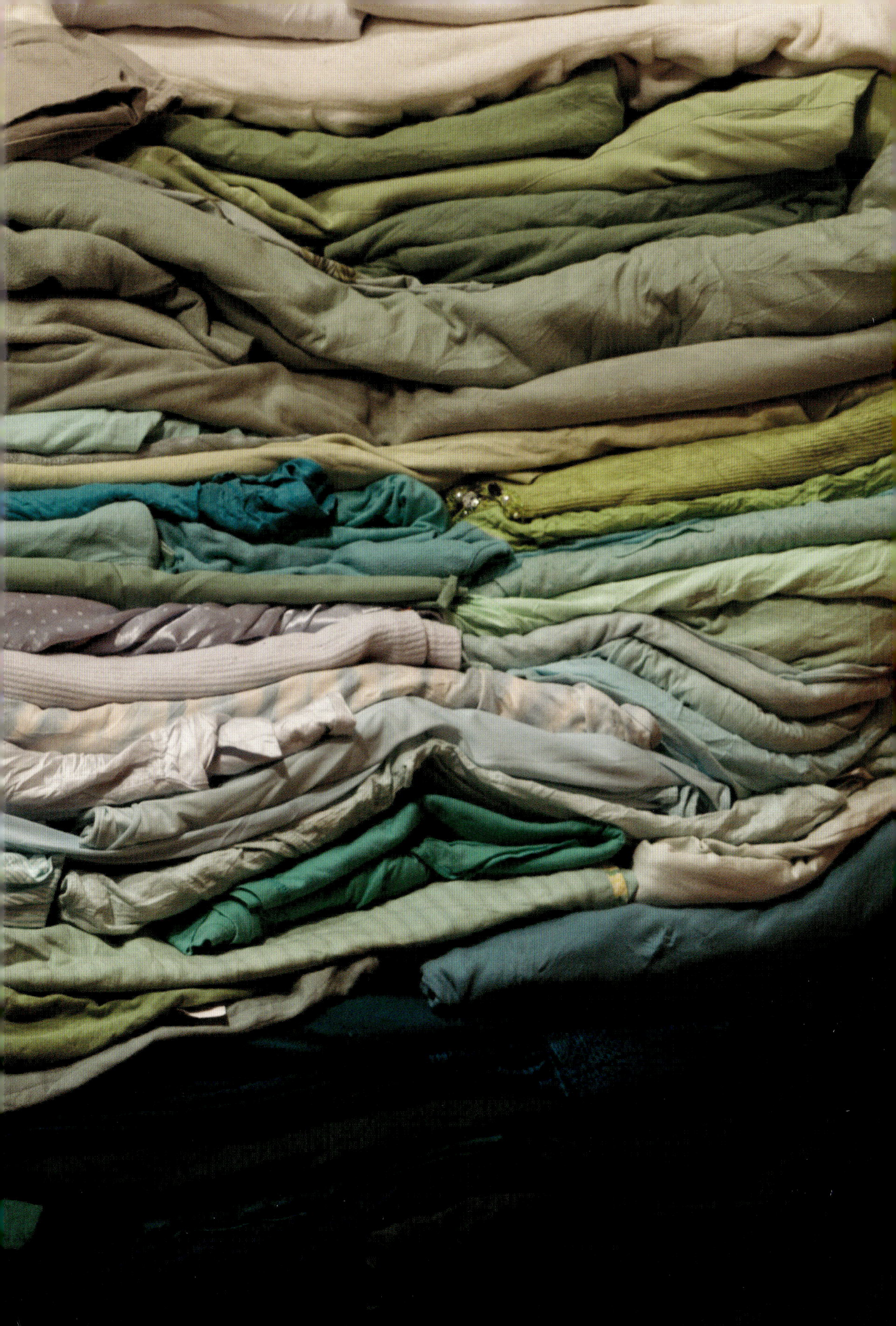

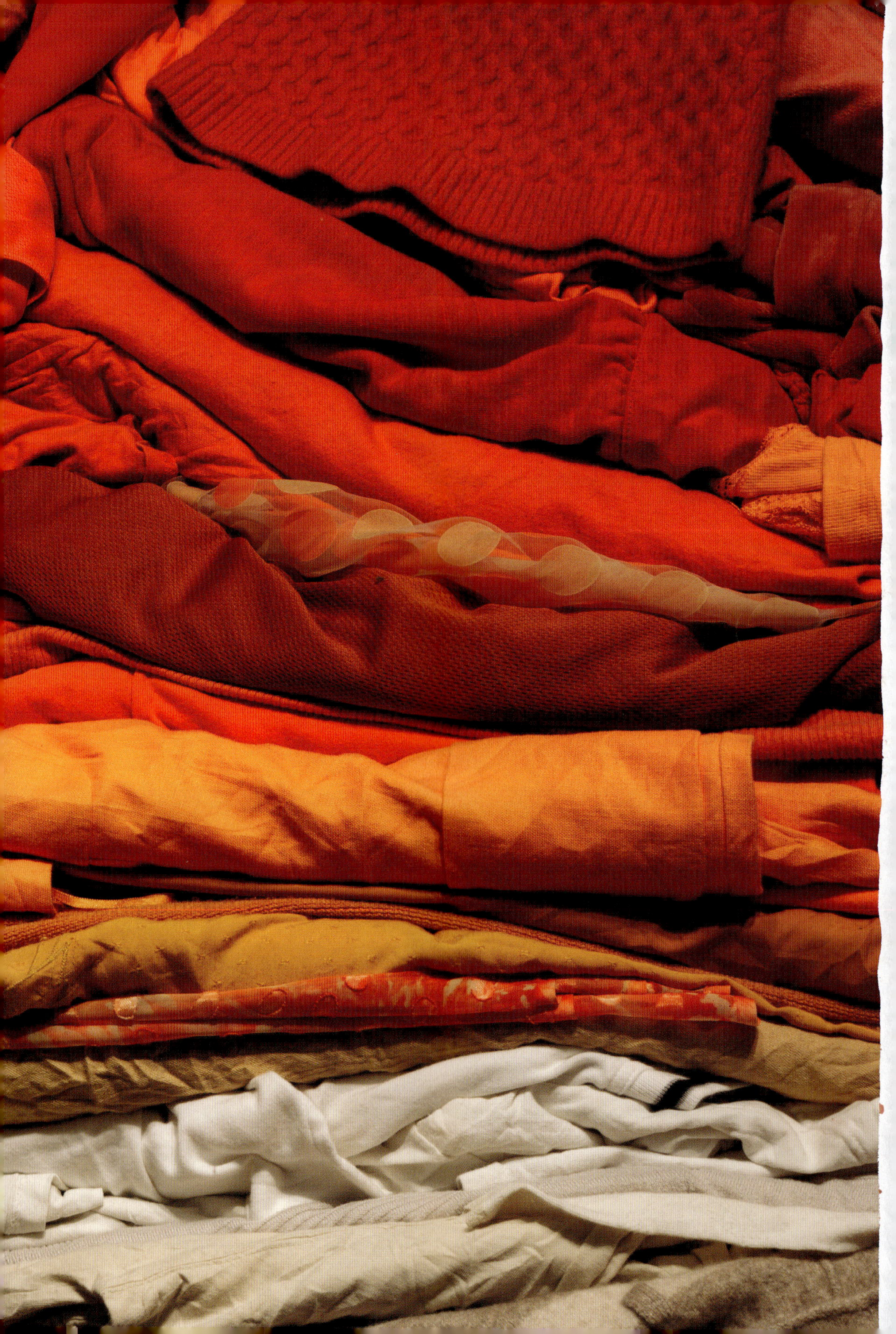